Enraged

Enraged

*Why Violent Times Need
Ancient Greek Myths*

EMILY KATZ ANHALT

Yale UNIVERSITY PRESS

New Haven and London

Published with assistance from the foundation established in
memory of Philip Hamilton McMillan of the Class of 1894,
Yale College.

Yale University Press books may be purchased in quantity for
educational, business, or promotional use. For information, please
e-mail sales.press@yale.edu (U.S. office) or sales@yaleup.co.uk
(U.K. office).

Set in Minion type by IDS Infotech, Ltd.
Printed in the United States of America.

Library of Congress Control Number: 2017930760
ISBN 978-0-300-21737-7 (hardcover : alk. paper)

A catalogue record for this book is available from the British
Library.

This paper meets the requirements of ANSI/NISO Z39.48–1992
(Permanence of Paper).

10 9 8 7 6 5 4 3 2 1

For Eduardo

ἔστι γὰρ ἡμῖν

σήμαθ᾽, ἃ δὴ καὶ νῶϊ κεκρυμμένα ἴδμεν ἀπ᾽ ἄλλων.

Contents

Acknowledgments

For their insight, inspiration, and constructive critiques, I am most especially indebted to Richard Garner, Donald Kagan, Kurt Raaflaub, and William C. Scott. This project has been percolating for a very long time. As an undergraduate at Dartmouth College, I first visited ancient Greece under the guidance and encouragement of Edward Bradley, Norman Doenges, Victor Menza, Christine Perkell, William C. Scott, Stephen Scully, James Tatum, and Christian Wolff. They introduced me not only to ancient Greek but also and especially to modes of study and inquiry that have enriched my life and brought me great joy and great solace. Their wisdom, enthusiasm, and pedagogical expertise remain the gold standard. I am similarly indebted to professors and colleagues at Yale University, whose kindness, generosity, and exemplary scholarship continue to inspire me: Robert Albis, Judith M. Barringer, Deborah Beck, Victor Bers, A. Thomas Cole, Richard Garner, George Goold, Judith M. Guston, John Herington, Donald Kagan, J. E. Lendon, Elizabeth Meyer, Sheila Murnaghan, Jerome T. Pollitt, Shilpa Raval, Joe Solodow, Gregory Thalmann, Elizabeth Tylawsky, Heinrich von Staden, Alysa J. Ward, and Gordon Williams. I also owe a great debt to Gregory Nagy for his influential scholarship and for his invaluable assistance in editing my first book (*Solon the Singer: Politics and Poetics*, 1993). For their wisdom and friendship, I am immeasurably thankful as well to colleagues at Trinity College: James Bradley, Mary Cornog, Richard C. Lee, Kenneth Lloyd-Jones, and A. D. Macro.

Since 2004, colleagues and students at Sarah Lawrence College have provided a most nurturing and exciting intellectual environment. A course-release grant from Sarah Lawrence gave me time to complete the manuscript. For their inspirational example and their advice and encouragement on this and other projects, I am particularly indebted to colleagues Cameron Afzal, Brom Anderson, Neil Arditi, Fred Baumgarten, David Bernstein, Bella Brodzki, Melvin Bukiet, David Castriota, Michael Davis, Isabel de Sena, Jerrilynn Dodds, Roland Dollinger, Charlotte Doyle, Glenn Dynner, Jason Earle, Joseph Forte, Melissa Frazier, Barbara Hickey, Barbara Kaplan, Eduardo Lago, Ann Lauinger, Eric Leveau, Nicolaus Mills, Nike Mizelle, April Mosolino, Sayuri Oyama, David Peritz, Tristana Rorandelli, Barbara Schecter, Sam Seigle, Judy Serafini-Sauli, William Shullenberger, Kanwal Singh, Fred Smoler, Philip Swoboda, Marina Vitkin, Charles Zerner, and Carol Zoref. Among many superb students, I would like to acknowledge specifically Daniel Nadelman, Rebecca Nadelman, and my extraordinary "Magnificent Seven" Greek students (2013–2015): Emma Duvall, Gal Eldar, Brian Fox, Michelle Houslanger, Julia Huse, Rebecca Shepard, and Lydia Winn.

Words cannot express my gratitude to physicians, family, and friends, who have sustained and encouraged me in sickness and in health. Francine Foss, M.D., saved my life, as quite literally no one else could have. I survived to write this book because of her genius, expertise, and kindness, along with that of Mary

Ann Fieffer, A.P.R.N., Diane Dirzius, R.N., Rose Mixon, R.N., and the many other talented, compassionate, and selfless doctors, nurses, and staff at Yale–New Haven Hospital.

For their wit, wisdom, generosity, and enriching friendship, I am also supremely grateful to Nancy and Scott Barcelo, Marion Caldwell and Tom Cicovsky, Mary Ann and Jim Carolan, Jeanne and Dan Dinaburg, Ellen and Brad Foster, Kopkun and Glenn Gardner, Terry Blonder Golson, Laura Jarett and Earl Giller, Jeffrey Mackie-Mason, Ruth and Lawrence Manley, Anne Craige McNay, Kathy Neustadt, Jane Orans (at whose glorious Quisisana Resort in Center Lovell, Maine, I have also written and edited extensively over many years), George Petty, Kathryn Roberts, Susan Roberts, Marjorie Schorr and Joe Gurvets, Phyllis and Howard Schwartz, Susan Schwartz, Janet and John Segal, Claudia and Paul Taskier, Daniela Varon, and Ken Winber.

My daughters Erica and Ariela and my mother Marilyn Katz read and commented brilliantly and tirelessly on drafts of the book from its earliest stages. Their insights and encouragement have been infinitely valuable. My brother Jimmy Katz not only gave me his turbo-charged bone marrow, he and my sister-in-law Dena Katz provided continuous, enthusiastic support as I recovered my health and resumed work. I am also grateful to my mother-in-law Nedda Anhalt and my cousin Marjorie Lynn for their affection and encouragement.

In addition, I owe many thanks to Sarah Miller, Susan Laity, Eliza Childs, Ash Lago, Laura Davulis, Eva Skewes, and the editorial staff at Yale University Press for their expertise and assistance in preparing this manuscript.

My greatest debt is to my husband Eduardo, whose brilliance, humor, and love preserve my life and my equilibrium. Eduardo's wise counsel delights, improves, and inspires me in all adventures and endeavors. Eduardo suggested that I turn my repeated dinner-table observations into something more constructive, and he continued to cheer me on as I labored like George Eliot's Casaubon on my own seemingly endless "Key to All Mythologies."

A Note on the Texts, Translations, and Notes

All adaptations, translations, and citations of the *Iliad, Ajax,* and *Hecuba* rely on the Oxford Classical Texts of D. B. Munro and T. W. Allen (*Iliad*), A. C. Pearson (*Ajax*), and G. Murray (*Hecuba*); translations are my own.

Homeric Greek is a literary composite of several dialects: primarily Aeolic and old-Ionic with some Arcado-Cyprian, Attic, and non-Greek forms as well as some neologisms. This combination would have sounded somewhat strange and elevated even to audiences in the sixth and fifth centuries BCE. Sections of the tragedies also very likely sounded formal and stilted to fifth-century audiences. I have tried to paraphrase and, at times, to translate the Greek (into prose, not poetry) as literally as possible, while still yielding sense in English. When possible, I have sought in the opening narratives to preserve some of the distance and elevated tone of the original Greek, particularly in the dialogue. To a contemporary reader, this may sound awkward at times.

Given the vastness of the scholarly bibliography, the notes are not intended to be exhaustive but, rather, representative of relevant scholarship in English and an impetus to further reading.

Enraged

Introduction
The Power of Stories

R age drives Achilles. Men and horses flee before him into the river. Leaping in after them, he cuts them all down. He captures twelve young Trojans alive, ties them up, and hands them to his companions to lead away to his ships. They will be a vengeance-price paid for the death of his best friend. Achilles will slit their throats and burn their bodies on his friend's funeral pyre.

One young Trojan warrior manages to escape from the river. Having lost his armor, shield, and spear, this young man is defenseless. He is also exhausted. As Achilles raises his spear, the young man rushes in underneath and grasps Achilles' knees. He begs Achilles to spare his life, and he promises a large ransom. He explains that he is only a half brother, not a full brother, of the man who killed Achilles' friend.

Achilles says that before the death of his best friend he spared many Trojans, capturing them alive and selling them. But now he will kill any Trojan he encounters, especially any sibling of his friend's killer. Once before, Achilles had captured and sold this very same young man, but now rage prevents him from finding value of any kind in human life. "Why do you beg and wail in this way?" Achilles demands

contemptuously. His white teeth flash against the smeared
blood on his face. "Don't you know that everyone dies, even
me, great as I am and half-immortal?"

Achilles' sword strikes between collarbone and neck,
and the young man falls forward on his face. His blood soaks
the ground. Hurling the young man's lifeless body into the
river, Achilles boasts triumphantly, "Let the fish feed on you!
Your mother won't lay your body out and grieve over you.
May you all die terribly, every single Trojan, until you pay
with your blood for my friend and for every Greek you killed
while I was not there to defend them!"

Like Achilles, the great Greek warrior of Homer's *Iliad,* we all
have the capacity for rage. Sometimes it dominates us. Sometimes
we dominate it. Rage fuels political movements and perpetuates
religious and economic disputes. It causes horrific violence,
and it disrupts or destroys families, communities, and states. It
prevents us from making good decisions because it obstructs
thought and discussion. When we are enraged, we easily mistake
anger for moral correctness; we think, "I'm really angry, so I must
be right." But an enraged response, regardless of the provocation,
is at best counterproductive and at worst catastrophic.

In the twenty-first century, we must move beyond violent
rage. Rage may be a natural reaction to injury, insult, or injustice, but indulging in rage and admiring it in others is a choice.
Whether we embrace or condemn rage in ourselves or in others
depends largely on the stories that we inherit and transmit. Our
culture's stories consciously and unconsciously shape the
choices that we make, the goals that we pursue, and the ways
that we treat one another.[1] History shows that the transition
from tribalism to civil society and the maintenance of civil

society both require individuals to restrain their own rage and to stop admiring rage in others. Ancient Greek myths encourage us to reject the primitive, tribal view of rage as a marker of the correctness of our cause. By exposing rage as shortsighted and self-destructive, these ancient tales enable us to recognize rage as a marker of illogical thinking and inadequate leadership.

In seeking to restrain rage and to promote constructive debate and the rule of law in the modern world, we are trying to reinvent the wheel while failing to consult the manual. From the eighth through the fifth century BCE, Greek myths accompanied and promoted the Greeks' historically unprecedented movement away from autocracy toward broader forms of political participation.[2] Some Greek *poleis*, "citizen-communities," replaced tyrants with oligarchs, that is, groups of powerful individuals. Some Greek *poleis* even developed democratic institutions and decided all or most political questions by means of a direct vote of all citizens.[3] Greek myths played a vital role in challenging the celebration of violent rage and in cultivating values and skills essential to rational, humane, compassionate relationships. In the sixth century BCE, Athens in particular experienced a remarkable transition from tribalism to civil society, from private vendetta to communal legal procedure, from physical violence to verbal debate.[4] In the twenty-first century, the global community must accomplish or preserve this same transition.

Maybe you are familiar with some ancient Greek myths. Maybe not. In this book, I retell a few of them in the hope that they can help us, as they helped the ancient Greeks, to see the costs of rage and violent revenge and to cultivate more constructive ways of interacting. Performed publicly as epic songs or tragic plays, ancient Greek myths exposed tyranny and violence as universal toxins capable of destroying perpetrator and victim alike. Greek myths reminded their audiences that human beings have better options for dealing with one another. Right now in the twenty-first century, Greek myths can arm us against the tyrants we might serve and the tyrants we might become.

During the ancient Greeks' extraordinary historical moment of political and social transformation, the mythical depiction of rage encouraged an increasing distaste for tyrannical brutality and cruelty.[5] The Greeks understood that violence can be necessary to preserve communal order and stability, and they never abandoned violence as a means of eradicating enemies and furthering their ambitions, as the history of the fifth century amply attests.[6] But their stories simultaneously affirmed the value of verbal debate. They even called into question the Athenians' own violent aggression, xenophobia, and exclusive sense of group identity.[7] The Greeks' success was only partial and imperfect, but their experience and their stories emphasize that only a change in attitudes can deter violent rage and the chaos it produces.

Recent political turmoil and devastating eruptions of violence worldwide attest that even the establishment of so-called free and fair elections does not alone produce or maintain stable, egalitarian governments or societies. Popular elections, law courts, even political term limits, cannot by themselves ensure that a government will promote fairness, justice, or a desirable, flourishing society. In practice, democratic procedures and institutions can easily serve tyrannical ends and promote atrocities. Nowhere in the history of the world have "free and fair elections" independently produced or constituted a successful, thriving, egalitarian society.[8] And yet, we continue to ignore the ancient Greeks' eloquent testimony, and so we are surprised each time a modern election results in increased violence rather than a civil transition or exercise of power.

The ancient Greeks did not abandon autocratic and oligarchic power structures and implement democratic institutions
overnight. Instead, over centuries their myths laid the ground-
work for humane social relationships and political interactions.
Ancient Greek myths emphasize the self-destructiveness of rage
and undermine the traditional equation of vengeance with
justice. They enable the audience to feel and see the costs of
violent revenge and the value of rational self-control. They
encourage the audience to see logical, predictable consequences of human choices and priorities, to acknowledge
other perspectives than their own, and to value reciprocal
obligations between individuals. They promote discussion and
debate as an alternative to violent conflict. In cultivating rational
thought and the capacity for empathy, ancient Greek myths
thwart the desire to celebrate or emulate those who succumb
to rage or commit atrocities.

Ancient Greek myths had broad political influence in their
own time, but in today's political climate ancient Greek literature, produced almost exclusively by "dead white males," can
be extremely polarizing.[9] Scholars at extremes of the political
spectrum often criticize one another for appropriating the
ancient texts to serve their own political and/or social agenda.[10]
To nonspecialists, the Greeks' use of slavery and their subjuga-
tion of women might seem to justify disregarding ancient Greek
culture. But the Greeks were not unusual in these areas. Human
rights and gender and racial equality are very recent ideals in
the history of the world. Slavery continued in the United States
almost a century after the ratification of the Constitution, and
women could not vote for more than fifty years after that. In
many parts of the world today, slavery and ethnic inequality
persist and women still lack equal rights and cannot vote. Even
in communities that claim to value universal human rights and

equality before the law, the reality often does not align with these ideals. In their own time, the ancient Greeks took the very first, giant, if wholly inadequate, step in the right direction. In our time, Greek myths can help us to close the gap between the reality and the aspiration. Ancient Greek culture demands our attention, despite its exclusions, because it initiated, although it never achieved, a movement toward individual autonomy and universal human rights that we ourselves have yet to accomplish.[11]

Ancient Greek myths offer a nonpartisan critique of rage, and they validate alternatives. They invite the audience to think deliberately about the effect of stories on human choices and goals. They naturally evoke objectivity and creativity, because the audience may have no vested interest in the story's outcome and can approach the issues without passion or partisanship. At the same time, these tales influence the audience's values and preferences. They encourage admiration for some behaviors and condemnation of others. They offer models to emulate or to avoid. Ancient Greek myths begin to redirect destructive human capacities and to promote constructive ones.[12]

Despite the crucial role that ancient Greek myths played in the development of Western culture, these stories remain foreign to many in the West, visible only dimly through the distorting lens of numerous popular adaptations. Many people first encounter Greek mythology, if at all, not in ancient Greek sources or even in stories told by parents or grandparents but in modern, synthesizing versions. Every retelling of a story is a reinterpretation, an adaptation to suit the needs of the moment. These ancient stories are no exception. Even the Homeric epics, the earliest surviving versions of ancient Greek myths, appear to be adapting still earlier versions of the tales, and the tragic playwrights are reinterpreting Homer.[13] Similarly, modern reinterpretations of ancient Greek myths reflect modern values and ignore changes in emphasis as the myths evolved over time. Modern versions obscure the historical development of the ancient Greeks' challenge to rage and violence.[14] In this book, I examine in succession the critique of rage in Homer's *Iliad*, an ancient epic poem originating perhaps 3,000 years ago, and in two fifth-century BCE Athenian tragedies, Sophocles' *Ajax* and Euripides' *Hecuba*. These three works expose the costs of rage and identify crucial prerequisites for the nonviolent resolution of conflicts, elements just as essential today as they were thousands of years ago. Each chapter begins with a narrative retelling of the relevant mythical tale, followed by a discussion of the story's themes and emphases and their importance for modern societies confronting the same issues. Some readers may be familiar with these stories, others less so. My aim is to make them accessible to everyone, although I hope that readers will want to read Homer's epics and the surviving Athenian tragedies in their entirety.

The ancient Greeks knew, as we do, the devastating seductions of rage, but long before the emergence of democratic ideas or institutions, ancient epic tales began to undermine confidence in the efficacy of rage and revenge and to promote a more far-sighted conception of self-interest. The *Iliad* and the *Odyssey*, two vast poems attributed to "Homer," were probably composed orally and were certainly transmitted orally for centuries before coalescing in the eighth century BCE into the form in which we have them. Performed publicly, with the singer accompanying himself on a lyre, Homer's epics were not written down until the sixth century BCE. We do not know who "Homer" was, and the question of the poems' authorship (called by scholars "the Homeric Question") essentially boils down to whether you want to call "Homer" the first poet who sang some tale that eventually developed into the *Iliad* or the sixth-century singer who dictated the monumental composition we know as the *Iliad* to the scribe who first wrote it down. More recent cultural examples of oral storytelling suggest that each storyteller or, in the case of Homeric poetry, each singer followed certain constraints (of plot, character, meter) but also had the artistic freedom to shape the story and phrasing himself. Musical composition offers only an approximate analogy: the composer follows his or her own creative impulses within the constraints of the key signature and other formal considerations. The epic poet's creative efforts were bounded still more by limits imposed by meter and tradition.[15] Widely performed not just at private dinners but at public festivals, particularly by the sixth century BCE, the Homeric epics shaped the attitudes not only of the wealthy few but of most, if not all, ancient Greeks.[16]

Evolving centuries before the emergence of democratic political institutions, the *Iliad* in particular critiques the misuse of power and questions the utility of vengeance. The narrative constantly invites reassessment of the characters' enthusiasm for violence. The *Iliad* depicts a firmly hierarchical, nondemocratic society, with individuals ranked by birth and wealth, but at the same time the epic cultivates the audience's capacity for critical reflection and rational judgment. This process begins to reveal the inadequacy of myopic, self-destructive priorities. Homer's characters strive to be *aristos,* "best," defined as excelling in warfare and in helping friends and harming enemies.[17] When wronged, they seek vengeance. But the narrative distinguishes the audience's viewpoint from the characters' perspective. It gives the audience access to the divine realm as well as to the experience of a broad range of individuals. The narrative even humanizes the Greeks' enemies. The broader perspective often permits the audience to see the characters' understanding as narrow and their priorities as limiting.[18] The narrative exposes the inadequacy of violent revenge and hints that empathy better serves an individual's self-interest. Above all, the *Iliad* enables the audience to recognize morality as the responsibility not of gods but of human beings. Immortal beings impervious to suffering do not need morality and cannot use it, but human vulnerability to suffering and death makes moral behavior among mortals both necessary and possible.

Hundreds of years after Homer introduced the concept of the audience as critical moral thinker, as the first generations of Athenians in the late sixth century BCE and throughout the fifth were learning to wield democratic government, Athenian tragic playwrights continued to cultivate the audience's capacity for critical moral judgment. The ancient Greeks understood, as by now we must, that traditional approval of violence will not magically morph into a preference for verbal debate with the advent of democratic institutions. Even as the Athenian democracy flourished throughout the fifth century, Athenians remained ambitious and aggressive. They sought power, often by violent means, and they knew that violence could be necessary to maintain and restore order.[19] But in revising and reinterpreting the archaic stories, the tragic playwrights challenged both ancient, traditional, nondemocratic values and also the newly emerging, radically democratic political ideals. Their plays remind us that, paradoxically, to challenge democratic values with verbal argument is to affirm them.[20] By retelling ancient, traditional stories in a new, dramatic form and with new emphases, Athenian tragedies continued to advance Homer's critique of rage. They emphasized the costs of violence and undermined the traditional equation of vengeance with justice.

In the twenty-first century, political theater often means political protest, and modern productions often use Greek tragedy to voice dissent or to further an anti-establishment political agenda. In its original context, however, Greek tragedy was an essential part of the fifth-century Athenian establishment. The plays were performed in public competitions produced and organized by government officials, financed by wealthy volunteers who saw this as public service, and judged not by experts but by average citizens selected at random. Ancient comedy could and did criticize and ruthlessly satirize specific individual politicians and policies, but tragedy did not voice dissent. Instead, it provided an opportunity for political reflection. It exposed problems and posed questions.[21]

Two fifth-century Athenian tragedies in particular, Sophocles' *Ajax* and Euripides' *Hecuba,* demonstrate that democratic procedures alone will not necessarily promote justice or success for individuals or for groups. Both plays commend verbal persuasion over physical violence but also expose the ambivalent potential of persuasive speech. Effective persuasion can produce injustice. It can rationalize atrocity. But effective persuasion can also promote a humane and far-sighted understanding of self-interest. Sophocles' *Ajax* emphatically affirms Homer's suggestion that compassion, rather than vengeance, better serves an individual's self-interest. This play also explicitly corroborates Homer's implication that it is supremely stupid for a human being to exult in or laugh at the suffering of another, even if the other is an enemy, since human fortunes are variable, and human beings are all vulnerable to suffering and death. Similarly, Euripides' *Hecuba* emphasizes the precariousness of good fortune and the self-destructiveness of greed, brutality, and cruelty. The *Hecuba* demonstrates that the failure to respect mutual obligations between the weak and the powerful destroys the powerful no less than the weak.

Today, after 2,500 years, ancient Greek myths still reveal essential prerequisites for human flourishing. Homer's *Iliad* promoted critical reassessment of the components of success and the responsibilities of power. Revising Homer's ancient stories 300 years later, as the world's first ever democracy evolved and prospered, fifth-century Athenian tragedies continued to question both old and new ideals of achievement and to challenge the tyrannical use of power. Although the Athenians continued to employ violence in their relations with outsiders, this ongoing process of critical reflection enabled them to resolve many internal conflicts without violence.

The *Iliad, Ajax,* and *Hecuba* remind us that successful relationships and constructive political decision making require us to take responsibility for our choices and the resulting consequences. We must acknowledge the essential humanity of political opponents and even enemies. We must hear and value multiple points of view. Only then can we hope that the best ideas might prevail. But the critique of rage in these ancient Greek stories does not grant every point of view equal value. Some ideas and some choices really are better than others. Ancient traditional ideals will inevitably subvert even democratic institutions and promote violence. Consequently, admiration for constructive competition, freedom, tolerance, and equality must replace traditional admiration for destructive competition, vengeance, and domination. The ancient Greeks' own experience was decidedly mixed. They continued to seek dominance and remained capable of violence without scruple, even as verbal debate largely prevailed within Athens. But their mythical tales cultivate the discernment and, above all, the desire to reject violence and intimidation and to substitute constructive verbal conflict. The Greeks initiated a movement away from violence without ever abandoning violence themselves. They put the ball in play, so to speak. We have yet to score the goal.

The ancient Greeks' ingenious efforts to address human limitations, develop constructive talents, and define the ideal society initially took the form of oral storytelling. As their culture began to exchange autocracy for broader political participation and hierarchical values for egalitarian ones, the Greeks kept telling and retelling their stories. Over centuries, ancient Greek myths emphasized that self-interest demands the ability to control anger, the capacity to differentiate vengeance from justice, and the farsightedness to exclude violence from the political process. We must rediscover these insights today. Our survival depends on it.

The story begins in the mists of myth, myths told and retold over centuries . . .

1

Passions and Priorities (*Iliad* 1)

I t might have been nighttime. You would have seen the undulating flames of torch fires and smelled the soul-crushing stench of smoldering corpses. In the glittering light reflected off polished bronze breastplates and blood-streaked shields, two men are arguing, their lips pulled back from their teeth.

"You have to give her back," the younger man tells the older one. His voice is calm, his eyes steady. His name is Achilles.

"She's mine!" screams the older man. This is King Agamemnon, leader of all of the Greek forces besieging Troy. Agamemnon commands his own warriors from Mycenae in Greece. Warlords from other Greek towns accompany him, each commanding his own fighters, but all have agreed that Agamemnon is in charge of the expedition as a whole. In ten years of sweat and screams and slaughter, they have been unable to breach Troy's massive city walls. They remain encamped on the coast, occasionally sacking villages and smaller towns nearby, plundering them for food and weapons, clothing and cooking utensils. And women.

They have crossed the Aegean from Greece to the shores
of Troy in order to recover Helen, stolen from Agamemnon's
brother by the Trojan prince called Paris. But the quarrel
tonight is about another girl, Chryseis, captured in the sack
of a nearby coastal town. This girl happens to be the daughter
of a local priest of the god Apollo, but when her father sought
her return, Agamemnon dishonored him and spurned the
offered ransom, although it was immense. He drove the
priest away with insults and threats. Now Agamemnon has
become enraged at Achilles' insistence that he return
Chryseis. "She was given to me as my share of the plunder,"
Agamemnon continues. "When we sacked her town. They
chose her for me. She's mine," he repeats.

Although much younger than Agamemnon, Achilles
shows no deference to the king. He, too, is a king, and at his
back are his own fighters, the Myrmidons, men he led out from
his hometown of Phthia. "Can't you see that the men are dying?"
he shouts. "That's why I called this assembly." The implication to
Agamemnon remains unspoken: you are in charge, so you
should have called this assembly. Evidently, you don't care about
all these men, even though they are here to help you and your
cuckolded brother recover his errant wife. "Our warriors are
dying from a terrible plague, and you just heard the seer tell us
that Apollo sent this plague because you dishonored his priest.
The plague will stop when you return the girl."

The other warriors press forward, trying to hear and
craning to see. You hear them all murmuring their assent. Even
Agamemnon, tone-deaf and self-involved as he is, can hear it,
and he repeats, "She's my prize." Although still shouting, he
now sounds less kingly, more desperate. "I like her better than
my own wife," he adds, almost to himself. Then he hesitates.
He looks around at row upon row of angry faces. Some look

ill. Others look fit and murderous. "I am ready to give her back," he says finally. "If that is better. I also want my people to be safe." But his frustration boils over: "Find me some other prize. I shouldn't be the only one of us to go without a prize!" And then, "Look!" he screams, glaring at the firelit faces of the men. "You all see me robbed of my prize!" Turning back to Achilles, he seethes with fury as he repeats, "Find me another!" "Your greed knows no bounds, does it?" the younger man responds coolly. "How can we give you another prize? They have all been distributed. Wait until we sack Troy. There will be plenty of prizes then. You will be repaid many times over."

"Oh, I see how it is," Agamemnon sneers. "You keep your prize and you force me to give up mine. I will give the girl back, but either you all will find a new prize for me, a girl of my own choosing, or I will take someone else's—yours, maybe, or a girl given to Ajax or to Idomeneus or to Odysseus." Suddenly, Agamemnon seems to remember that he is, after all, king. "We will discuss this later," he says. "For now I will send Chryseis back to her father. Ajax or Odysseus can take charge of her, or Idomeneus, or even you yourself, Achilles. We will return her to her father and then make sacrifice to try to appease Apollo."

But by now Achilles has stopped listening. He is stuck on the absolutely outrageous remark Agamemnon tossed off in passing. Achilles' sudden anger makes him seem even taller and larger. His jaw clenches as he spits out his words. "You are threatening to take MY prize, you shameless, greed-obsessed dog?" he screams. "Do you think that anyone will obey you ever again? I didn't come here to sack Troy because I hate Trojans," he continues. "I have no hatred for them. I came here for you, you stupid dog-eyed sack of shamelessness." He hurls epithets without sense or logic. "I

came here to honor you and your brother. And now you are
threatening to take away my prize? Are you out of your mind?
I always do the lion's share of the fighting, and I get the
smallest share of the spoils. You know what? I'm going home.
I have no interest in staying here and being dishonored while
helping you increase your wealth."

"Fine. Run away," Agamemnon responds. He sounds
fierce and confident, but you suspect that he is bluffing.
"There are others to honor me. I hate you. You just like to
quarrel. Go home and be king of the Myrmidons. And while
I am sending my prize Chryseis back to her father, I am going
to your shelter to take for myself the beautiful Briseis, your
prize. I will show you who is in charge here! Let the next man
try to contend with me. I'll show you."

The next instant, you see Achilles reaching for the sword
at his side. His hand closes on the silver hilt, and he begins to
draw the gleaming blade from its sheath. Then, unaccountably,
he freezes. For a long second he stands motionless. You can see
why, but no one else can: the goddess Athena has suddenly
grabbed Achilles by the hair. She is talking to him. She is
telling him to wait, telling him to restrain himself. She is
advising him to withdraw from the fighting. If he does, the
Greeks will realize how badly they need him. He will
eventually win even greater prizes if he controls himself now
and doesn't kill Agamemnon. This all happens in an instant.
Only Achilles and you can see and hear it.

Then Achilles jams the sword back into its sheath. "You
empty wine sack with the eyes of a dog and the heart of a
deer!" he shouts, his face so close to Agamemnon's that the
older man takes a step back. "You are a coward. You take away
the prizes from any man who dares to speak up to you. You
are a king who eats up his own people. Well, I swear this to

you: someday soon you and all the warriors gathered here today will long for me. When man-slaying Hector cuts you down in vast numbers before the walls of Troy, you will be powerless without me. Then you will miss me. Then you will need me. Then you will regret that you did me no honor, that you did not honor the *aristos*, 'best,' man among you." Achilles continues, "Take the girl. I won't stop you. But just try to take one other thing of mine from beside my ship, and all here will see your blood flow around my spear point." And then, as if present among them, you see Achilles stride furiously away from the assembled men. You see the warriors' troubled faces in the firelight as they watch Achilles walk swiftly back along the beach, heading toward his shelter and his ships. His own men follow him, and you see the smug satisfaction on Agamemnon's face. And something else: fear.

A Story of Human Choices

"Rage," the *Iliad*'s very first word, launched the Western conversation about how we do and should conduct ourselves and treat one another. "Rage," Homer's narrator begins, "sing, goddess, the devastating rage of Achilles, son of Peleus, which made countless sufferings for the Greeks and sent many mighty souls forth to the Underworld, and made the men themselves prey for dogs and all birds" (*Il*. 1.1–5).[1] The story begins with the quarrel between Agamemnon and Achilles. By any humane modern calculation, these men are a disaster. Both treat women as property, and both prize above all else honor, military success, and the acquisition of more power and more material possessions than anyone else has. There is nothing remotely restrained, egalitarian, or farsighted about the values of these two powerful kings.[2] Their priorities are very primitive. There might once have been a real Agamemnon and a real Achilles. We do not know. We only know that stories about them and others like them began to be told more than 3,000 years ago.[3] Agamemnon and Achilles are both proud of destroying towns and capturing women and other property. They immediately become enraged if anyone slights their honor. Each claims to be *aristos*, "best," of the Greeks. But do we admire them? Can we admire them? That is the revolutionary question that Homer's tale asks. Thanks to Homer's narrative, we know a lot more than Agamemnon and Achilles do. The *Iliad* will show us the devastation their value system brings upon themselves and others.

Most remarkably, this epic tale of men and gods owes its existence to no particular man or god. Greek storytelling from its inception had no defined obligation to an autocratic political or religious authority. The *Iliad* originated in oral tales that were told and retold for centuries before they coalesced, sometime in the eighth century BCE, into a single monumental epic. This epic continued to evolve as oral poetry until it was written down in the sixth century BCE. The absence, for centuries, of a fixed, monumental text meant that the ancient Greeks kept shaping and reshaping their ideas about the way the world works and the role of human beings in it.[4]

Lacking a commitment to a particular political or religious authority, the *Iliad* as a whole does not express the will or requirements of a supernatural being. The narrator does begin by addressing a divinity, but this divinity has no role or agenda in human life or in the world of the *Iliad*'s characters other than as a source of poetic inspiration or poetic memory. In the opening line, "Sing, goddess, the devastating rage of Achilles, the son of Peleus" (1.1), the narrator asks the Muse for the poem's subject matter. The "goddess" is the Muse of epic poetry, and the Muses were the divinities responsible for artistic inspiration in general.

In the *Iliad*, the Muse appears to serve as the embodiment or personification of poetic inspiration or memory. Unlike a king or a god, the Muses demand no payment, obedience, or worship, and they offer no promise of reward in exchange.[5] Undeniably, other gods besides the Muses are everywhere in this story. But contrary to what we might expect, these ever-present gods do not, in fact, determine the substance of events. The *Iliad* emphasizes instead human choices and actions and the consequences of these choices and actions.[6] Focusing on *menis*, "rage," the epic's first word, the opening identifies the tale's central themes: anger and conflict, starting with the quarrel between Agamemnon and Achilles and all the suffering stemming from it. Most important, the narrator seeks the causes, asking, "Who, then, of the gods sent them together to do battle in strife?" (1.8). This interest in cause and effect is logical and rational, even scientific. The simple answer to the question is "Apollo," since the god sent the plague that prompted the quarrel between Achilles and Agamemnon. But as the story develops we can see that this answer is completely inadequate. Apollo's intervention does not come out of the blue. It turns out to be the consequence of a series of human decisions, and the consequences of Apollo's intervention also develop from human choices and actions. Apollo is just one link in the chain of causality.[7] Why did the quarrel start between Agamemnon and Achilles? Because Apollo sent a plague against the Greeks while they were besieging Troy. Why did Apollo send the plague? Because Agamemnon, as leader of the Greek forces, dishonored Apollo's priest when that priest asked the Greeks to return his daughter, captured in a raid. Why did Agamemnon refuse to return the girl? Because he felt like it. That was his choice.

Achilles becomes directly involved because he calls an assembly in order to try to discover why Apollo has sent the plague. That he, and not Agamemnon, calls the assembly shows that other leaders besides Agamemnon have the power to call an assembly. It shows, too, that Achilles cares about the suffering warriors and that Agamemnon has less concern for the distress of his people than he might. Agamemnon could have called this assembly, but he chose not to.[8]

As the assembly proceeds, we see that there is nothing egalitarian about the decision-making process and participants do not enjoy equal freedom of speech. Before the seer will explain why Apollo is angry, he must first ask Achilles for protection because he knows that he is going to make Agamemnon angry. And he does make Agamemnon very angry. Agamemnon is willing to give up the girl only if he gets some other girl in return. He likes the girl he has, but he considers that all female captives, like any captured property, have the same function: establishing his status among the other Greeks. And so he wants recompense if he is going to give up the girl.[9]

Achilles turns Agamemnon's general notion of recompense specific. There are no prizes left undistributed, he says. Wait until we sack Troy. Then there will be lots of stuff (1.122ff.). But Agamemnon refuses and insists that he will take someone else's prize. "Yours," he tells Achilles, "or Ajax's or Idomeneus's or Odysseus's" (1.137–138). At this point, Achilles chooses to make the problem his own by saying, in effect, "I came here to win honor for you and your brother Menelaus. I have no personal grievance against the Trojans. And now you are threatening to take *my* prize?!"

OK, Agamemnon decides. That's a good idea. I'll take *your* prize (1.181ff.). And the plot of the *Iliad* is off and running. The point is that the gods did not cause this quarrel; the choices of two hot-headed, status-obsessed human beings caused it.[10] We can also notice that although the poem begins in the tenth year of the war, the issue in this quarrel between Agamemnon and Achilles replicates the one that first began the war: one man's choice to steal another man's woman. Achilles himself will point out this connection later on (9.336–345). There is a tale behind the theft of Helen that makes the goddess Aphrodite the cause of the Trojan War. Aphrodite promised to give Helen to Paris if he judged her more beautiful than Hera or Athena.[11] This tale, called "the Judgment of Paris," shows that Paris made a choice. As the *Iliad* begins, Agamemnon's theft of Achilles' prize, in evoking Paris's prior theft of Helen, emphasizes that the relevant participants could easily have made better choices.

Now, it is also quite true that when Achilles is trying to decide whether to pull his sword and kill Agamemnon, the goddess Athena swoops down and grabs him by the hair to stop him (1.188ff.). She advises him to withdraw from the fighting and insists that he will win even greater prizes if he does (1.207ff.). We might interpret this as overt divine intervention, but no one can see Athena except Achilles (1.198). And us. So we might instead understand Athena as a personified explanation for the invisible reasoning process going on inside Achilles' head, a process of calculation that no mortal in the story, except Achilles, witnesses. Athena is, after all, goddess of wisdom, strategy, and skill.

Homeric scholars call this "multiple determination" or "double motivation."[12] That is, Achilles decides not to kill Agamemnon, *and* Athena pulls his hair to stop him. Throughout the *Iliad*, we can see the gods functioning as explanations for internal, invisible, psychological processes, as Athena does here, or as causes of otherwise inexplicable events that we might attribute to chance or luck. Why does a man suddenly take it into his head to do something? Because a god impels

him. Why does one arrow strike its mark and another go
astray? Because a god or goddess guided it toward the goal or
deflected it away. The narrative encourages the audience to
distinguish events that are not fully in human control from
human choices that are.[13]

Rage as a Political Problem

In emphasizing the role of human choices from the outset, the
Iliad begins by exposing the problem that rage poses for the
community. The confrontation between Agamemnon and
Achilles, their obsession with honor, their short fuses and willingness to indulge their own anger will have adverse effects for
the community that has chosen to honor them. Both Agamemnon and Achilles claim to be the "best" of the Greeks, and so
their quarrel immediately raises the political question Which
of these two kings actually deserves to be a leader of men?[14] This
question compels two others: Which qualities should the community decide to honor? What will be the consequences for
everyone else? When Achilles swears by the scepter, the symbol
of political authority conferred by cultural tradition (1.233ff.),
he calls himself the "best" of the Greeks (1.244). (The Greek
word is *aristos,* the root of the word *aristocracy,* or rule by "the
best.") Later, the elder statesman Nestor says that Agamemnon
boasts that he himself is the best by far of the Greeks (2.82).
Achilles had also said earlier that Agamemnon claims to be the
best (1.91).[15] Each of these two leaders considers himself the
"best," raising the question for the audience: What is "bestness"
in human achievement? What should a community want in a
powerful individual? This kind of question begins to make
broader political participation both possible and necessary. If
a ruler is understood to be a divinity or divinely ordained, the

question cannot be asked. It can only be asked in a society with various powerful individuals competing for supremacy.[16] The conflict between Agamemnon and Achilles pits the conventionally accepted authority figure, Agamemnon, against the exceptionally talented warrior, Achilles.[17] Agamemnon is in charge of the expedition as a whole, the collection of Greek forces besieging Troy. But Agamemnon is not a god or the son of a god. He is not the best warrior or military strategist. In fact, he is tactless, insensitive, self-serving, and shortsighted.[18] But everyone accepts his leadership. Except Achilles. Achilles leads his own forces, called the Myrmidons, and everyone agrees that he is the finest warrior who has ever fought before the walls of Troy.

Agamemnon and Achilles do not resort to violence against one another, but their anger and intransigence will have devastating consequences for their people. As it happens, these "leaders of men" care most for their own honor and glory.[19] The needs of the community factor only incidentally into their calculations. After refraining from killing Agamemnon, Achilles angrily calls Agamemnon "a king feeding on his own people" (1.231). He accuses Agamemnon of being shortsighted (1.337ff.), and subsequent events will confirm this; you might be tempted to sympathize with Achilles as a principled rebel standing up to an unjust king.[20] Achilles' anger does encourage us to recognize that conduct, not merely status, should determine honor.[21] But Achilles' decision to withdraw from the fighting spells death for countless numbers of Greek warriors, Achilles' allies in this war.

Agamemnon and Achilles both display the irresponsible selfishness that frequently characterizes people with extreme power. In most modern nondemocratic societies, and even in democratic ones, powerful rulers often show little concern for the welfare of the people over whom they rule. The *Iliad,* however, posed the question more than 3,000 years ago: What obligations does a powerful ruler or leader have to his people? This question begins to undermine the brutal, selfish use of power and to promote more thoughtful citizens and more responsible political leaders.

Such a challenge to tyrannical authority can arise only in a human community. It can have no meaning, for example, in the autocratic society of the gods. After the quarrel, as Achilles remains angrily beside his own ships, refusing to attend Greek assemblies or to participate in the war, the scene shifts to an assembly of the gods on Mt. Olympus. Homer invites the audience to consider the contrast between the conflict at Troy between the mortals Agamemnon and Achilles and conflict on Olympus between the gods Zeus and Hera.[22] While two powerful mortals in vying for supremacy make life worse for the human beings over whom they rule, conflict in the divine realm has no lasting adverse consequences for the gods. The society on Olympus is firmly autocratic, and Zeus has no obligation to the gods he rules over. Other gods may voice dissent, but they fear Zeus's anger and his absolute power. When Hera objects to Zeus's decisions, he simply silences her (1.565ff.). Once Zeus's autocratic power ends the quarrel, harmony and the enjoyment of bodily pleasures prevail on Olympus: the gods feast together happily (1.595ff.), and Zeus and Hera go to bed together (1.610–611). By contrast, the quarrel among mortals is not so easily resolved.[23]

By juxtaposing the contentious mortal leadership of Agamemnon and Achilles with the absolute authority of Zeus, the *Iliad* suggests that force can be necessary to preserve order. But at the same time, Zeus provides an inadequate model for mortal political leadership. His tyranny may constrain conflicts among immortals, but no mortal can hold equivalent power over other mortals.[24] Unlike human beings, Zeus is not subject to time and the vagaries of fortune, illness, aging, and death. Zeus maintains his authority by violence and intimidation, but durable human authority cannot depend on the brutality of a specific "strong man," whose power is limited by his lifespan. The analogy between the mortal quarrel and the divine one begins, perhaps, to undermine the audience's confidence in the long-term efficacy of a mortal ruler's violence and intimidation.

Western civilization thus begins with the problem of passion, specifically the problem of anger and the problems of lust (for sex, for power, for battle, for possessions) and ambition (for status, for public recognition). Anger, that most basic human emotion, causes grief, pain, and destruction. Homer knew, and we know it too, that anger makes us say and do things we never would in calmer moments. It produces outcomes we never would choose or want. It distorts our ability to consider our own or anyone else's real interests. The same goes for lust. In its grip, we often feel that we are not in our "right mind." Lust for sex, lust for power, lust for battle, and lust for material things produce conflict, war, suffering, and death. Ambition is more complicated. It gets us out of bed in the morning. It fuels ingenuity and achievement and human progress. And it, too, brings us into conflict with one another and makes us do foolish, destructive things.

We may not need Homer to tell us any of this, but the *Iliad* offers us a model, a sort of mock-up structure to help us think long and hard, and dispassionately, about some potent causes and consequences of anger, lust, and the double edge of ambition. As conscious and self-conscious beings, we often deny the extent to which anger and lust and naked ambition dictate our behavior, but even the most casual glance at contemporary domestic and international events confirms that this is so.

Critically, though, we have no particular vested interest in the individuals in Homer's story or the outcome of the events the poem describes. The *Iliad* presents the tale objectively, inviting us to view it from the perspective of both the Greeks and their adversaries the Trojans. We can see ourselves in these people. We can appreciate their strengths and their limitations. We can briefly set aside our own angers, lusts, and ambitions. We can temporarily sidestep our destructive energies and engage our constructive ones. "Give me a lever and a place to stand," Archimedes famously announced, "and I will move the world." Homer gave the ancient Greeks—and us, too—a place to stand.

The *Iliad* tells the story of a great war, "great" in the dual sense of "glorious" and "immense." The epic narrative gives the audience a different perspective on events than Homer's characters have. As the story proceeds, it will compel us to consider whether the benefits of warfare justify the costs, whether warfare evokes the best in us or embodies the worst in us, whether warfare reveals magnificent human achievements or constitutes a failure of the human intellect and imagination. By showing us the causes and consequences of anger, lust, and ambition, the *Iliad* also compels us to consider what qualities we require in a leader and what attributes we must cultivate in ourselves.[25]

For Agamemnon and Achilles, these questions do not arise. Both men exemplify, with complete confidence and certainty, the values of a hierarchical society, an aristocratic society, ruled by a small group of select individuals. Excellence in warfare is their idea of highest achievement. They value courage, strength, resolution, and above all success—but exclusively in the context of war. Talent and success in war indicate the gods' favor and win honor in the community. Agamemnon holds power because communal consensus has given it to him, and he holds the scepter, emblem of his political authority, to prove it. But this power over other leaders appears to have been pro-visional. It is only for this particular expedition. Why are the other warriors willing to accompany Agamemnon on his expe-dition to recover his brother's wife? According to tradition, the other leaders had sworn an oath to defend the rights and honor of Helen's husband and to fight to recover Helen from the Trojans.[26]

We can recognize this value system: family and friends first. Help your friends and harm your enemies. Be the best fighter you can be. Earn the honor and respect of others for your martial prowess. Most important, avenge wrongs done to yourself and others. Even now, in our own violent times, this remains the credo of many groups and subgroups the world over.[27] But in the *Iliad,* this definition of human achievement does not go unchallenged. Is martial valor the be-all and end-all of individual accomplishment? The full measure of a human life fully lived? What are the consequences of prioritizing honor and celebrating rage? Precisely which qualities and ex-ploits deserve honor?

Valuing military success above all, Homer's characters welcome the expedition against Troy as an opportunity to display their great fighting ability and win eternal honor. The epic tales themselves provide this glory and honor in the form of eternal remembrance. Desire for immortal glory makes both Greek and Trojan warriors welcome death in battle. "If we could live for-ever," one Trojan warrior famously tells another in the middle of the *Iliad,* "there'd be no point to risking our necks in the fighting. But given that we are going to die, it is better to die with glory than without it" (12.310–328). Those are, of course, the two options.[28] The fact of mortality motivates human achievement because epic tales permit mortals a kind of immortality by pre-serving for all time men's great exploits in warfare.

But in preserving tales of great human exploits, the *Iliad* also calls into question the characters' narrow definition of great achievement as success in warfare. The epic introduces prerequisites for the restraint of violent rage and for the development of broader political participation, ideas that eventually made even democratic government possible: the *Iliad* shows that human choices and actions powerfully affect what happens to human beings. Moreover, the dire consequences of competition between powerful men for honor and supremacy suggest that everyone else ought to think about what such powerful men should be honored for. The *Iliad* thus begins to suggest that no community can succeed by honoring exceptional individuals whose indulgence in rage and ruthless pursuit of honor causes them to neglect or imperil those who depend upon them.

The narrative perspective in the *Iliad* reveals a really remarkable awareness that there is not just one possible perspective on events, but that there are, in fact, many possible perspectives. Instead of glorifying the characters' susceptibility to rage, instead of validating their hierarchical, zero-sum values, their celebration of warfare, their lust for power, women, material possessions, and honor, the *Iliad* gives the audience a different perspective than the characters have. The characters' priorities begin to appear not entirely optimal. The ancient Greeks never fully managed to reject violent conflict resolution, even among themselves, but they did gradually begin to experiment with nonviolent alternatives, particularly within *poleis,* "citizen-communities." By introducing a critical distance between the experience of the characters and the perspective of the audience, the *Iliad* long ago began to devalue rage and to encourage the development of more constructive ideals. It might do so again.

2

Them and Us (*Iliad* 6)

The war intensifies between the Greeks and the Trojans. Spearheads clang against breastplates, and helmets thud to the ground as warriors fall. You hear the screams of men, horses, and mules. Dust rises everywhere, and everywhere the earth is stained with blood. A bronze spear point shatters a forehead, another pierces a man through the side. The Greeks seem about to force the Trojans to retreat back behind their walls.

But here comes Helenus, a son of the Trojan king, Priam, to talk to his brother Hector. Helenus is the best of the Trojans at interpreting omens from bird signs. He now reminds Hector that their people rely most on him and one other warrior because they are the two best Trojans in fighting ability and in intelligence. (You notice how fixated the characters all are on being "best.") Helenus advises Hector to rally the men and make sure they hold their battle positions, especially by the city gates. Helenus and the others will continue fighting, but Hector must return to the city and tell his mother Hecuba and the Trojan noblewomen to sacrifice to Athena. The women must beg the goddess for pity and protection from the onslaught of the terrifying Greek warrior Diomedes, whom no Trojan fighter can defeat. Helenus does not attribute these instructions to a bird sign or omen, but he specifically states that the women must make an offering of Hecuba's best and largest robe and twelve yearling heifers.

Without hesitation, Hector follows his brother's instructions. Leaping from his chariot, armor and all, he races among the Trojan fighters, urging them to keep fighting and to hold out against the Greeks while he returns inside Troy to tell the elders and the women to sacrifice to the gods.

It does not strike you as a very good plan, but it never occurs to Hector or to anyone else that the Trojans inside the city would surely have thought long ago to pray and sacrifice to the gods. Do they really need one of their two best fighters to leave the thick of battle and tell them to do it? Even if the message were necessary, why must Hector deliver it himself rather than sending a lesser warrior or even a servant? Surely Hector is more useful on the battlefield. Why does he not confront the Greek warrior Diomedes himself? The impracticality of this plot development alerts you to a surprising fact: you are about to see one of the two greatest enemy fighters not in action on the battlefield but at home within the walls of his own city.

Hector leaves the battlefield at a run, still wearing his gleaming bronze helmet and carrying his massive shield of bronze and cowhide. The shield's bottom edge clangs against his bronze shin guards, and its top edge strikes the bronze breastplate at his neck. It cannot be easy to run with such a huge shield.

As Hector races toward Troy, you do not follow. Remaining on the field of battle, you suddenly see the great Greek warrior Diomedes encounter the Trojan fighter Glaucus. You know that the Trojans fear Diomedes terribly.

You have seen him kill many men already, and you now expect
another scene of carnage. Surely Diomedes will slaughter
Glaucus as efficiently as he has killed so many other Trojans.
But, no, something very strange happens. As the two
powerful men move toward one another, instead of hurling his
spear, Diomedes asks Glaucus to identify himself. "Who are
you?" Diomedes shouts across the dusty, blood-streaked
distance that separates them. "Are you mortal or immortal?
Because if you are an immortal, I will not fight with you, but if
you are a man, come closer so that I can kill you more quickly."
No warrior in this story has ever said this to an opponent
before, so you know that something special is about to happen.

In response, Glaucus sounds surprisingly philosophical.
"Why do you ask my lineage?" he wants to know. "Men are like
leaves," he says. "The leaves grow, and then the wind blows
them to the ground. But then in springtime the tree grows
more leaves. It is the same with men: one generation flourishes
while another passes away." On the surface, this analogy seems
to make sense. Lots of leaves, lots of men. New ones coming
into existence all the time. What is one more or less? What
could one individual possibly matter since one warrior is just
like any other? But you notice that the analogy has reversed
the time sequence: the leaves die, then regrow; people flourish,
then die. So, instead of reassuring you that one more dead
warrior is no big deal, this analogy reminds you that unlike
the leaves which grow back just the same in spring, dead men
never do return. A leaf is like any leaf, but each man is not like
any other. Every human being is unique and irreplaceable. You
realize with surprise that you derived this profound insight by
thinking about the words of an enemy.

Glaucus seems to know that his analogy hints at the
unique worth of each individual because he immediately

proceeds to relate his own distinctive lineage. At length. He lists
exploits of celebrated ancestors, going back six generations.
When Glaucus finishes, Diomedes stabs his spear straight into
the ground and announces that his own grandfather was once
host to Glaucus's grandfather. These two grandfathers
exchanged guest-gifts. This means that their descendants
Diomedes and Glaucus are "guest-friends" too. Diomedes says
that there are plenty of other Trojans for him to kill and plenty
of other Greeks for Glaucus to slaughter, if he can. "Let's not try
to kill each other," Diomedes says. "But instead let's swap armor
so that everyone will know that you and I are guest-friends."

Leaping from their chariots, the two enemies shake
hands and bind themselves to one another by pledges of
mutual trust. Suddenly, the narrator intrudes, speculating
that Zeus must have taken away Glaucus's sense for the
moment, since he gave up gold armor for bronze, gold armor
being almost ten times as costly as bronze. But you might not
agree. Bronze is much stronger than gold. In battle, which is
really the more valuable metal? You might even begin to
consider what exactly makes something valuable. Is it just
what people say? Or are there objective standards of
usefulness? You might also reflect that instead of being cut
down by the unconquerable Diomedes, Glaucus walks away
with his life. Who really gets the better deal?

By now, Hector has reached the Scaean Gates, the main
gates of Troy. As he enters the city, the women run to ask how
their loved ones are faring in the battle. Hector tells them all
to pray, but the narrator reminds you that for many the
prayers will be futile.

Hector enters the immense dwelling of King Priam. It
has lovely covered walkways of smooth stone and fifty
connecting bedrooms also of polished stone, one for each of

Priam's fifty sons and their wives. Facing these, on the
opposite side of the inner courtyard, are another twelve
connecting bedrooms, one for each of Priam's twelve
daughters and their husbands. Priam's grand palace shows
you that the Trojans are refined and civilized. The
construction of such a magnificent structure required
immense technological skill and artistry. Priam and his sons
and sons-in-law value the institution of monogamous
marriage, just as the Greeks do. Each man lives with his own
wife, and the wives are all modest, honored, and respected.

Hector's mother Hecuba and her eldest, most beautiful
daughter come to greet him. Addressing her son tenderly,
Hector's mother wonders why he has left the battlefield. She
is sensitive and deeply empathetic. She understands that her
son must be exhausted from fighting. She does not pester
him with questions. She assumes that he has decided to pray
to Zeus from the highest point of Troy. She offers him wine
for making libations to Zeus and then for drinking so that he
can regain his strength.

Hector politely refuses. Respectfully, he explains that
drinking wine may weaken his fighting spirit. He also
considers it shameful to pray to Zeus while still covered with
battle gore. He repeats Helenus's instructions: his mother
must lead Troy's noblewomen to Athena's temple, dedicate
her most beautiful robe, and sacrifice twelve heifers. The
women must ask the goddess to pity the Trojans and protect
them from the onslaught of the terrifying Greek warrior
Diomedes, whom no Trojan fighter can defeat. (You recall
that you just saw Diomedes' terrifying, unstoppable onslaught
checked by conversation and the respect for the obligations of
guest-friendship.) Hector says that he will go find his brother
Paris to try to get him to listen to him. In fury and frustration,

Hector adds a wish for Paris's death, lamenting that Zeus made Paris grow up to become a source of woe to the Trojans.

Hecuba wordlessly obeys. She chooses to dedicate to Athena her most beautiful robe of extraordinary craftsmanship, a gift from her son Paris. The Trojan women assemble, and you accompany them to the temple at the top of the city, where they supplicate Athena with prayers. They offer the robe and the twelve heifers if, in exchange, Athena will shatter Diomedes' spear and let him fall dead before the Scaean Gates. But Athena refuses. The narrator tells you this. The women of course cannot know it yet.

Meanwhile, Hector goes in search of Paris. He finds the great lover contentedly holding (and no doubt admiring) his own exquisitely made breastplate, shield, and bow. The lovely Helen sits nearby supervising her maidservants at their work (weaving, presumably, the emblem of proper, industrious female activity). Helen herself is not working. You see that while the other Trojans are fighting and dying for the sake of this stolen woman and her handsome lover, he sits happily at home enjoying his shining armor and his beautiful, idle mistress.

Hector sees this, too. Speaking harshly, he rebukes Paris. He tells him that it is neither morally nor aesthetically "fair" for him to keep his wrath in his heart while all the other Trojans are fighting a war on his behalf and initiated by him. Trying to motivate Paris, Hector reminds him of the standards of their society. He says that he knows that Paris himself would fight any other Trojan who failed to participate in the bloody struggle to save the city. You realize that if Paris needs this reminder, he has not really internalized this all-for-one-and-one-for-all mentality.

Paris accepts the rebuke mildly and admits that Hector is right. He says that he has been depressed. At Helen's urging he was just about to rejoin the battle. He will accompany Hector back to the battlefield, if Hector will just wait for him to put on his armor.

But Hector does not respond, and now Helen addresses Hector tenderly. She obviously likes him. Filled with self-loathing, she wishes that she had never been born. She blames the gods for her situation and wishes that she were the wife of a better man than Paris. Recognizing that Hector is doing the lion's share of the fighting on their behalf, Helen invites him to come in and sit down and rest. She is highly critical of herself and of Paris, but she blames Zeus for her predicament. Most astonishingly, she almost seems to realize that she is herself a character in the story you are hearing. She insists that Zeus's purpose in giving Paris and herself this evil destiny is, in fact, to make them a subject of poetic song for people of the future.

Answering Helen gently, Hector is courteous and kind. But unlike his irresponsible brother, he is impervious to Helen's seductive charms. He acknowledges her care for him but smoothly rejects her offer, insisting that he must return to battle as the Trojans need him. He urges Helen to get Paris moving. Maybe he will be able to catch up with Hector while he is still in the city.

Hector now goes to find his wife and child, knowing that this may be his last chance to see them. His wife Andromache is not at home, nor is she with her sisters and sisters-in-law at the Temple of Athena. Terribly distraught, she has taken her little boy to the city wall, having heard that the Trojans were hard pressed.

Hector races back through the streets of Troy to the Scaean Gates, where his wife, richly dowered Andromache, runs to him. A nurse follows carrying Hector's little boy. He is called Astyanax, meaning "ruler of the citadel," but his father calls him Scamandrius, a nickname based not on politics but on geography, meaning perhaps "little one living beside the Scamander River." Hector smiles at his little son but says nothing. Andromache, standing near, weeps copiously.

Grasping her husband's hand and addressing him by name, Andromache insists that Hector's fighting strength will destroy him. She accuses him of having no pity for his child or herself, soon to be widowed. The Achaians will soon kill him, and then she would rather be dead, since without Hector she will have nothing. Achilles killed her father and her seven brothers. Achilles also captured her mother and released her for a ransom, but she died later in the halls of her own father. For Andromache, Hector is everything: father, mother, kinsman, and husband. She begs him to pity her and remain on the wall so as not to leave her a widow and his child an orphan. She urges him to draw up the Trojans to defend the wall at its weakest point.

Hector refuses this request, just as he refused the requests of his mother and Helen. He is polite and kind but resolute. He has been pondering these matters, too, and he shares Andromache's concerns. But, he says, he would be terribly ashamed for the Trojans to see him evading the war like a coward. And his own heart will not let him, ever since he learned to be brave and to fight always among the leading Trojan men, striving to achieve great public recognition and immortal glory for himself and for his father.

Hector explains this without optimism. He knows Troy will fall and King Priam and his people will be destroyed. Hector imagines the scenario vividly. "But," he continues, "the thought of the death of my father, or my mother, or my many courageous brothers does not cause me as much grief as the pain I feel imagining you being led away by some bronze-clad Greek, as you weep bitterly, and he deprives you of your freedom." Hector describes Andromache's bleak future as a slave woman in Greece, compelled against her will to weave at the loom of another woman and to lug buckets of water from Greek springs.

Hector is a vivid storyteller. He says that on seeing Andromache enslaved and in tears, some imaginary Greek will say, "This is the wife of Hector, the preeminent Trojan fighter, who did battle defending Troy." Hector's fantasy of Andromache's life after his death seems self-indulgent to you. It is no kindness to Andromache to describe to her this vision of her grim future. And this last comment certainly suggests that Hector is thinking of himself, not her. Undoubtedly, it reassures him to imagine that his name and reputation will outlast him.

But what about Andromache? "You will feel worse, hearing this," he assures her, "being the widow of a man so capable of defending you from slavery." You begin to see the terrible irony: if Hector is so capable of preventing Andromache's enslavement, why, then, in this imagined future, is she a slave? Missing the irony completely, Hector continues, "But may I die and the earth cover me before I learn of your outcry and of your being dragged away into captivity." You find Hector's wish completely illogical: he wishes to die before he learns of her enslavement but, of course, the only way that Andromache will become a slave is if Hector dies first.

Hector reaches for his child, but the little boy cries and clings to his nurse. His father's bronze armor and horsehair helmet crest frighten him. His alarm makes his father and mother laugh. Removing the helmet and setting it, all gleaming, on the earth, Hector kisses his dear son and swings him in his hands. He asks the gods to give his son the same prominence among the Trojans as he himself has. May they give his son as much strength as his father and let him rule over Troy by force. One day, Hector says, "Let someone say, as he returns from battle, 'This man is much better than his father.'" Hector prays that the gods will allow his son to kill his enemies and his mother to rejoice.

His prayer finished, Hector returns the baby to his mother's arms. Andromache is both laughing and weeping, and Hector speaks pityingly to her. "Why do you grieve excessively?" he asks. "No one will kill me if it is not according to Fate. No one can escape his fate, not the coward or the brave man. Go into the house now and attend to your own work, your weaving. And order your maidservants to do their work. Warfare is the concern of all the men of Troy, but of me especially," he concludes, as he picks up his helmet.

Andromache, silent, tears falling, heads toward home. She keeps turning around to look back at her husband. Hector never turns to look back at her.

Humanizing the Enemy and Evoking Moral Judgment

In showing the great enemy warrior Hector inside Troy and interacting with his loved ones, the *Iliad* begins to promote the capacity of its audience, as individuals, to acknowledge and respect the essential humanity of every other individual. The *Iliad* is a Greek tale, but it is not a one-sided, self-congratulatory account of the Greeks' conquest of Troy. Far from merely celebrating a great Greek victory, the *Iliad* begins to cultivate the audience's awareness of multiple perspectives on events. Surprisingly, the narrative shows many battle scenes from the Trojans' point of view and also poignant, intimate scenes among Trojans as well as Greeks. The audience gets a glimpse of the

war from the Trojans' perspective, and the surprisingly humanizing depiction of Hector within his city emphasizes the special
value of this enemy warrior to those nearest and dearest to him.
By detailing Hector's relationships with his family, the narrative
makes him seem familiar and fully comprehensible. The audience can see that Trojans are just like everyone else: each of us
is unique and uniquely valuable to our own people.

The *Iliad* offers this variety of perspectives on events, but it
does not suggest that all perspectives are equally correct. Rather,
the recognition of multiple perspectives makes moral judgment
possible, and the narrative from the outset invites all members
of the audience to exercise theirs. Before seeing Hector inside
Troy, we come to appreciate that the Trojans have already violated two moral standards that are of central importance to
Homer's Greek characters. The Greek warriors care deeply about
the responsibilities incurred by oaths. They also respect a complex
system of reciprocal obligations between guests and hosts known
as *xenia,* "guest-friendship." For the Greeks, these moral obligations are not merely arbitrary conventions. They are absolute
necessities, since Zeus, the great ruler of the cosmos, guarantees
both oaths and "guest-friendship." Zeus punishes anyone who
violates an oath or transgresses against the obligations of guest-
friendship.[1] In fact, the claim that Zeus is the guarantor of oaths
and guest-friendship may simply be a way of saying that violations
of these moral standards have predictably adverse consequences.

The Greeks' siege of Troy itself derives, implicitly, from a
Greek decision to respect an oath and a Trojan decision to violate the rules of guest-friendship. Asserting that Agamemnon's
kingly authority derives directly from Zeus, the narrative alludes
to a tale, well known but surviving today only in sources later
than Homer, that many Greek warlords swore an oath to help
recover Helen. Zeus therefore constitutes the source of

Agamemnon's authority because he guarantees oaths. The siege of Troy exemplifies the Greeks' willingness to honor their oath.[2] By contrast, the Trojans are under siege because the Trojan prince Paris opted to violate his obligations under *xenia*, "guest-friendship," by stealing Helen, the wife of his Greek host. A guest definitely violates his obligation to his host if he runs off with the host's wife. As the catalyst for the massive, lengthy, and devastating Trojan War, Paris's theft of Helen emphasizes that a violation of *xenia* has predictably adverse consequences.

Paris's egregious failure to respect the obligations of guest-friendship causes the war, and the Trojans' subsequent failure to honor an oath prolongs it. Following the quarrel between Achilles and Agamemnon, the Greeks and Trojans agree to a truce and a one-on-one fight between Helen's Greek husband Menelaus and her Trojan lover Paris in order to determine who will keep Helen (*Iliad* 3). Both sides swear to abide by the result. But when this fight proves inconclusive, the Trojans are the first to violate their oath and break the truce. This puts them morally in the wrong. Again. Just as Paris's theft of Helen put the Trojans morally in the wrong in the first place.[3]

Conversely, the narrative also offers a positive moral example of the benefits of choosing to respect the obligations of guest-friendship. A remarkable tale of an encounter between two opposing warriors bisects the narrative account of Hector's return to Troy. This vignette delays the portrait of Hector inside his city and perhaps increases the audience's anticipation for it. When the Greek Diomedes and the Trojan Glaucus meet in battle and realize that their grandfathers were guest-friends, they exchange armor and do not fight one another.[4] This episode emphasizes that a decision to respect obligations under the guest-host relationship has the power even to unite two enemies.

Intervening in the narrative as Hector races toward his city, the exchange between Diomedes and Glaucus reminds the audience that the decision to honor one's obligations requires conversation, judgment, and choice. In the nondemocratic world of Homer's characters, identity and allegiances are inherited. Both men understand the question "Who are you?" to mean "What is your lineage? Who were your father, grandfather, and great-grandfather?"[5] These biological relationships entail specific responsibilities. But the encounter reveals that individuals must decide to respect inherited obligations and choose to uphold them. Inherited identity does not determine the guest-friend relationship; it just makes the relationship possible. By talking, Diomedes and Glaucus discover that their ancestors were guest-friends and therefore they must be too. But they both must agree to respect their obligations under this system. While Homer's characters accept the notion that inherited identity determines obligations, Homer's audience can appreciate that such acceptance is a choice.

And there it is, suddenly visible to the audience in this brief vignette amid the chaos and carnage of a catastrophic conflict, the alternative to raging bloodlust: conversation, rational thought, and the decision to honor a moral obligation. For Homer and his original audiences, inherited status predetermined human relationships. But the interaction between Diomedes and Glaucus allows the audience to glimpse a model of moral decision making that would, centuries later, prove crucial to democratic politics: opponents exchange information; they respect one another; they make wise choices.

Successful human relationships and broad political participation require not only an appreciation for the value of discussion and rational choice but also an ability to value the lives and experiences of others. Homer's portrait of this battlefield encounter between two fierce enemies encourages the recognition that every individual human life (even an opponent's) has unique worth. The meeting begins with the beautiful analogy between generations of leaves and generations of men.[6] Because the speaker reverses the terms of the analogy (leaves die and then new ones grow; men flourish and then die), the analogy emphasizes not the similarity between leaves and men but the crucial difference: leaves are essentially indistinguishable from one another, whereas men are not. New leaves in spring replicate the ones lost in fall. New human beings do not replicate dead ones. No one leaf has unique value to anyone. No leaf grieves at the loss of another. But this is not the case with men. Each human being is distinctive and irreplaceable.[7] Although the *Iliad* was composed by a Greek (or Greeks) and for a Greek audience, the catalyst for this profound insight is not a Greek warrior but a Trojan one. It turns out that encounters with the perspective of others, even enemies, can be illuminating.

By the time the audience sees the Greeks' enemy Hector inside his city, we can already appreciate that moral standards involve judgment and choice. We recognize that choices have consequences, and we have been reminded that human individuals are not indistinguishable from one another in the way that leaves are. Because Hector seems fully human and even familiar, we may find ourselves assessing him and evaluating his choices. He has followed his brother's instructions without question, apparently trusting his brother's ability to deduce reliable omens from bird signs (6.75). Hector simply assumes that his brother's advice has a divine source and therefore must be sound, but he never asks his brother to confirm this assumption. We might criticize Hector's unquestioning credulity, especially since the effort to appease Athena fails, as we learn

in advance, although the Trojans follow Helenus's instructions
to the letter. As one of the two best Trojans not only in fighting
but also in deliberation (6.79), should Hector have made certain
that Helenus had grounds for his advice? Perhaps this exposes
a Trojan weakness—if one of their best thinkers accepts his
brother's instructions without question. But we also must admit
that anyone might easily make such an assumption in the heat
of battle. And Hector's immediate willingness to follow his
brother's advice suggests that he takes his own responsibilities
very seriously. He is eager to do whatever is necessary to preserve
his people.

The Warrior and His Community

Despite the possible criticism of Hector's judgment (and, by
implication, the judgment of all Trojan warriors, since Hector's
judgment is supposedly the best), Homer's portrait of Hector
evokes admiration more than condemnation. Leaving the
battle, Troy's greatest defender (6.77–80) runs with his enor-
mous shield. Its metal rim bangs against the armor at his neck
and ankles as he runs. It is, obviously, much easier to run without a shield, but Hector does not drop his shield and run as a
coward or a defeated warrior would. (Shields could double as
stretchers for wounded or dead men, and Spartan mothers
famously sent their sons off to battle with the injunction, "Come
back with your shield or on it," that is, don't leave it on the
battlefield and run like a coward.)⁸ Homer emphasizes that
Troy's best fighter is not fleeing. He is going to give the message.

But the contrived nature of the situation alerts us to the
storyteller's technique. Instead of encouraging us to suspend
disbelief, Homer engages our critical judgment at every turn.
The Trojans within the walls should not need this message, and

Hector should certainly not be the one to deliver it. The audience recognizes this as a plot device offering a view of this great warrior within his city, interacting with his mother, brother, sister-in-law, wife, and son. Similarly, Helen's prescient understanding that she and Paris will be the subject of future epic tales (6.357–358) reminds us of the dual function of these stories.[9] For the characters, they provide a kind of immortality. For the audience, they provide an education.

Above all, the depiction of the enemy warrior interacting with his family suggests, surprisingly perhaps, that Trojans are just like Greeks. The repeated instructions to pray to Athena and the numerous references to Zeus all indicate that these enemy Trojans pray to the same gods as the Greeks do.[10] Homer characterizes Hector as polite, refined, and compassionate. He is as concerned for his relatives as they are for him. His mother cares for him just as any Greek mother cares for her son. Hector criticizes his brother for not defending Troy (6.329–330), just as any Greek might criticize his brother for not fighting to defend his homeland. Hector is tender with his wife and son (6.440ff.). They depend on him as every Greek family depends on its males. Hector and Andromache laugh at their son's fear of his father's helmet crest (6.471) as Greek parents might laugh. Hector's nickname for his son provides yet another subtle, humanizing detail. Calling him Scamandrius or "little one living beside the Scamander River" rather than Astyanax, "lord of the citadel," Hector shows a father's natural appreciation for his son as the little boy he is now, not as the ruler of the city he might one day become.

Hector's relatives also seem human and real. When his mother Hecuba comes to greet him, the narrator calls her "kindly giving" (or "bountiful"), and we see that she is generous and undemanding. She understands that Hector is tired from the fighting. She offers him rest and wine to restore his strength. She is surprised that he has left the battlefield, but she obeys his instructions without comment. Hecuba's kind, humane nature will not survive this terrible war. By the end of the *Iliad,* immense suffering will distort the essential character of this sensitive, empathetic, and generous woman. Shockingly, toward the end of Homer's epic, she will utter the monstrous wish that she could eat her enemy's liver raw (24.212–214). Hundreds of years later, Euripides revisited Hecuba's story in his tragedy the *Hecuba.* In that play, as we will see in chapter 6, Euripides shows that terrible suffering can cause even a generous, kindly person to succumb to rage, become monstrous, and lose her humanity. Euripides' *Hecuba* emphasizes that people in power and especially victors in war have the obligation to treat those in their power humanely. For Homer, however, Hecuba's story simply epitomizes the complete instability of fortune. Once a prosperous queen and mother of fifty valiant sons, Hecuba will become a childless widow, enslaved to a Greek master. Exemplifying the precariousness of good fortune, Homer's Hecuba reminds us that success and power may be transitory. Centuries before Euripides' reinterpretation of Hecuba's story, Homer's original audiences already might deduce from Hecuba's example that self-restraint and compassion in times of victory and success could be a good idea.

In addition to humanizing the enemy and perhaps promoting self-restraint and compassion, these scenes of life within the walls of Troy delineate the spheres of men and women: warfare and politics for men; domestic activities, weaving, and child-rearing for women. Andromache's concern for her husband's safety makes her leave her home and go to the ramparts of the city. The meeting between husband and wife takes place at the city wall, the border between the domestic realm and the battlefield.[11] Blood-stained and wearing his fear-some armor and helmet, Hector seems incongruous within the city walls, and his little son's fear of his father's terrifying appearance (6.466–470) underscores the inherent opposition between Hector's role as loving father and his role as murderous fighter.[12]

Hector is polite, and he seems to care for his wife and son, but his concern is not really about them, because he thinks of them as markers of his own status. His detailed description of Andromache's future life as a slave (6.450ff.) cannot possibly reassure her. From the perspective of the twenty-first century, we might find that Hector lacks a modern, egalitarian sensibility. We may criticize his acceptance of separate roles for women and men. We can condemn his view of women and children as possessions or status symbols rather than as individuals in their own right with valid feelings and concerns of their own. But Homer's original archaic Greek audiences (and even some twenty-first-century readers) could see that Hector's marital relationship is not, perhaps, so very different from their own.[13]

In considering his wife and son as status markers, Hector shares the traditional, hierarchical priorities of Homer's characters (and, undoubtedly, Homer's original audiences). Just like Greek warriors, Hector defines supreme achievement as success in battle. Articulating this ancient, limited definition of success, he wishes that his son may become a greater warrior even than his father, succeeding in battle and bringing joy to his mother as a result (6.476–481). This narrow conception of achievement encapsulates Hector's role in Troy.[14] But Hector's martial valor will bring his own mother only grief.

Hector, of course, fails to perceive the paradox. His sense of honor and his sense of obligation require him to put himself at the forefront of the fighting. He must risk his life to defend his family and his people. But if he dies in defense of his city, and he suspects that he will, he will deprive his family of their defender. His death means their destruction.[15] His obligations to himself, his family, and his city do not quite align. He can earn immortal glory by fighting to defend both family and city, but he cannot die gloriously on behalf of his city (a warrior's noblest form of death in the opinion of Homer's characters) and still survive to defend his family.

As a result, although Hector utters traditional sentiments, his own predicament begins to undermine the audience's traditional certainties. The tale of Troy predates our *Iliad*, and even Homer's original audiences undoubtedly knew its outlines. Dramatic suspense comes not from the "what" but the "how" of events. The *Iliad* deftly foreshadows Hector's destruction and the fall of his city. Hector knows Troy will fall (6.447–463), and we see his helmet in the dirt (6.473). Hector places it there himself, and this emphasizes his own complicity in the matter. Hector's awareness of the likelihood of his own death in battle (6.365–368) underscores the limitations of his value system. He knows that his own sense of honor and responsibility will very likely kill him and destroy his family. And he can do nothing to prevent this. His military excellence, his definition of success, and his loyalty to his family and city will inevitably destroy him, his family, and his city.[16]

Hector's military talents and objectives will not save him or his community, but Homer also meticulously details Hector's many other admirable qualities. His brother Helenus reminds him that he is one of the two Trojans who are best in deliberation as well as in fighting ability (6.79). Hector's withdrawal from battle and his return to Troy show that he is a loving, responsible son, brother, friend, husband, and father. Homer's descriptions of Hector's relationships illustrate with great sensitivity and poignancy how very much his kindness and sense of responsibility matter to others.

Despite displaying an impressive kindness and sense of responsibility, however, even Hector himself reduces high achievement to excellence in warfare. In his prayer for his son, Hector does not ask the gods to make the little boy grow up to be kind, compassionate, and responsible. He prays that the gods grant him the same prominence and strength as his father has among the Trojans. He prays that the gods allow him to rule over Troy by force and be an even better warrior than his father. He prays that the gods grant that the little boy grow up to kill his enemies and make his mother rejoice. Defining success in these terms, Hector articulates the value system that he and his people share with their Greek adversaries.

Even an audience sharing Hector's value system will be oddly troubled by his story. Hector's example illustrates the tragic consequences of defining highest achievement as valor in battle. This value system guarantees a mutually destructive relationship between the high achiever and his community. Prioritizing the talent for warfare, Hector cannot see the problem, but the audience must. Hector's obligation to fight and die in defense of his people paradoxically ensures both their destruction and his own. Hector imagines the grief of his wife Andromache as "the widow of a man so capable of defending you from slavery" (6.463), and he claims that he would rather die than see her dragged off into slavery (6.464–465). But of course his death is a necessary prerequisite to her being dragged off into slavery. Later Hector will encourage his companions by insisting that there is no loss of honor if a man dies in defense of his homeland, since he will save his country, his wife, his children, and his property if the Greeks go away in their ships to their own homeland (15.494–499). But this is not logical. There may be no dishonor in dying in defense of one's homeland, but it is not going to make the Greeks *more* likely to sail away home. In the end, as Homer's original audience always knew (and I have ruined the suspense for you, so you know, too), Hector does die and Troy does fall. The audience can see that Hector's definition of success does not serve him or anyone else very well.

Human communities can derive greatest benefit from, but are also most vulnerable to, their most talented and exceptional members. The quarrel between Achilles and Agamemnon exposes the need, therefore, for everyone to think very carefully in deciding which human talents and achievements deserve the greatest honor. Which goals should we strive for? Which abilities should we prize in our leaders and cultivate in ourselves? Hector's predicament illustrates the consequences of choosing poorly: his community has chosen to confer the highest honor on a set of qualities that will destroy both him and themselves. Homer's original audiences always knew, and we will soon see, that Hector, most capable and honorable as he is, will scrupulously accomplish this "achievement."

Homer's earliest archaic Greek audiences might have been surprised to see enemies depicted as equally civilized and refined as they. Twenty-first-century readers may be similarly unaccustomed to seeing their own enemies as fully human, beloved by their mothers, brothers, wives, and children. The *Iliad* introduces the idea that even dire enemies may be just like us, with thoughts and feelings and concerns not unlike ours.[17]

But the *Iliad*'s portrait of the shared humanity of participants on both sides of the Trojan War does not equate all choices and actions. Appreciation for the essential humanity of all participants constitutes, rather, the necessary prerequisite to good moral decision making. Hector and his people share the ideals of the Greek characters and undoubtedly of Homer's original audiences and of many potential audiences still. But Homer's audience understands that the Trojans are under siege because Hector's brother Paris violated his responsibilities as a guest. And we see Hector inside his city only after we have seen that the Trojans have violated an oath. We (any audience, ancient or modern) may, therefore, begin by judging Hector as a Trojan, a foreigner, not one of "us." But we must conclude by judging ourselves. Anyone who shares Hector's priorities must find his story disturbing. Hector's tale illustrates the consequences of opting to honor talents that will ultimately prove self-destructive. The *Iliad* confronts its audience (any audience, not merely a modern one with egalitarian, humanistic sensibilities) with the responsibility to reassess the conviction that the capacity for violence deserves the highest honors that the community can confer. As we will see in chapters 5 and 6, ancient Greek tragic playwrights later took that ball and ran with it.

3

Cultivating Rational Thought (*Iliad* 9)

The battle turns, and the Trojans begin to prevail. But as darkness falls, Hector realizes they cannot press their advantage. Ordering an assembly, he advises the Trojans to cease their attack and prepare a meal. But they must also keep watch to prevent the Greeks from sailing away unscathed. Hector wants to injure the Greeks so much that they will fear to attack the Trojans ever again.

You find yourself back in the Greek encampment on this same night. The mood is grim, as every man feels panic and chilling dread. Lacking Achilles' help, the Greeks have had little success, and many brave men have perished. The Trojans have driven them back against their own deep fortification ditch. The heart in each man's chest feels torn up, as when blasts of the north and west winds, coming suddenly from the wild regions of Thrace, stir up the sea, and the black wave towers up and strews much seaweed from the salt surf.

You know that Zeus has resolved to help Achilles by aiding the Trojans. Two goddesses, Hera and Athena, tried to intervene to protect the Greeks, but Zeus threatened them and commanded them to stop. Zeus's power is absolute; the two goddesses can only sit apart and mutter their opposition to Zeus's plan. Zeus proclaimed that more Greeks will die at Hector's hands tomorrow. This will continue until Achilles rejoins the battle, and that will happen only when the Greeks are pressed back against their ships, fighting over the corpse of Achilles' best friend, Patroclus.

As the Trojan watch fires burn brightly all too nearby, Agamemnon has called the disheartened Greeks to assembly. Tearful and self-pitying, Agamemnon abruptly announces, "Zeus won't let me win. We should just go home."

The great Diomedes immediately protests. "I will do battle with you first, since you are thinking foolishly," he tells his king, "since it is *themis*, 'traditional, appropriate, right,' in an assembly for one man to oppose another who is thinking foolishly." This young warrior's bold opposition to the king surprises you. Challenging the king can be dangerous: in a previous assembly, you watched a lowborn warrior get struck down and humiliated for criticizing Agamemnon (2.243–277). But apparently a verbal challenge to the king of kings by another preeminent warrior remains within customary bounds.

Agamemnon's defeatism infuriates Diomedes. Opting to give up the siege, Agamemnon has offended Diomedes by suggesting that the Greek warriors lack fighting spirit and defensive valor. No, Diomedes retorts, Agamemnon himself is deficient. Zeus gave him the scepter and made him honored above other men but failed to give him defensive valor, the greatest power. "If you are so eager to go home, why don't you just go?" Diomedes demands. "There is the way for you. Your ships stand near the sea. But we will stay until Troy falls. Even if everyone else flees homeward, I and my friend Sthenelus will remain and fight until we sack Troy."

Diomedes' audacity astounds you, but the other Greeks shout approval. The aged Nestor praises Diomedes for strength in war and skill in deliberation, calling him "best in council among all men his own age." No Greek will find fault with Diomedes or speak against him, says Nestor. "But," he continues, "you should listen to me, Diomedes, because I am old enough to be your father. Friendless, lawless, homeless is that man who loves horrible civil strife."

Turning to Agamemnon, Nestor reminds him that he is "most kingly." He should distribute the feast to the elders, providing wine and welcome as is fitting, since he rules over all. "Of many men gathered together," Nestor reminds King Agamemnon, "obey whichever one advises the best plan." You recognize this as sensible advice for a king to follow. You realize that it is also, in general, a very good idea.

Nestor again points out the obvious: the Greeks are currently in dire need of a good plan, since their enemies are burning many watch fires near their ships. Nestor's intervention defuses the confrontation between Diomedes and Agamemnon. Taking his advice, the Greeks set guards between the ditch and defensive wall and prepare dinner.

Inside Agamemnon's shelter, the elders have finished eating, and Nestor tactfully resumes. He calls Agamemnon "most honored by the gods" and "lord of men, since you are lord over many peoples." He reminds Agamemnon that his authority comes from Zeus, explaining, "Zeus has put into your hands the scepter and the judgments of tradition, so that you can make deliberations with them." Nestor's statement echoes, almost word for word, a statement you remember Odysseus making previously. Soon after the quarrel between Achilles and Agamemnon, Agamemnon inadvertently provoked the Greeks to abandon the siege of Troy. As they fled toward their beached ships, Odysseus intervened. Beating the

men back into assembly, he reminded them that there must
be just one king "to whom Zeus has given the scepter and the
judgments of tradition, so that he can make deliberations
with them" (cf. 2.206 and 9.99).

Making the claim then, Odysseus sought to recall
Agamemnon's subordinates to their responsibilities. But in
repeating the claim now, Nestor is recalling Agamemnon to
his. Nestor's statement makes you realize that this ideal that
there should be just one king is reciprocal. It entails
obligations not only for the men, but for the king, too. Nestor
tells Agamemnon, "It is necessary for you to speak or to listen
and to make sure that another man can speak and be heard,
whenever the heart urges someone to speak for the good. But
whatever you command will depend on you." Agamemnon
might choose to interpret this simply as flattery, but you
recognize that Nestor is reminding him of his responsibilities.

Neither modest nor self-effacing, Nestor maintains that
no one's opinion is better than his own. He criticizes
Agamemnon for ignoring his earlier advice not to take Achilles'
prize girl Briseis against Achilles' will and against the advice of
everyone else as well. "Yielding to your own great-hearted
passion, you dishonored the best man, one whom even the
immortal gods honor," Nestor admonishes. "But what's done is
done," he continues. "How can we remedy this situation even
now? Let us consider how, by appeasing Achilles, we may
persuade him with pleasant gifts and gentle words."

Agamemnon takes the rebuke surprisingly well. He accepts
Nestor's assessment of his own foolish behavior, sort of. "Aged
elder," he admits, "you did not say anything false in speaking of
my *atē*, 'divinely sent ruinous folly.'" But you reflect that Nestor
never accused Agamemnon of *atē*, a word signifying a disastrous
foolish action with a supernatural cause. He accused him of

"yielding to his own great-hearted passion." Agamemnon seems not quite willing to admit responsibility for his own stupid decision. "I was deluded. I myself don't deny it," he says, evidently preferring to see his colossal error as something that happened to him rather than something he chose to do.

By now Agamemnon has recognized that Achilles is worth more than many men to the Greek army. "Since I was deluded, persuaded by miserable thoughts," he says, "I will make amends and give boundless gifts." He lists an astounding number of magnificent things: tripods, gold, cauldrons, race horses, seven women, plus Briseis herself, whom Agamemnon will return, swearing that he never slept with her. Agamemnon promises to give Achilles all this at once. Later, after Troy falls, he will allow Achilles to carry off as much gold and bronze as his ship can hold. He will let Achilles select twenty of the loveliest Trojan women. If they return safely to Greece, Achilles can marry whichever of Agamemnon's daughters he prefers and be his son-in-law. Agamemnon adds further "reconciliation gifts," promising to honor Achilles as much as his own son. He will give more than any man ever gave for his daughter: he will give Achilles seven rich citadels to rule with his scepter, including all their people, livestock, and lands.

Agamemnon promises all this, if Achilles will cease from his anger and "be subdued." "Hades, God of the Dead, is relentless and not to be prevailed over," Agamemnon proclaims. "Therefore, he of all the gods is most hateful to mortal men." Having implied that Achilles' refusal to give up his anger makes him as hated as death itself, Agamemnon concludes by insisting that Achilles must submit to him because he is far more kingly and also can boast that he is much older.

The elders consider Agamemnon's offer worth taking to Achilles and agree to send a delegation consisting of Phoenix,

Ajax, and Odysseus, accompanied by two heralds. You notice, though, that among all of the sumptuous gifts, Agamemnon has included no apology.

Agamemnon's emissaries find Achilles inside his shelter singing epic tales and accompanying himself on a lyre. (You have never seen another of Homer's warriors singing, and you never will again.) You know Achilles as wrathful, quick tempered, and acutely sensitive to slights to his honor, but now, having opted out of the fighting, he sits in his shelter and sings. He must be singing very old stories that predate the *Iliad.* Or is he composing new songs to celebrate and immortalize his own achievements? You find this sad. Who will sing of Achilles' exploits if his continued absence from battle brings destruction on his own people?

Achilles hosts Agamemnon's ambassadors generously, bidding his dear companion Patroclus to prepare food and drink. He never asks why they have come. He must know. After everyone has eaten his fill, Odysseus begins speaking. Wishing his host well, he insists that Achilles is not inferior in the "equally divided feast," either in Agamemnon's shelter or here now. You feel the tension. Is Odysseus trying to reassure Achilles of his status? Describing the Greeks' predicament, Odysseus urges Achilles to rejoin the fight, warning that he will regret it if he fails to preserve the now-exhausted Greeks.

Odysseus reminds Achilles that his father, in sending him off to Troy, advised him to control his anger and avoid quarrels. If he did, his father said, he would win more honor from the Greeks. You wonder if this is true (and if so, how Odysseus could possibly know it), but you recognize it as the sort of thing an anxious father of a hot-headed son might say. You see that Odysseus is a resourceful and persuasive speaker.

Telling Achilles to stop being so terribly angry now, Odysseus meticulously lists Agamemnon's offer: tripods, gold, cauldrons, race horses, the seven women, and Briseis, plus Agamemnon's promise to swear that he never slept with her, and his promise to grant Achilles, after they sack Troy, all the gold and bronze his ship can hold and the twenty loveliest Trojan women. Odysseus includes Agamemnon's offer to make Achilles his son-in-law when they return to Greece. He includes the seven citadels that Agamemnon will give Achilles, with kingly authority over them. "All of this Agamemnon will accomplish for you," Odysseus assures Achilles, repeating Agamemnon's words, "if you cease from your anger."

Then Odysseus stops transmitting Agamemnon's message and introduces a plea of his own. Even if Achilles cannot stop hating Agamemnon and his gifts, he says (Odysseus must suspect the gifts will not do the trick), he should at least have compassion for the other Greeks. They suffer terribly and will honor him like a god. Trying to entice Achilles with the prospect of killing the arrogant Trojan Hector, Odysseus says that Hector believes no Greek can equal him in battle.

But you remember that there was more to Agamemnon's message. Agamemnon ended by saying that Achilles must not merely give up his anger but must "be subdued" (or "be reduced to subjection"). Agamemnon implied that Achilles should not behave like the relentless, hateful Hades. He ended by asserting his own superiority in kingly status and age. Tactfully refraining from repeating Agamemnon's conclusion, Odysseus has substituted ideas of his own.

Achilles must be shrewder than Odysseus thinks, because you sense that he knows that Odysseus has left something out. "I will speak my mind," he begins angrily. "For hateful to me as the gates of Hades is that man who hides one thing in his thoughts but speaks another." Enraged at the very fact of Agamemnon's authority and his clumsy manner of wielding it, Achilles intuits (correctly, as you know) that Odysseus has left out Agamemnon's tactless reassertion of his own status and power. Nothing could infuriate Achilles more.

"No one, not Agamemnon or anyone else, will persuade me, since I never got any thanks for fighting relentlessly against enemies!" Achilles shouts, incensed at the injustice. "The man who remains behind gets the same share as the one who fights very hard. The coward and the brave man receive equal honors. The lazy man and the active man die equally. There's nothing in it for me, when I've endured many sufferings in my heart and risked my life. Like a mother bird forever feeding her young but receiving only suffering herself in return, I've been fighting endlessly, enduring blood-filled days and sleepless nights." Achilles recently sacked twenty-three cities near Troy. He brought back vast amounts of treasure, while Agamemnon waited beside his ships. "Agamemnon distributed all the prizes to everyone else," Achilles rails, "but from me alone of all the Greeks he has taken for himself and holds my heart-pleasing bedmate."

Another thought strikes Achilles. "You know what?" he continues. "Let him delight himself sleeping with her. Why do Greeks even have to fight with Trojans? We only came here because Agamemnon's brother Menelaus wanted his wife Helen back. Doesn't everyone love his own wife? That is how I feel about Briseis, even though she was acquired by my spear. But now, since he took my prize and he deceived me, let him not try me again, knowing him as I do. He will not persuade me."

Achilles appears to understand the full cost of his absence. Curtly advising Odysseus to make plans with the other leaders, he reminds Agamemnon's envoys that when he himself took part in the fighting, Hector hardly dared to emerge from Troy. Achilles almost killed him once. "But now," Achilles says, "I don't want to fight Hector, and I'm going home." He will sacrifice to the gods tomorrow, load his ships, and be home in Greece in three days, if Poseidon, god of the sea, will allow this.

Following this announcement, Achilles continues to rant about Agamemnon for a long, long time. "He took my prize! He cheated me! He doesn't even dare to come look me in the eye! Tell him what I say so the others will be angry with him. I will never work with him again. I hate him! His gifts are hateful to me. He won't persuade me even if he gives me I don't care how many times as many gifts as these." (Here Achilles lists infinite amounts, including all the possessions in Egyptian Thebes and gifts as many as there are grains of sand.) "No amount of material gifts is worth the life of a man!" Achilles yells. He knows that he is destined either to die young, fighting here in Troy and winning eternal glory, or to live a long, inglorious life at home. Now, thank you very much, he will choose the latter.

Achilles tells the others to leave but invites Phoenix to stay the night. Phoenix tearfully explains his own predicament if Achilles leaves Troy without him. He reminds Achilles that Peleus, Achilles' father, sent him off to Troy to accompany the youthful Achilles and make him "a speaker of words and a doer of deeds." As a young man, Phoenix had quarreled with his own father. He escaped to Achilles' home, where Peleus took him in, loved him like a son, and made him rich and powerful. Childless himself, Phoenix helped to rear Achilles. He reminds Achilles of the dire consequences of *atē*, "ruinous folly," the same divine spirit that Agamemnon blamed for his own disastrous and shortsighted decision to take Achilles' prize.

Reiterating all the gifts that Agamemnon has offered, Phoenix argues that a refusal puts Achilles morally in the wrong. In ancient times, he says, when furious anger would come to someone, he would be open to gifts and could be prevailed upon by words. Phoenix now launches into a lengthy tale about a great warrior named Meleagros.

Meleagros's father failed to honor the goddess Artemis sufficiently, so she sends an immense boar to ravage his orchards. Meleagros assembles a huge hunting party from various cities. After killing the boar, the men fight over the prize of its head and skin. One group, Phoenix says, besieges Meleagros's city and his people. As long as Meleagros keeps fighting, his people succeed. But Meleagros becomes enraged at his mother after she curses him for the death of her brother. Did Meleagros kill his uncle? Or does his mother somehow hold him responsible? Whichever it is, Meleagros withdraws from battle. (The elements of this tale begin to sound familiar to you.) Under siege, the noblemen and Meleagros's father beg him repeatedly to come out and ward off the attack. They offer him extensive gifts. His mother, sisters, and dearest companions all beseech him. But Meleagros keeps refusing, saying he will not fight until the enemy attack his very own bedchamber. As the enemy breach the city's walls, Meleagros's wife details the coming horrors: the men slaughtered, the city in flames, the women and children enslaved. This last supplication works. Meleagros gets up and puts on his armor. "Yielding in his passion," says Phoenix, "he warded off the evil day from his people." But, Phoenix continues, "they no longer gave him the many lovely gifts, but even so [or "to no purpose"] he warded off the evil."

You definitely find this story familiar. A war with a trivial cause. A besieged city. A great fighter defending his people but then becoming angry and refusing to fight. Supplications and the offer of gifts so that he will return to the battle and protect his people. The fighter's persistent refusal . . .

Phoenix tries to make sure that Achilles gets the point. There would be no sense in defending the Greek ships after they are already burning, he reminds him. "Take the gifts the Greeks are offering you now. If you wait and enter the fight too late, you will no longer be held in equal honor, even if you ward off the attack."

But even this plea fails.

Do you see something pure and admirable in Achilles' refusal to be bought off by such a stupid, selfish, irresponsible, unrepentant leader as Agamemnon? Or do you think Phoenix has made a valid point? Is remaining angry really in Achilles' own best interest? What should he do? If he stays angry, he harms the Greeks and himself. If he yields, it is like admitting that he was wrong to get angry in the first place.

Achilles answers Phoenix respectfully, without the rage he directed at Agamemnon and Odysseus. He claims not to need the honor men can give him since he has enough from Zeus. He criticizes Phoenix for preferring Agamemnon to himself, but he generously offers the older man half of all he owns and invites him again to stay the night. In the morning they will decide together whether to return to Greece or remain in Troy. Phoenix's entreaty has evidently had some effect. Earlier Achilles said he was definitely going home. Now he appears to be wavering.

Last to speak is the great warrior Ajax, renowned for his extraordinary defensive valor. The narrator has repeatedly called him a mighty "bulwark" or "defensive wall" for the Greeks. A blunt, direct man, Ajax has heard enough. He turns from Achilles. "Let's go," he tells Odysseus. "We will not accomplish anything by words. Achilles has made the heart in his chest ferocious. He cares nothing for the friendship of his

companions, even though we honored him most of all. He has
no pity. A man will accept payment for even a murdered brother
or child. The killer pays the penalty and stays in the community,
and the other man restrains his heart and bold passion. But
Achilles is making all this fuss on account of one single girl."

Ajax turns to address Achilles. He finds his problem
incomprehensible. "You're upset about one girl," he says, "but
we're offering you seven. And much else besides." He urges
Achilles to make his heart kind, reminding him that under
his roof right now are the Greeks who are nearest and dearest
to him.

This plea fails, too.

Achilles agrees with Ajax but cannot yield. "My heart
swells with anger," he insists, "whenever I remember how
Agamemnon treated me rudely among the Greeks, as if I were
some interloper. But you go and give him this message."
Achilles will not consider returning to battle until Hector
attacks Achilles' own ships and his shelter. That's it. Meeting
over. Agamemnon's representatives each pour out a libation to
the gods and wordlessly return to their ships. Only Phoenix
remains with Achilles. You find yourself thinking of Meleagros.
He finally did defend his people, but he waited until the last
minute. He gained no gifts, no honor, as a result. Does Achilles
not see the warning that the tale of Meleagros provides? Does
Achilles no longer want gifts and the honor they represent?
Maybe all he really wants now is to be angry.

Reassessing the Characters' Priorities

By showing various perspectives on events, the *Iliad* continu-
ously evokes the audience's capacity for critical moral judgment.
Homer's characters remain obsessed with honor and status as

they strive to be *aristos,* "best." Nestor recalls that Achilles' father
sent him off to Troy with the reminder "to be always the best
and more eminent than others" (11.784).[1] But since the characters' choices produce undesirable results, the audience begins
to question whether their achievements and priorities really are
optimal. Fury at being dishonored has caused Achilles to stop
defending the Greeks. His and Agamemnon's obsession with
honor and status prevents reconciliation.[2] The powerful king
cannot undo his error, and his offer of gifts only further enrages the great warrior. Agamemnon's inability to persuade
Achilles to rejoin the battle leaves their community vulnerable
to enemy attack.

Prioritizing his own honor, Agamemnon remains an inef-
fective and self-defeating leader. He has learned from experience
and is now willing to return the girl, but he fails to accept full
responsibility for his earlier decision. He realizes that Achilles'
supreme fighting abilities are essential to the Greek war effort,
but he cannot tolerate the challenge that this poses to his own
authority. The immense number of reconciliation gifts, his offer to make Achilles his son-in-law, his insistence that Achilles
submit to his authority all indicate that he still fails to see the
essential problem. The best warrior, Achilles, will not subordinate himself to a less powerful, less intelligent man even if
other kings have sworn to accept Agamemnon's authority and
his scepter comes from Zeus.[3]

Agamemnon fails to go in person to talk to Achilles.[4] He
fails to offer anything approaching an apology. Achilles resents
the very fact that Agamemnon is in a position to offer these
excessively extravagant gifts. His rage derives precisely from
Agamemnon's unfounded arrogance, wealth, and gift-giving
power.[5] We may understand Achilles' reluctance to submit to
Agamemnon's authority, but his stubbornness makes little sense.

In opposing Agamemnon, Achilles is also, by his own standards, defeating himself. If he persists in refusing to fight the Trojans, Agamemnon will die or return home in shame, yes, but Achilles will return home without glory, too.[6]

Achilles' stubbornness seems self-defeating, but he appears neither thuggish nor stupid. He welcomes Agamemnon's envoys politely. He provides generous and appropriate hospitality. He accurately perceives that Odysseus has not transmitted Agamemnon's message in its entirety (9.157ff. vs. 299ff.) and is not deceived by Odysseus's clever suppression of its most offensive part, Agamemnon's insistence that Achilles subordinate himself to him.[7]

But despite Achilles' impressive physical and intellectual abilities, we see that his continued refusal to fight on behalf of the Greeks harms his own community. Achilles cannot capitulate to Agamemnon. He cannot swallow his rage at the insult to his honor. As a leader, Agamemnon appears inadequate, but Achilles' refusal to compromise his own principles proves dire for his people. They need him desperately, but he does not seem to care. The narrative prompts the audience to consider the costs of Achilles' rage and the irrationality of his desire to be honored by the very people he is failing to protect.[8]

Cultivating Critical Reasoning: Identifying Parallels and Contrasts

As Achilles' rage pursues its destructive path, the *Iliad* overtly calls attention to the capacity of stories to develop the audience's aptitude for logic and critical thought. The ability to reason logically constitutes an essential prerequisite for individuals in any community striving to identify and empower the "best" leaders and to determine and implement the "best" ideas.

Numerous stories throughout the epic invite the characters and also the audience to draw comparisons with elements in the narrative as a whole.[9] Phoenix tells the tale of Meleagros (9.525–599); Nestor tells lengthy tales of his own youthful exploits (11.669–761). Such stories promote logical reasoning and critical judgment by offering models to emulate or avoid.

The tale of Meleagros, like Achilles' story itself, urges listeners to compare the protagonist's choices and experience to decisions and outcomes in their own lives. Why should Achilles care what happened to Meleagros? According to Phoenix, Meleagros exemplifies the danger of staying angry too long, of finding reconciliation too late. Meleagros ultimately does defend his people, but they are no longer willing to give him any gifts (9.599). Meleagros's anger, his resistance to supplication, and his belated change of heart might provide a cautionary example for Achilles (9.553–555).[10]

Achilles' inability to draw the necessary conclusion, however, exemplifies how *not* to interpret a story. He fails to identify with Meleagros, although the audience easily sees the parallels. He fails to perceive the moral of Meleagros's story, or he chooses to ignore it. Achilles' example suggests that you interpret a story incorrectly if you fail to see its relationship to your own life.[11]

The obvious analogy between Achilles and Meleagros alerts us to other analogies. Homer's similes, the frequent narrative assertions that something is "like" something else, constitute the epic's most frequent and powerful stories-within-the-story.[12] Crucial to the effect of Homer's poetry, the similes not only add color, texture, and emotional impact to the narrative, they also develop the audience's ability to identify parallels and contrasts. Similes offer a story-within-the-story that often only the audience gets to hear.[13] The similes help to distinguish the characters' perspectives from the perspective of the poem as a whole, and they cultivate critical and logical reasoning ability in the audience.

Similes liken events in the narrative to events in the natural world.[14] They liken struggles between individual warriors or groups of warriors to animals both wild and domestic, and they juxtapose (often jarringly) warfare with other human activities, such as hunting or agriculture or other peacetime activities.[15] For example, the tale of Achilles' refusal of Agamemnon's gifts begins with that evocative image likening the feelings inside the Greek warriors to turbulent winds blasting from the wild regions of Thrace (9.1–8). Agamemnon attacking Trojans is compared to a lion (11.113ff.) and a raging fire (11.155ff.). A simile of farming illustrates a night raid on the Trojans by Odysseus and Diomedes (10.351–356). For the audience, the similes also incorporate a full range of human experience into the *Iliad*'s account of a few days during the course of a ten-year war.[16]

Above all, the similes are like questions on college aptitude tests, asking the audience to identify logical analogies: Achilles is to lion as Trojans are to hunters. Each analogy offers a logic puzzle. Each awakens and sharpens our critical faculties by inviting us to find parallels and contrasts. For example, a simile likens the great Greek warrior Ajax attacking Trojans to a lion furious with hunger but driven off by men's spears. So, too, Ajax reluctantly retreats (11.547–556). The comparison to a ravening lion emphasizes Ajax's strength and fierce resolve but also his natural limits.[17]

An analogy may also expose a contrast. Defending their fortifications, for example, the Greeks fling rocks onto the Trojans below. These stones drop "like snowflakes" (12.156–160).[18] Perhaps the stones fall as frequently as flakes in a snowstorm, but scarcely anything could be less like the skull-crushing force of a heavy stone hurled from a high rampart than a snowflake.

If only the stones were falling like snowflakes, you can imagine the Trojans thinking. Stones hurled from the top of a wall most emphatically do not fall like snowflakes. Stating that they do implies that they have completely reversed their role. This reversal in the analogy highlights the reversal in the narrative: as a consequence of Achilles' withdrawal from battle, the Greeks no longer besiege the walls of Troy. Instead, Trojans now besiege the Greeks' defensive fortifications. This shocking reversal powerfully equates attackers and defenders. They have swapped roles; they can so easily swap roles.[19]

A simile may highlight both similarities and contrasts. An analogy between Agamemnon and Zeus, for example, invites us to consider all the ways in which Agamemnon is and is not like Zeus. In the night, after the failed embassy to Achilles, a wakeful Agamemnon debates many things within his own turbulent thoughts, as when Zeus causes rain or hail or snow to fall on farmlands or constructs "the great mouth of destructive war" (10.3–10). The parallels seem obscure. Agamemnon, following a series of inept and self-defeating decisions, now struggles to decide what to do in a difficult predicament. Zeus hurls down severe weather and fashions war for men. Where is the connection? Evidently, both rulers act with autocratic obliviousness to the needs and concerns of human beings, but Zeus does not agonize over his decisions. Agamemnon must. Zeus actually has absolute autocratic authority. Agamemnon can only wish that he did.

Images of farming emphasize the most poignant contrast of all, the contrast between peace and war. For example, a simile of reaping grain depicts opposing ranks of fighters cutting one another down. Battle lines of Trojan and Greek warriors slaughter one another just as, the narrator explains, "reapers drive their furrow through a field of wheat or barley belonging to a wealthy man, and the handfuls of grain cut by the sickle fall thickly" (11.67–71). The image implicitly equates Greeks with Trojans, as both sides equally reap and are reaped. But reaping grain produces food to sustain life, whereas the slaughter of men quite obviously destroys life.[20] Another simile likens two half brothers, fighting side by side, to a pair of oxen ploughing (13.701–708). Here, too, a life-*destroying* collaborative process within the narrative evokes a life-*sustaining* collaborative process outside of the narrative. In likening fallen warriors to mere handfuls of cut grain and successful slaughter to cultivation, these analogies evoke a devastating picture of colossal waste.[21]

The similes invite us to reexamine our certainties. What is valuable in human achievement? Warfare? Farming? Another image exposes the morally ambivalent role of human technological ingenuity. The narrator likens the fighting between Greek and Trojan warriors to a perfectly straight chalk line drawn by an expert carpenter as he cuts wood to build a ship (15.410–413). This simile aligns the murderous, but equally balanced, intentions of opposing warriors with the technology of shipbuilding. The analogy reminds us that the value of any technology depends on how it is used. Ships are good if used for good purposes. Ships increase travel, exploration, and experience. They promote material exchange and the acquisition of wealth. But if no carpenter had ever built a ship, Paris might have stayed at home in Troy instead of sailing off to Sparta and abducting Helen, and no ships could have brought the besieging Greeks to the shores of Troy. Earlier, the narrator described the death in battle of the man "who had constructed for Paris the balanced ships that began the troubles, which were an evil to the Trojans and to himself" (5.62–64).[22] The surprising analogy of warfare to shipbuilding underscores the ambivalent potential of all human ingenuity. What will ensure that human energy, ingenuity, and creativity achieve good purposes?

In enlisting our critical faculties and moral judgment, the similes, like all of the tales in the *Iliad,* prompt us to assess the characters' priorities and our own. They help us to determine what is good and admirable. Homer's characters prize victory in battle, but many similes directly evoke sympathy for the fallen or discomfort at the unfairness of an unequal combat.[23] When the narrative likens Agamemnon slaughtering two brothers to a lion slaughtering two defenseless fawns (11.112–121), the audience may begin to feel less certain than the characters do that such slaughter deserves honor. The analogy emphasizes the vast gap between Agamemnon's abilities and his opponents', but does that enhance or diminish Agamemnon's achievement? What is so courageous or impressive about butchering a couple of defenseless fawns?[24]

Raging like a lion or wild boar and slaughtering many enemies may be worthy of praise and honor in the world of Homer's characters, but similes claiming that the warriors are like such beasts invite the audience to consider whether it really is optimal behavior for a human being. Is it really something to brag about? Menelaus points out that boasting over slain victims is something that leopards, lions, and wild boars *do not do* (17.19–23).[25] So although the similes frequently liken human behavior to animal behavior, they also call this equation into question.

Yes, Ajax is like a raging lion hungry for food (11.547–556), but is he really? Does a lion have a choice to forgo food? Does Ajax have no other options than to slaughter Trojans? You may argue that the Greeks must recover Helen, but did Paris have to take her from Greece in the first place? Yes, human beings can behave like animals, but must we? Organized warfare and systematic slaughter for the sake of honor are certainly not behaviors found in animal species. Such a simile reminds us that human beings have destructive talents that far exceed the destructive talents of animals.

But we also have constructive talents that make us unique. Above all, we have the ability to communicate using words. The narrator likens the Trojan forces, warriors gathered from all parts of the region, to a bunch of bleating sheep "because," the narrator explains, "there was not one speech or language common to all, but their tongue was mixed, and the men were called together in large numbers from many places" (4.433–438). In this analogy, it is precisely the absence of the ability to communicate through language that makes warriors like animals.[26]

By developing logical reasoning skills in the audience, the similes and other stories within the story distinguish the perspective of the audience from the perspective of the characters and begin to cultivate the audience's ability to evaluate the characters' choices and priorities. The process affects not just modern readers who may have a cultural aversion to warfare and violence or a general preference for peace. The process also affects anyone (including a listener in the eighth to fifth centuries BCE) who might share the priorities of Homer's characters. Stories and similes in the *Iliad*, by developing the audience's capacity for logical thought, call into question the characters' definition of what is honorable and worthy of glory. Whether or not Achilles himself comes to question or even to reject the traditional ethical system, the narrative highlights for the audience the propensity of the system to promote conflict and thwart reconciliation.[27]

As Achilles sits on the sidelines refusing to fight, we see the destructiveness of his anger and intransigence. His rage and his concern for honor and status are causing his own people to die in vast numbers. Can we admire Achilles' inflexibility? It does not seem to serve him or anyone else very well. Experiencing the similes, can we share Achilles' conviction that success in battle is the highest form of human achievement and worthy of the highest honor?

Redefining Great Achievement: The Interdependence of Individual and Group

The *Iliad* as a whole, the stories-within-the-story, and the similes all evoke the audience's moral judgment and make it difficult to share the characters' tremendous enthusiasm for warfare. But it is also true that Homer's characters prioritize not only success in physical combat but also success in debate; they recognize the power of words as well as the power of deeds.[28] Achilles' friend Patroclus makes a distinction between the goals and results of things men do with their hands (e.g., kill one another) and the goals and results of the things men do in counsel and in council (e.g., advise one another and determine whose plan is best) (16.630). Similarly, Nestor praises Diomedes for his martial talents and also for his skill in *boule*, "counsel/council" (9.53–54). Phoenix tells Achilles that when Achilles was young he "did not yet know of war that levels all alike or of verbal combat, where men become distinguished" (9.440–441). He reminds Achilles that Achilles' father sent Phoenix with him to Troy to teach him "to be both a speaker of words and a doer of deeds" (9.440–443).[29] The characters understand that success requires achievement in both physical and verbal conflicts.

Since success requires verbal as well as physical talents, Homer's characters value the ability to use words effectively. When Odysseus criticizes Agamemnon's plan to flee from Troy

under cover of night, Agamemnon asks for someone else to
speak up, someone "who might relate better counsel" (14.107).
Stepping forward to speak, Diomedes first establishes his lineage, insisting that he is born "from a noble father" (14.113), and
he proceeds to identify his father, grandfather, and great-
grandfather and their exploits. He concludes his personal genealogy by claiming, "You must have heard of these things, if
indeed they are true. Therefore, declaring me lowborn and
unvaliant, you could not dishonor any word I say, if I speak
well" (14.125–127). Diomedes' aristocratic lineage justifies his
right to speak in the assembly, but he still has to speak well if
he is to succeed.[30]

Just as they value excellence in speaking ability, Homer's
characters also value the responsibility to listen to others. Reminding King Agamemnon that holding power entails the responsibility to listen, Nestor explains, "It is necessary for you to
speak a word or to hear one and to accomplish this also for
another man, whenever the heart urges someone to speak for
the good. But whatever you command will depend on you"
(9.100–102). Think of it, 3,000 years ago, maybe more, a warrior
in a story insisting on the obligation of a powerful ruler to listen
to opposing viewpoints. Think how crucial that concept is for a
stable, functioning society and how modern governments rou-
tinely violate it (not merely single dictators, small ruling juntas,
or even large collectives styling themselves "the popular will,"
but also political leaders in technically "democratic" governments). The exercise of tyrannical power requires the suppression
of verbal dissent. Conversely, openness to verbal criticism distinguishes a healthy, constructive political process.

Agamemnon not only listens to Nestor's criticisms, he
reverses his previous position. Reminded that he ignored good
advice in taking Achilles' prize, Agamemnon now recognizes

that he was senseless then, and he is willing to make recompense. Today, such receptivity to counterarguments and processing of new information, the reversal of a previous decision, might bring Agamemnon the label of "flip-flopper." But we see that even if he cannot quite accept responsibility for his own poor decision, still he can learn from experience and from the criticism of others.[31] Any political leader must have this capacity. How else will the "best" ideas prevail?

Able to learn from experience, Agamemnon now sees (as we do) that the Greeks need Achilles' talents as a warrior, but Achilles' encounter with Agamemnon's envoys also emphasizes that the superior warrior needs the group just as much as the group needs him—maybe more. Enraged, Achilles no longer wants to fight on behalf of the Greeks, "since," he proclaims, "I never got any thanks for fighting relentlessly against enemy men. The portion is the same for the man who remains behind as for the one who fights very hard. There is no distinction in honor between the coward and the brave man. The lazy man and the active man die equally" (9.316–320). Achilles reasons that since everyone dies, there is no point in fighting if martial achievement brings no honor. Achilles likens himself suffering hardships on behalf of the Greeks to a mother bird suffering in order to bring food to her young (9.323–327).[32] For Achilles, the relationship has all been one-way. His anger and resentment and his sense that the group has not fulfilled its obligation to him by honoring him appropriately indicate just how much the successful warrior needs the group to appreciate, celebrate, and honor his success.

Without honor conferred by the community, the great achievements of the exceptionally talented individual have no meaning. While Achilles' rage still prevents him from fighting, Nestor tells a lengthy tale of his own battle exploits and the glory he won from his people, concluding with the prediction, "But Achilles will get the benefit of his *aretē,* 'excellence,' alone. Indeed I believe that he will weep afterward very much, when his people are destroyed" (11.762–764). Homer's characters view *aretē,* "excellence," as the opposite of cowardice (e.g., 13.275–291). *Aretē* derives from Ares, god of war. In the *Iliad* it means "prowess" or "valor" or "courage" in warfare.[33] Nestor's comment suggests that *aretē* in isolation, without communal validation, has no value. The warrior cannot gain glory unless his people survive to confer it.

Conversely, while the warrior's *aretē* cannot earn glory from the community at the expense of the community, honors conferred by the community can impel the warrior to great deeds on the community's behalf. In the furious heat of battle, the Trojan Sarpedon suddenly pauses to reflect on his motives and his relationship to his people (implausible, yes, but it gets your attention). Sarpedon asks another fighter, a fellow Lycian, Glaucus, why their people honor them like gods and give them pride of place and extensive lands. These honors, he says, oblige them to fight nobly in the forefront of battle so that others will say that they are indeed noble. "Therefore," Sarpedon explains, "we must stand among the foremost Lycians and encounter the raging battle, in order that thus someone of the thickly armored Lycians may say, 'Not without glory do these kings rule throughout Lycia and eat the rich flocks and the choice, honey-sweet wine. But also, as it appears, their fighting force is noble, since they do battle among the foremost Lycians'" (12.315–321). Sarpedon identifies a mutually reinforcing circle: because they receive honor from the community, they must behave so as to deserve and justify that honor.[34]

Sarpedon briefly considers the alternative. What if they opt not to fight and win honor and glory in battle? "Friend," he tells Glaucus, "if you and I, fleeing this war, should be forever ageless and immortal, I would not fight among the foremost men, nor would I send you off to the man-ennobling battle. But as it is—for the death-spirits draw near, thousands of them, which no mortal can escape—let us go. Either we will attain glory because of someone, or someone else will attain it because of us" (12.322–328). Sarpedon understands that since we all die, either we die with glory or we just die. If human beings did not die, there would be no point in striving to earn glory. Sarpedon recognizes that the fact of human mortality makes fighting and dying in battle necessary, since it is better to die with glory than without it.[35]

Unlike the audience, Sarpedon never doubts that fighting and dying in battle deserve the highest glory, but he identifies the constructive potential of our mortality. He recognizes that if we were immortal, there would be no point in pursuing glory. Gods do not die, and so their choices and actions have no lasting consequences for themselves. Because human beings do die, every human choice, every human action matters.[36] Remarkably, Homer attributes this profoundly motivating and empowering insight not to a Greek warrior but to a Trojan enemy.

But why, really, is it better to die with glory than without it? Because your glory can live on after you are gone. If people continue to remember your great achievements, then you have a kind of immortality. Tales of your great exploits can permit you to transcend death. Epic poetry, such as the *Iliad* itself, immortalizes in song extraordinary deeds deserving of immortal remembrance. But which deeds, which stories, deserve retelling by present and future generations? What behaviors should the community admire or condemn?

If a great warrior fails to defend his people, there will be no one left to sing of his deeds ever after. Therefore, the possibility of immortality in the form of being remembered and celebrated for great achievements requires the "best" individual to care about everyone else. He needs them as much as they need him. By definition, he cannot achieve immortal glory without them. When the embassy arrives at Achilles' shelter to try to convince him to rejoin the fighting, they find him playing the lyre and singing tales of *klea andron,* "the glorious achievements of men" (9.189), the precise subject of Homer's epic tales. No other warrior in Homer's stories ever plays the lyre or sings epic poetry. Has Achilles chosen to sing of his own deeds or the deeds of warriors before him?[37] Has his anger at Agamemnon blinded him to the fact that if the Greeks all perish there will be no one left to sing of his great achievements?

The Durability of Stories

In defining, honoring, and preserving human achievements, stories are far more durable than other human constructions. Defensive walls, for example, succumb to natural forces of destruction. When the Greeks first build fortifications to protect their encampment and ships, the god Poseidon fears that this wall's *kleos,* "glory" (the singular of *klea*), will last forever and people will forget the wall of Troy, which Poseidon and Apollo constructed (7.451–453). But Zeus promises that after the Greeks depart, Poseidon can destroy their fortifications, wash the pieces into the sea, and efface the wall and ditch completely (7.461–463). And we know this will occur.

Poseidon's concern symbolically associates the Greek fortifications with the walls of Troy, and Homer's description of the future destruction of the Greek wall, like the description of its construction (7.433–442), has an equalizing effect. The destruction of the Greeks' defensive ditch and wall foreshadows and substitutes for the destruction of Troy, which the *Iliad* does not include (12.10–35).[38] Human constructions, even massive, mighty walls, are not very durable, whether built by Greeks or by Trojans. In the middle of the epic, describing the Trojans' assault on the Greeks' walls, Homer suggests an assault on a besieged city, including a lengthy description of the Greeks' strong, high, bolted double doors (12.453–463). Hector crashes through, and some Trojans "leapt over the wall, while others poured in at the well-made gates, and the Greeks were put to flight" (12.469–470). We see this happening to Greeks; we know that it will happen to Trojans when the Greeks eventually do sack Troy.[39]

The implicit equation of the Greeks' defensive fortification with the walls of Troy removes any possibility of interpreting the *Iliad* as a simplistic tale of the triumph of noble Greeks over evil Trojans. There are not exactly "good guys" and "bad guys" in this story. There are just "guys" (and a very few girls) who do good and bad things. The *Iliad* does not celebrate the destruction of Troy as a great military triumph or stunning moral victory. It is a disaster, a disaster illustrating the fragility and impermanence of human constructions.

Time may obliterate the walls, but the stories of human constructive and destructive achievements can endure and can teach new generations. Poseidon long ago washed the Greeks' defensive fortifications into the sea. Wind and dust have buried Troy under layers of earth and subsequent human constructions. But the *Iliad* survives. The durability of stories means that the glory that the community confers can transcend time and permit an individual to gain a kind of immortality.

In memorializing human achievements and transcending the limits of individual human lifetimes, the *Iliad* promotes an interdependence between the individual and the community.

The high-achieving individual must help to preserve his people, so that their stories will commemorate his achievements forever. Conversely, the community must define the constituents of high achievement. Which behaviors deserve glory? Which offer instead negative examples? Despite his impressive talents, Achilles irrationally prioritizes his own honor at the expense of his people. His anger and sense of entitlement blind him to their needs and his own. Violent times inevitably offer countless examples of similarly irrational and myopic but powerful and influential individuals. The *Iliad* precludes the possibility of admiring or celebrating them.

Determining What Is "Best"

The *Iliad* promotes the audience's ability to reason logically and identify parallels and contrasts. Homer makes us consider the specific capacities that human beings do not share with lions, leopards, and wild boars: technology and language. The epic asks us to think about how best to employ these capacities. The recognition that the high-achieving individual and the community need one another gives everyone the responsibility to define "bestness." What goals should we strive for? What achievements should we celebrate in others?

Homer's characters restrict *aretē*, human "excellence," to military excellence. Pursuit of glory makes warriors willing to risk their lives in battle.[40] Achilles' destructive and self-destructive rage results naturally from this value system: the existing power structure failed to give him honor commensurate with his achievements. But the *Iliad* makes the audience ask: What should a society celebrate in its high achievers? How do you determine "best"? "Best" at what? "Best" for whom? The *Iliad* shows that an individual's supreme excellence in fighting and killing and his preoccupation with material markers of status does not necessarily serve the interests of his community.

Effective decision making requires, as Nestor reminds Agamemnon, that when many voice their opinions, you should always select the best one. Such a simple concept and so difficult to implement, for what criteria do you use to determine what is "best"? In the twenty-first century, we might choose to demand other talents from our best and highest achievers, ingenious, practical problem solving, for example, or the ability to communicate good ideas to others. What if the community especially honored those who excelled in compassion and in generosity? The *Iliad* encourages us to reconsider what we choose to prize most.

4

Violence, Vengeance, and a Glimpse of Victory (*Iliad* 10–24)

Troy still stands, but its attackers are under siege. The Greeks fight for their lives as the battle roils around their ships. The chaos feels total, the noise overwhelming. The hand-to-hand combat is stomach-turning and relentless. In vivid flesh-piercing, bone-crunching detail, spear points find vulnerable gaps between chin and chest guard. They shatter eye sockets and mouths. Brains and teeth mingle in the blood and dust. One warrior falls like a lovingly nurtured olive tree uprooted by wind. Another, dying, leaves a dear young wife at home and grieving parents. You imagine his family's terrible sorrow. As one young fighter falls dead, his head lolls to the side, like a poppy nodding under the weight of spring rainfall. The vivid delicacy of this image surprises you. By evoking flowers and the life-giving rain of springtime, the analogy makes you feel sad for the young man. He will never see spring flowers again.

At Achilles' request, Zeus promised to let the Trojans prevail for a time, and he continues to prevent other gods from intervening to help the Greeks. Zeus announces the events to come: Achilles will make his companion Patroclus stand and fight. Patroclus will kill the Trojan Sarpedon. In revenge, Hector will kill Patroclus. In return, Achilles will slaughter Hector. Eventually, the Greeks will seize Troy. But for now, Apollo gives Hector strength. The blood and carnage continue, and Achilles remains on the sidelines, refusing to help his fellow Greeks. They are weary and downhearted, but the Trojans are optimistic.

Now you see Achilles' closest friend, Patroclus, standing before Achilles. Tears run down his cheeks like spring water flowing down a rock face. A kind, empathetic man, Patroclus grieves for the suffering Greeks. Their best fighters are wounded, and Achilles is their only hope. Patroclus criticizes him for his inhuman hardness. "It is as if your parents were the sea and the cliffs," says Patroclus. "You are so unsympathetic to the Greeks' plight. At least let me borrow your armor and lead your warriors into battle," Patroclus implores. "The Trojans may mistake me for you and retreat. This will give the Greeks some respite."

Still enraged over Agamemnon's insult to his honor, Achilles will not fight until the battle reaches his own ships. But he reluctantly agrees to let Patroclus wear his armor into battle. He instructs his friend to drive the Trojans back from the Greek ships but warns him not to attack Troy. Achilles fears that one of the gods will destroy Patroclus. He wishes they two together could slaughter every Trojan, demolish Troy, and be the war's only survivors. You realize that Achilles' rage makes him care for only this one friend and no one else. But Zeus has told you what will happen to Patroclus.

Wearing Achilles' armor, Patroclus kills many Trojans and drives the others back toward Troy, but he does not of course heed Achilles' advice to withdraw afterward. He kills

Zeus's son Sarpedon, whom even Zeus cannot save because Sarpedon is mortal. (Hera reminds Zeus that if he saves Sarpedon, other gods will want to save their own sons and feel resentment. Evidently, many warriors are sons of gods, but they are still mortal.) As Patroclus keeps fighting, disregarding Achilles' warning, the narrator observes that "Zeus's mind is ever stronger than a man's." Surely nothing else could explain Patroclus's failure to follow Achilles' instructions.

Patroclus kills nine Trojans on each of three assaults on Troy, but on his fourth assault, Hector, helped by Apollo, strikes his helmet from his head. Achilles' massive helmet with its horsehair crest rolls in the dust. Zeus gives it to Hector to wear. Patroclus, now completely vulnerable, receives many wounds before Hector drives the final deathblow deep into his belly. As Hector vaunts over him, Patroclus, dying, predicts Hector's death at Achilles' hands. Hector thinks that he himself may kill Achilles. But you know better.

Learning of Patroclus's death, Achilles rolls, inconsolable, in the dust, tearing his hair and rubbing mud into it. His companions and servants all weep. Patroclus was much beloved.

Later, alone on the shore, Achilles encounters his divine sea-nymph mother. He wishes that he had never been born and no longer wants to live unless he can get revenge by killing Hector. With sadness, his mother insists that after Hector's death Achilles' own death is certain. (You recognize Achilles' fate as a predictable consequence of most vengeance killings, as each avenger soon becomes the victim of another.)

Achilles does not care. He failed to defend his companion and now must avenge his death. After a fervent but hopeless wish that "contention would perish from both gods and men," Achilles abruptly decides to give up his anger at Agamemnon.

Out of necessity, he will subdue his passion. He will kill Hector. If, in consequence, he himself will die soon, so be it.

Since Achilles now has no armor, his mother asks the craftsman god Hephaestus to make him some. Fashioning the armor for Achilles with supernatural artistry, Hephaestus depicts on the shield the whole of human experience, including earth, sea, sky, and all the constellations, all bordered by the river Ocean running around the shield's edge. In the center, Hephaestus shows a city at war and a city at peace. Battles, skirmishes, assaults, and deceptions engulf the city at war. All is confusion, chaos, death. The city at peace has marriage festivals, peaceful arbitration, rich fields, grain harvests, an overseeing king, a vineyard, grazing cattle. Men with swift dogs hunt marauding lions. There are beautiful meadows, flocks of sheep in roofed pens, young women and men dancing and others delightedly watching. These scenes remind you of so much in human life that is absent from the blood-soaked plains of Troy.

Receiving this divine armor and furious to avenge Patroclus's death, Achilles has moved on from his previous motive for anger, but Agamemnon continues to blame Zeus and *atē*, "divinely sent ruinous folly," for his quarrel with Achilles, insisting, "Zeus took away my understanding." But he promises to give Achilles the gifts he offered before. "Fine," says Achilles, his thoughts elsewhere. "Give the gifts or don't give them. I don't care. We're wasting time. It's time to wage war. Now."

Odysseus reminds Achilles that the men must take food and wine first in order to have strength to fight. Agamemnon says that meanwhile Odysseus can go get the gifts. But anger still consumes Achilles. (Agamemnon's gifts, even the return of Briseis, the girl Agamemnon took initially, evidently mean nothing to him.) "No," he says. "We should fight now. We can eat afterward." Odysseus persuades him to allow the others to eat, but Achilles refuses food or drink until he has avenged Patroclus's death. As Achilles continues to grieve for his friend, you alone see the gods give him ambrosia and nectar, immortal food and drink, so that he will have strength for battle.

Donning his divine armor, Achilles gleams like the sun. He tells his horses to be sure to return him safely after the battle. You are surprised to hear him address his horses but even more amazed when one replies. If the divine armor, and the ambrosia and nectar, did not alert you previously, you recognize now that the situation is not normal. Achilles has become something other than human. His horse not only promises to return him safely from this battle, he also prophesies Achilles' death, which is fated to come soon. "I know," says Achilles. "Why tell me? I don't care. I will not stop until the Trojans get enough of war."

Now, abruptly, this story becomes not just abnormal but surreal and cataclysmic. The gods go down among the mortals assisting whomever they please, Greek or Trojan. The gods are divided in their passions. All is terror. Zeus makes the sky resound with thunder and remains on Olympus to enjoy the show.

Like Zeus, you watch Achilles' rampage. Apollo keeps protecting Hector, but countless other Trojans fall before Achilles' raging fury. He thrusts his spear through one man's brain, then through another's back. His sword slices someone's neck. Shockingly, Achilles kills a man who grasps his knees in supplication. You have seen mighty warriors spare men who clasped them by their knees and begged for mercy. You know that Achilles himself used to take prisoners and sell them back to their people for a hefty ransom. But now Achilles will hear no supplication. He will take no prisoners. He cuts a man's head from his neck. He stabs another in the belly. All die before his furious onslaught.

Like a wildfire fanned by winds and ravaging a mountainside, burning all the woods, Achilles is everywhere, as if he were some divine power. He is covered in blood. His horses and chariot, racing across the body-strewn plain, crush fallen men and armor beneath them. The narrator says Achilles is "pressing on to earn *kudos,* 'glory,' his unapproachable hands stained with gore." Achilles is not pursuing *kleos,* the immortal glory of present and future generations remembering and retelling great exploits. No, Achilles pursues *kudos,* the glory that only the gods bestow. Maybe the gods think that Achilles' current behavior deserves glory. Do you?

Men and horses flee before Achilles into a river. Leaping in after them, he cuts them all down. He is like a monstrous sea mammal terrifying every fish and eating all he can. He captures twelve young Trojans alive, ties them up, and hands them to his companions to lead away to his ships. They will be a vengeance price paid for Patroclus.

Lycaon, a son of King Priam, escapes from the river. Not long ago Achilles had captured him and sold him into slavery. But a wealthy friend ransomed the young man, and he returned home. Achilles recognizes him now. Lycaon has lost his armor, shield, and spear; he is defenseless and exhausted. As Achilles raises his spear, Lycaon rushes in underneath and grasps his knees. He begs Achilles to spare his life, and he promises a huge ransom. He explains that he is only a half brother, not a full brother, of Hector, who killed Patroclus.

Unmoved, Achilles says that before Patroclus's death he spared many Trojans, capturing them alive and selling them. But now he will kill any Trojan he encounters, especially a child of Priam. "Why all the fuss?" he asks the young man.

Achilles is grinning a terrible sort of grin, his white teeth flashing against the smeared blood on his face. "Don't you know that everyone dies, even me, great as I am and half immortal?"

Achilles' sword strikes between collarbone and neck, and Lycaon falls forward on his face. His blood soaks the ground. Hurling the young man's lifeless body into the river, Achilles boasts triumphantly, "Let the fish feed on you! Your mother won't lay your body out and grieve over you. May you all die terribly, every single Trojan, until you pay with your blood for Patroclus and every Greek you killed while I was not there to defend them!"

Continuing his rampage, Achilles soon angers the river god by killing one of his sons. "Achilles," the river shouts. "You are stronger than other men, and you do more evil. Stop clogging me up with bodies." But Achilles does not stop. And now—this is really bizarre—Achilles fights with the river itself. Surrounded by a wave, he grabs for an elm tree to save himself, but he rips it out of the ground. Escaping the whirling water, he races for the plains. He is frightened now. But the mighty river god rises up and pursues him. Fast as Achilles is, the god is gaining on him. Sometimes Achilles turns to fight, but the river batters him, wearing him out. Achilles prays to the gods, and Poseidon and Athena reassure him. They advise him to keep on fighting, drive the Trojans back behind their walls, and kill Hector. They promise him victory.

But the river calls to his brother, another river, to help him obliterate Achilles. Finally Hephaestus, urged by Hera, sets the river on fire, inflaming the corpses and the fish as well as the trees and bushes beside the river. Hera sets winds to fan the flames. And the river god gives up. He cannot fight Hephaestus and his fire, so he backs down. What does he care if Achilles sacks Troy? Hephaestus quenches the fire, and the waters slide back into their proper course.

Hera, Hephaestus, and the two river gods rest. But the other gods redouble their efforts. All earth and sky clang with the din of combat. "And Zeus laughs," the narrator says, "watching the gods contending in strife." Yes, Zeus is enjoying this chaos. Maybe you are too, sort of. It is exciting. What must it be like, though, for the human participants?

The Trojans retreat inside their city's walls. (Apollo tricks Achilles into chasing him instead of Trojans. This alone could explain, you realize, the surviving Trojans' ability to escape Achilles' rampage.) Hector stays outside before the Scaean Gates. His parents beg him to come inside and fight from behind the walls, but Hector struggles with divided thoughts. He speaks only to himself, but you hear him. He realizes he should have heeded his brother's advice to take the Trojans back inside the city when Achilles first rejoined the fighting. Now Hector is ashamed to face the Trojans who depend on him. It would be better to kill Achilles now or die trying.

Hector briefly considers approaching Achilles unarmed and offering to return Helen and everything Paris also stole in carrying her off from Sparta. (Surely this offer could have been made ages ago?) Hector considers offering all the treasures Troy now holds, too. But he realizes that Achilles is just as likely to respond by killing him, defenseless as he would be, like a woman. No, Hector determines to contend with Achilles as soon as possible and see who wins.

But Achilles is approaching. Suddenly, terror seizes Hector, and he turns and runs. Achilles chases him three times around the entire city. Like a dove fleeing before a hawk, Hector runs past the lovely springs where Trojan women used to wash clothes in peacetime. The two men run as if in a footrace with a tripod or a woman set as the prize. Achilles, though famous for his swiftness, cannot catch Hector, and the long chase scene enables you to put yourself in Hector's sandals. Sprinting flat out, Hector fights for breath. You imagine his terror and despair.

Like a man in a nightmare, Hector cannot escape his relentless pursuer. The gods will not save him. Apollo helps him initially but then abandons him. On the fourth circuit around Troy, Athena tells Achilles to stop for breath while she, disguised as Hector's brother, persuades him to stand and fight. As the two warriors come together, you expect the combat to begin, but first the two converse. Hector wants them both to swear that whoever wins will return the loser's body to his own people, after stripping the armor, of course. This strikes you as reasonable—but only for Hector. Achilles knows he will win. He has no need to hedge his bet. More than that, he is beyond human compacts or oaths of any kind. "Just as men and lions can make no agreements, just as lambs and wolves can have none, so, too," Achilles tells Hector, "can there be no friendship or oaths sworn between you and me."

You have seen Achilles refuse to eat. (How terribly unnatural that is. Everyone has to eat.) You saw him receive divine nectar and ambrosia and converse with his horse. You saw him put on immortal armor and fight with two river gods. But his rejection of oaths, his refusal to agree to Hector's reasonable request, this most of all convinces you that Achilles' bloodlust for revenge has destroyed his humanity.

All of the killing has not satisfied Achilles; it has only made him angrier. As he cut down innumerable Trojans, Achilles blazed ever more fiercely in his rage. Now, confronting Hector, he shows no mercy. After an exchange of spear throws (Hector's gets stuck in Achilles' shield and he loses it; Athena returns Achilles' spear to him), Achilles attacks like an eagle picking off a lamb or a bunny. He is furious at the sight of his own armor, stripped from Patroclus's corpse and now worn by Hector, his murderer. Without hesitation, Achilles drives his massive ash spear straight through Hector's neck.

As Hector drops in the dust, dying, Achilles boasts loudly, promising to make his corpse prey for dogs and birds. Gasping for breath, Hector begs Achilles to return his body to his parents for burial. His parents will give Achilles ample gifts in exchange.

But you see that it is hopeless. Achilles has won, he has killed his most hated enemy, but he remains consumed by fury. He will not permit Hector a proper burial. He only wishes he could chop him up and eat him raw. He will accept no amount of gifts as ransom. No, the dogs and birds will feast on Hector, Achilles proclaims.

Hector's spirit leaves reluctantly for the house of Hades, and the Greeks return to their ships. Achilles ties the corpse to his chariot by the ankles and drags Hector's beautiful body through the dust. The Trojans, and Hector's parents especially, grieve for Hector as if for Troy itself, already fallen. Andromache is inconsolable. Watching from the wall, as Achilles drags her husband's body in the dirt, Andromache faints, throwing off her shining headband, Hector's gift to her on her wedding day. Everyone knows the city will not survive Hector's death. Andromache imagines her own grim future, and her son's, with Hector gone.

While the Trojans grieve for Hector, the Greeks mourn Patroclus, and Achilles' fury continues unabated. He has avenged his friend's death by killing his killer, but still he rages. He is still preparing to slaughter on the funeral pyre of

Patroclus the twelve young Trojans he captured earlier. He is still devising ways to outrage Hector's corpse. Achilles refuses to wash the battle gore from his body and hair. He still refuses to eat. What was the point of all the bloodshed, you wonder, if it did not make Achilles feel any better?

While the other men take dinner and go to sleep in their huts, Achilles lies alone on the beach until sleep overtakes him. As he sleeps, Patroclus's ghost reproaches him for not yet having given him a proper funeral. On waking, Achilles prepares the funeral for his dear friend.

The Greeks build a huge pyre and on it Achilles places two of Patroclus's dogs whose throats he has slit. He kills also the twelve captured young Trojans and places them on the pyre, too. You note that killing Hector has not made Achilles change his mind about this. He murders the young men as easily as he kills the dogs. His farewell to Patroclus shows that he is still enraged and still planning to give Hector's body to birds and dogs to defile. You know that Aphrodite and Apollo are keeping the dogs away and protecting Hector's beautiful corpse in spite of Achilles' mistreatment. Afterward, while Achilles sleeps, the Greeks gather Patroclus's bones, bury them in an urn, and construct a huge grave mound over it.

Now Achilles holds funeral games in his friend's honor. These games come as a great relief after so much bloodshed. You admire the warriors' skill in the chariot race and in contests of boxing, wrestling, throwing, and archery. The footrace has prizes for all, even for the last-place finisher. Achilles furnishes the prizes from his own stash. He supervises the games and judiciously resolves disputes. Distributing prizes fairly and generously, he seems to set the tone for all. When the winner of the chariot race objects to him giving second prize to the last-place finisher, Achilles agrees to give the loser instead something else from his own ship. When Menelaus, second in the chariot race, accuses the winner of illegally fouling him, the winner agrees to give him his prize. Agamemnon stands up to contend with Meriones in the spear-throwing contest, but there is no competition. Achilles assures Agamemnon that everyone knows he is *aristos,* "best," at spear throwing. (You wonder if this is true.) Agamemnon lets Meriones take the first prize and agreeably takes the other.

It is all very surprising. You have seen warriors quarrel and kill for such prizes. Now they are casually giving them away to one another? Achilles' admiration for the competitors' efforts and his generosity seem to set a constructive example for the others. You have never seen this side of Achilles. He is confident, authoritative, judicious, and magnanimous. The man who once flipped out at losing one girl is giving away numerous possessions without a second thought. He resolves disputes peacefully. Even Agamemnon accepts Achilles' pronouncements without objection. All seems orderly and pleasant when Achilles is in charge and Agamemnon also feels his own excellence acknowledged.

After the games, everyone returns to his own ship for dinner and the pleasure of sleep. But Achilles remains weeping and unable to sleep. The interlude of Patroclus's funeral games, agreeable as it was for everyone else, has eased his grief no more than his rampage of revenge killings had. Achilles paces the beach until dawn.

At first light, Achilles harnesses his horses to his chariot and resumes ceaselessly dragging Hector's body around Patroclus's tomb. Apollo protects the corpse, complaining to Zeus that Achilles has destroyed compassion and has no respect or mercy in him. Zeus instructs Thetis: "Tell your son that the gods are all angry with him, especially me. He may perhaps fear me and release Hector for ransom." You notice that Zeus does not order Achilles to return the body.

Thetis delivers the message, and Zeus sends the messenger-goddess Iris to King Priam instructing him to go alone to Achilles, taking gifts "which may move his heart to compassion." Through Iris, Zeus assures Priam that Achilles is not senseless and will spare a suppliant. You realize that Priam could never otherwise have had such a wildly improbable idea, and you have seen how Achilles has been treating suppliants recently.

Priam readies the ransom. He is eager to go but also apprehensive. His wife Hecuba considers him out of his mind even to think of approaching Achilles, a man who has murdered so many of his noble sons. Hecuba is sure that Achilles "eats raw flesh and is not trustworthy." She wishes that she herself could eat Achilles' liver raw. "That would be vengeance," she insists. You notice the hypocrisy: she accuses Achilles of the monstrosity of "eating raw flesh," but in the next breath she is wishing she could, too. You marvel at how Hecuba has changed from the kindly, generous mother who greeted Hector on his return from battle. Her suffering and her desire for vengeance have done something terrible to her.

Despite Hecuba's objections, Priam gathers immense, shining treasure: cloaks, clothing, blankets, talents of gold, tripods, cauldrons, goblets. A good omen precedes Priam's departure, but his people mourn for him, as if he goes to his death. No one expects him to return alive.

Incredibly, under cover of night, Priam gets past the Greeks' ditch and defensive wall, traverses the encampment, and reaches Achilles' shelter. Zeus sends the god Hermes as guide. (How else, you think, could a solitary old man have managed this journey?) Claiming to be one of Achilles' companions,

Hermes reassures Priam that the gods have been protecting his son's body, despite Achilles' efforts to defile it. Hermes puts the watchmen to sleep, opens Achilles' massive courtyard door, and brings in the ransom. Then Priam is on his own.

Slipping unnoticed into Achilles' shelter, Priam grasps Achilles' knees and kisses the terrible, murderous hands that have killed so many of his sons. Achilles gazes at Priam in wonder just as people gaze on a murderer once seized by *atē*, "ruinous folly," who comes to supplicate a rich man. (The analogy seems peculiar. Achilles is the killer, not Priam. How is this suppliant requesting pity from a murderer like a murderer seeking forgiveness for his crime?)

Choosing his words carefully, Priam urges Achilles to think of his own father, who must be about Priam's age. With Achilles absent, his father is now defenseless. "Your father is surely hoping," says Priam, "that someday he'll see his son returning from Troy." (You know that he never will. And you know that Achilles knows it, too.) "I had fifty sons myself," Priam continues quietly, "but most of these were killed in the war. And you killed the one who remained to defend the city. I have come to ransom him now, bringing infinite gifts. Respect the gods, Achilles, and pity me, as you remember your own father. But I am even more pitiable. I have endured what no other earthborn mortal ever yet has: to come in supplication to the man who has slain my children."

Will Priam's words anger Achilles further? Will he coldly murder Priam as he has recently killed other suppliants? No, Priam has made Achilles think of his own father. You watch, stunned, as he takes Priam by the hand. You see the two men grieve together, Priam for his son, Achilles for his father, and then for Patroclus. As they weep, you realize that they have both lost so much, but Achilles grieves for a present loss and also for a future one, imagining the pain his own father will feel at losing him.

Achilles marvels at Priam's courage in risking his life to come to him. He recognizes that the gods do not suffer, whereas suffering defines mortal life. "Zeus gives everyone a mixture of good and bad in life, except for those to whom he gives all bad," Achilles says. "Good fortune is impermanent, and there is no point in grieving over loss. You have lost your sons," he tells Priam. "My father is going to lose me." You notice that Achilles does not distinguish friend from enemy. All mortals suffer and die, friend and foe alike.

But Achilles remains dangerous and potentially explosive. He becomes irritable when Priam asks him to accept the ransom and return Hector's body for burial. "Don't provoke me," he tells Priam. "I'm thinking about it. I had a message from Zeus." He warns Priam not to anger him. He is still grieving and could lose his temper and fail to honor Priam's suppliant status. He might transgress against Zeus's commands. Achilles understands his own capacity to violate Zeus's wishes. Zeus has suggested the proper course of action. It is up to Achilles to choose.

Abruptly, he does. He leaps up like a lion but does not attack Priam. He tells his serving men to bring in the ransom and bids his serving women wash and prepare Hector's corpse. Achilles realizes that if Priam sees his son's body uncared for, he might succumb to anger and then Achilles would retaliate by killing him. Imagining Priam's feelings, Achilles prudently elects to return the body only after it is properly prepared. He promises to return Hector's body the next morning and bids his men prepare a meal. The two enemies now eat together, staring at one another in amazement. You also marvel, seeing Priam eating with his son's killer and Achilles eating with the father of the man who killed his best friend. You know that this is the first meal Achilles has eaten since Patroclus died.

Achilles tells his servants to make up a bed for Priam outside, sheltered by the porch roof and unseen by other Greeks who might kill him if they knew of his presence. He promises to hold back his own fighters for the twelve-day period that Priam requests for Hector's funeral. Priam lies down on the bed prepared for him outside, and Achilles sleeps inside beside Briseis. You recall that this is the first time Achilles has slept, too, since Patroclus died. Eating, sleeping—these normal human activities mark Achilles' return to humanity.

But Priam does not dare sleep the night within the Greek encampment. What if Achilles changes his mind? Achilles is still an enemy, still violent, still dangerous. He might even kidnap King Priam for ransom. Slipping away in the middle of the night, unseen, Priam takes his dead son's body back to Troy.

But you saw that for an instant the human capacity for pain and sorrow removed all distinctions between even the most bitter enemies. For one brief moment Achilles understood that suffering unites him and Priam as human beings. You realize that Achilles has glimpsed something that felt better than rage, better than killing. And you have seen it too.

A Moral Critique of Warfare

Achilles' brief moment of insight and empathy, startling as it is, does not emerge from the *Iliad* without precedent. In fact, Achilles' extraordinary behavior at the end of the epic epitomizes the *Iliad*'s portrait of war. Achilles' compassion shocks Priam and even surprises Achilles himself, but the narrative has repeatedly prepared the audience for it. The *Iliad*'s depiction of warfare constantly evokes the audience's critical judgment and undermines any conviction the audience may have that success in battle constitutes the highest human achievement. Similes in the narrative and descriptions of warriors dying in battle prompt the audience to sympathize not with victorious fighters but with their victims.

The warriors within the tale can ignore the fact that their opponents are men like themselves with ambitious goals to accomplish and loving families to mourn their deaths, but the audience cannot. Long before Achilles reenters the battle and embarks on his destructive rampage, the narrative enables the audience to see the deaths of defeated warriors as sad and wasteful. Long before Achilles recognizes the fundamental equality of all human beings in their capacity to suffer and die, the narrative has demonstrated this to the audience repeatedly. Although Homer's warriors value vengeance, Achilles' example ultimately undermines the audience's confidence that revenge accomplishes anything at all. In discovering the value of empathy, Achilles does not intuit a new standard of "bestness." Rather, he corroborates an ideal implicit in the narrative all along.

The *Iliad*'s bone-crunching, guts-flying descriptions of hand-to-hand combat may seem primitive to a modern audience, but the violence can also make this ancient tale seem recognizably familiar; warfare remains a feature of modern life as well.[1] The relentless, gory battle scenes can make modern readers miss the point. Some readers see only evidence of a timeless human attraction to violence. Oddly, some readers find comfort in thinking, "Ah, human nature has always been like this. Violence and wars are in our DNA." They see nothing more in the *Iliad*. But the great danger in reading anything is that you see only what you want or expect to see. If you fail to read carefully, you find in the text nothing but confirmation of your prior assumptions. The *Iliad* does not affirm or condone the human capacity for violence, destruction, and chaos. The *Iliad*'s characters celebrate warfare as the finest human achievement; the narrative does not.[2]

The *Iliad*'s detailed account of the horrors of war is also a critique of the morality of warfare and a celebration of the value of each individual human life. In describing the death of a warrior, the narrative often includes poignant details of the man's background and his unique value to his family. The dead are not nameless fighters. They are somebody's son or brother or husband. Vivid similes emphasize the sad, wasteful destruction of a young man slaughtered in his prime.[3] An archer misses Hector, for example, but strikes another man, "a noble son of Priam, in the chest with an arrow. His wedded mother, from Aisyme, the beautiful Kastianeira, like to the gods in her build, bore him. And he, once struck, nodded his head to one side, weighed down by his helmet, as a poppy in the garden, weighed down by its fruits and spring moisture, nods its head to one side" (8.302–308).[4] This delicate image makes it difficult for the audience to experience the killer's joy or satisfaction. Instead, the simile makes us feel the tragic, senseless loss of an innocent young man. (He was not even the archer's intended target.) The references to the young man's mother and father also prompt us to imagine their loss and the grief they will feel.

Like the simile of the broken poppy, other similes evoke the sadness and wasteful destructiveness of warfare. As another Trojan retreats, Menelaus drives the point of his weapon through the man's "tender neck." He falls with a thud, and his armor clatters upon him. His hair, bound with gold and silver, is "like the Graces" but also "stained with blood." Dead, the man is "like the blooming, lovely, luxurious shoot of an olive tree which someone nurtures in a lonely spot and gives abundant water. And breaths of all the winds agitate it. And it swells with its white blossom.

But then, suddenly, a tempestuous wind wrenches it out of its planting hole and lays it out on the ground. Such was Euphorbus, the son of Panthous and a man good with the spear, when Menelaus, son of Atreus, killed him and stripped his armor" (17.45–60).[5]

This analogy of the dying Euphorbus to a lovely, well-cared-for olive tree suggests not the glory of his Greek killer's achievement but the counterproductive, wasteful destruction of a human life. Similarly, the narrator details another dying Trojan's entire biography and then explains that "he fell like an ash tree which, on the peak of a mountain and visible from far away on every side, once cut with the bronze, brings its tender leaves to the ground" (13.170–180). As another warrior falls, we learn that he was the "dear son of Zeus-nurtured Aisyetes" and "son-in-law of Anchises," and also the husband of Hippodameia "whom her father and queenly mother loved in their heart." Moreover, this Hippodameia, the man's wife, "excelled every girl her age in her beauty and her actions and her intelligence. For this reason also the best man in broad Troy married her" (13.427–433). Dying, this Trojan distinguished by such an admirable wife "called out hoarsely, transfixed by the spear, and falling with a thud. And the spear stuck fast in his heart" (13.441–442). This same man was Aeneas's brother-in-law and took care of Aeneas when he was little (13.465). Another Trojan dies "pitiable, aiding his citizens, away from his properly wedded wife, from whom he saw no pleasure, but he gave many things for her" (11.242–243).

Persistently distinguishing the audience's perspective from the killer's, the narrative emphasizes both the gore of bloodshed and the resulting sadness and loss. Targeting a Trojan trying to capture the body of Patroclus, Ajax, "darting through the throng, struck him in close combat through his dog-skin helmet with its cheeks of bronze. And the helmet, thick with horsehair, broke around the point of the spear, being struck by the great spear and the stout hand. And his brain ran up from the wound along the eye socket, bloody. And right there his martial might was dissolved. And then from his hands he let fall to the ground, to lie there, the foot of great-hearted Patroclus. And near to him, he fell face-first upon the corpse, far from fertile Larisa, nor did he give recompense to his dear parents in return for their rearing him. But his lifetime was brief, as he was laid low by the spear of high-spirited Ajax" (17.293–303). Ajax may feel proud of this conquest, but the narrative prevents the audience from sharing his enthusiasm. We imagine instead the grief of far-away parents.

The details in these descriptions of death emphasize the contrasts between the values of the characters and the perspective of the audience. Warfare, for the characters, provides the opportunity to win glory. But the similes and little vignettes evoke the experience of the victims and validate the lives lost. These are all Trojans dying, in the examples above. These are enemy fighters, but their deaths are not a catalog of glorious Greek victories. Instead, they are stories of wasteful destruction and sad loss. Spears and arrows mutilate fine bodies in numerous and horrific ways. As they fall in death, warriors clutch at the ground (e.g., 11.425, 13.508). The dying men have loving fathers, mothers, and wives. Parents weep (e.g., 13.658). Even Nestor's account of his own martial exploits emphasizes the importance of individual lives lost. Nestor identifies a victim's father-in-law, for example, and describes his wife in detail, her beauty, her knowledge of medicine (11.737ff.). The *Iliad* makes us see all dying warriors, not just Greek ones, as fully human and important and their deaths as tragic.[6]

Death in the *Iliad* comes with horrific finality, in powerful contrast to stories' capacity to transcend death and confer immortality. The Homeric conception of the afterlife includes no possibility of serene paradise. Achilles, visited by the phantom or spirit of the dead Patroclus, realizes that "there is some spirit and phantom even in the halls of Hades, but the mind or thoughts are entirely not in it" (23.103–104). The gory details of physical destruction and the absolute finality of death make all the more attractive that possibility of gaining immortal remembrance via epic poetry celebrating a warrior's splendid achievements.[7]

Undermining the Enjoyment of Others' Suffering

By individualizing dying warriors and enabling the audience to experience the sadness and wastefulness of their deaths, the *Iliad* prevents us from sharing the achievement or exultation of the slayers. But the sheer volume of descriptions of slaughter in the *Iliad* and the graphic, bloody, horrific details of pierced bodies and smashed bones can be overwhelming, even numbing.

The gods, however, experience delight in watching the destruction of human life. Zeus sits "exulting in his *kudos,* 'glory,'" while "looking upon the city of the Trojans and the ships of the Greeks and the gleam of the bronze and men destroying and men being destroyed" (11.81–83). Zeus enjoys watching men dying in battle, telling Poseidon at one point, "I will remain sitting on the cleft of Olympus, where, seeing, I will delight my thoughts" (20.22–23).

To be fair, Zeus also enjoys watching gods fight; he "laughed with joy in his dear heart when he saw the gods contending in strife" (21.389–390). Athena, too, laughs after she defeats Ares, but of course there are no lasting consequences for Ares since he is a god. He is the war god, in fact, so we may smile at the incongruity as we watch Aphrodite, goddess of love, lead him safely out of the fighting (21.408ff.). For gods, warfare has no lasting consequences or real meaning. It is just a form of entertainment.[8] But for the human characters within the poem, warfare is hardly a charming pastime. Combat is life or death. Success or failure in battle is everything.

The gods' delight in watching human warfare prompts us to consider our own role as spectators viewing this story. Like gods, we are immune to the fighting occurring within the tale. Our current safety from the violence depicted in the story permits any pleasure or thrill we may get from watching it. But Zeus's example also reminds us that we are not gods. Whether we are hearing or reading a story like the *Iliad* or watching some television or film depiction of warfare or violence, our invulnerability at that moment is only temporary. In our real lives we are, of course, always vulnerable to violence and destruction. The gods' ability to enjoy watching horrific violence and remain untouched by it reminds us that this perspective is possible only for immortals.

Homer's gods thus provide a negative standard against which to measure our own reaction to watching "men destroying and men being destroyed." We may find the violence in the *Iliad* overwhelming or unpleasant. Or maybe not. By showing us the gods' amusement in watching human beings maim and kill one another, the *Iliad* also considers the possibility that we, too, might simply find pleasure and entertainment in viewing the violence. This possibility presents a tremendous danger to any society. If we accept narrated or simulated violence as exciting, admirable, or even simply entertaining, why would we choose to control our own rage or substitute verbal competition for physical combat in real life? Unlike the Judeo-Christian conception of divinity (and unlike the misleading impression some modern sources may promote about Greek gods), Homer's gods are not a model of goodness for human beings to strive to emulate. Their actions and reactions do not set an example that human beings can or should try to follow.[9] Since the gods live forever, death has no meaning or consequence for them. Precisely because mortals do die, death for us is catastrophic and absolute. Watching other people suffer and die may be somehow thrilling, but it also must remind us of our own vulnerability, losses, and eventual death.

The *Iliad* helps to counteract the seductions of rage and violence by continually reminding the audience that we are not gods. We are all equal in our mortality. We all make choices and must endure the consequences. The characters continue to define human excellence as success in killing, but the audience experiences the tragic defeat and loss of each individual victim. We see that every individual life matters and that death is the inevitable and absolute end, for us as for them.

Challenging the Value of Vengeance

While the audience sees the gods' counterexample and the human costs of the characters' definition of achievement, the characters themselves continue to identify violent revenge as the only admirable reaction to injury or loss. Lacking the foresight and breadth of vision that the narrative affords the audience, the characters exult in an enemy's destruction. One Trojan warrior, defending the body of his brother, and having killed a Greek attacker, "exulted terribly, calling afar, 'Boastful Greeks, insatiable of threats, surely now the labor and misery won't be ours alone, but at some time you also will die in this way. Consider how your Promachos sleeps, subdued by my spear, so that the blood price for my brother, at any rate, may not in any way go unpaid long. Therefore also any man prays to leave behind in his halls a blood relative as a defender against battle'" (14.478–485). This warrior, like others in the *Iliad*, understands vengeance as the only satisfying response to violent injury.

But the narrative suggests otherwise. As the capstone to all of the preceding descriptions of slaughter, Achilles' example, especially, undermines any confidence the audience may have in the value of vengeance and promotes instead the possibility of empathy. The theme of vengeance dominates the story in the final third of the epic, since a series of revenge killings powers the plot: wearing Achilles' armor, Patroclus kills Hector's friend Sarpedon; Hector takes revenge by killing Patroclus; the desire for revenge then drives Achilles to kill Hector; Achilles accepts his own imminent death as long as he can kill Hector first (18.98, 115).[10] His fury at Hector enables him to surmount his anger against Agamemnon. We see that Achilles begins to suspect that his rage has not served him well thus far, for he wishes that strife and anger would vanish entirely from the lives of gods and mortals (18.107–111). But nevertheless he determines to avenge Patroclus's death by killing Hector and winning glory for himself (18.121).

Achilles' desire for revenge prevents him, at this point, from feeling empathy for his enemy. He thinks of the grief of Patroclus's father and that of his own father (18.324ff.), but in the next breath he is planning to behead Hector and twelve glorious children of the Trojans (18.334ff.). Achilles imagines the death of his own father and son as not worse than the death of Patroclus (19.321–327). But the intensity of his rage prevents him from pursuing this insight to its logical conclusion. The thought of the grief of his own losses does not permit Achilles to think of the future grief of the parents of his intended victims.

Initially, Achilles cannot see beyond his own need for revenge. Viewing the immortal armor that Hephaestus has fashioned for him only increases his anger (19.15ff.). He gives up his fury at Agamemnon only in order to satisfy an even greater rage for vengeance (19.67).[11] He has learned nothing from his previous experience indulging his anger, but the audience sees clearly that he managed only to further the destruction of many fellow Greeks, including his beloved Patroclus.

Achilles' rage blinds him to the consequences of his actions, but the audience sees that the pursuit of revenge destroys Achilles' humanity. Although he is half mortal and half immortal, since his father is a human being and his mother is a divinity, the many supernatural details in this part of the story indicate that the passion for vengeance robs Achilles of his human attributes. He receives divine armor (18.130–144, 468–616), and he refuses to eat until he has exacted revenge (19.199ff.). When Odysseus insists that it is natural for human beings to grieve for their dead and then eat, that is, then go on living, Achilles agrees to let the other men eat but refuses to do so himself (19.216ff., 305). Achilles receives nectar and ambrosia, the food of the gods (19.352, 5.341–342), and gods address him not in disguise but directly (21.286). His horses actually speak to him (19.408).[12]

These supernatural elements mark Achilles' departure from humanity, and we see the dehumanizing process escalate as Achilles succumbs to his passion for revenge. He slaughters Trojans indiscriminately. Pitiless, he even butchers men who supplicate him at his knees (20.465; 21.67). The narrator likens Achilles, consumed by rage, to "fiercely blazing fire" (20.490) and to smoke from a blazing city (21.522). Repeatedly, he is identified as *daimoni isos,* "like to a divinity" (e.g., 20.495, 21.18, 21.227).[13] Merciless, Achilles captures twelve young captives alive to be "a blood price" for his dead friend (21.27). Achilles admits that he had mercy before Patroclus died and used to ransom live captives. Now, he says, what is the point? We will all die anyway (21.100ff.). He vaunts over killing a defenseless victim who has begged for mercy, and he feels that his desire for vengeance cannot be sated until all Trojans are dead (21.133–135).[14]

This depiction of Achilles' loss of humanity in the pursuit of vengeance puts the audience at a critical remove from Achilles' own perspective. Warfare offers Achilles and all warriors the opportunity to win *kleos,* "glory," by displaying *aretē,* "martial excellence or valor," and the characters exult in their ability to kill their enemies. But the narrative explicitly prevents the audience from agreeing that success in killing epitomizes human excellence, that this deserves our highest admiration or commendation. Greek has two words that can be translated as "glory": *kudos,* the glory that the gods bestow, and *kleos,* the glory that human beings confer (i.e., the glory that epic poetry celebrates and commemorates). Describing Achilles' rampage, the narrator insists that Achilles was "pressing on to earn *kudos,* 'glory,' and his unapproachable hands were stained with gore" (20.502–503). And as the Trojans fled, "Achilles pursued eagerly with his spear. Strong rage ever held his heart, and he was striving to win *kudos,* 'glory' " (21.542–543). These repeated references to Achilles' bloody pursuit of *kudos,* the glory that the gods bestow, make the audience question whether this behavior deserves human approval. The gods may value such "achievements," but do they deserve the glory (*kleos*) that we choose to confer on one another by celebrating and memorializing deeds worthy of praise and admiration?[15]

The *Iliad* has posed this question before, compelling the audience to distinguish deeds unworthy of human approval from worthy ones. An earlier use of *kudos,* the glory that the gods confer, undermines traditional confidence in the value of harming enemies regardless of the methods employed. Greeting Odysseus upon his return from a nighttime raiding expedition, Nestor calls him "much-praised Odysseus, great *kudos,* 'glory,' of the Greeks" (10.544). But what has Odysseus accomplished on this night raid? The audience has watched him and Diomedes sneak up on and ruthlessly massacre a group of sleeping warriors. We saw them kill a Trojan captive while that captive grasped their knees and begged for mercy (10.447–457). By calling Odysseus "great *kudos* of the Greeks," Nestor suggests that the *gods* approve of Odysseus's exploits. But are they worthy of *kleos,* the approval that human beings can confer on one another? That is up to us to decide. Merciless butchery of defenseless men hardly seems particularly courageous or impressive. English obscures the distinction, but in Greek Nestor's greeting of Odysseus as "great *kudos,* 'glory,' of the Greeks" rings terribly hollow. The bloody deeds of the night raid seem distinctly shabby, not especially worthy of human praise or glory (*kleos*).[16]

Later in the epic, prompted to question whether Achilles' murderous pursuit of divine approval (*kudos*) actually deserves human admiration and commemoration (*kleos*), the audience comes to see the spectacular futility of Achilles' exploits. His lethal rampage, narrated in horrific detail in three full books (20–22), does nothing to ease his anger or soothe his grief. Hector's death neither satisfies Achilles nor restores his humanity. Achilles boasts over his dying enemy (22.330), but he continues to rage, wishing only that he could eat Hector raw (22.345). He despoils the body (22.395). Achilles says that he has killed Hector as he promised, but we see that he is still "devising shameful deeds" for Hector's corpse (23.24). Achilles remains angry and continues to behave inhumanly, refusing to wash until he has held a funeral for Patroclus (23.37ff.). He gains no satisfaction from murdering the twelve young captive Trojans on Patroclus's funeral pyre, as still "he was devising evil deeds in his thoughts" (23.176).

Achilles' murderous rampage fails to satisfy him, and the narrative ensures that it gives the audience no vicarious satisfaction either. In the final confrontation with Hector, we do not, as we might expect, experience Achilles' delight or pleasure in finally exacting vengeance on his friend's killer. Instead, the narrative takes us inside Hector's head as he awaits Achilles' onslaught and debates what to do (22.100ff.). Hector's flight around the walls of Troy feels like our own nightmare (22.100ff.).[17]

Hector tries to strike a deal with Achilles, asking that they agree that whoever wins will return the loser's corpse to his people. But we see that Achilles' desire for revenge has driven him beyond the reach of civilized compacts. No Geneva Convention–style standards are possible for him. Achilles' complete rejection of Hector's civilized and reasonable request, his angry dismissal of any possibility of concord or agreement (22.261–267), shows that his desire for revenge has dehumanized him completely. Agreements, love, oaths are features of human society, consequences of the human capacity for verbal communication. The desire for vengeance, by making these all impossible, has made Achilles not merely bestial but monstrous.[18] The *Iliad* prompts us here not to identify with Achilles but to judge him.

Unlike Achilles, we witness his "achievements" from the perspective of his Trojan victims for the narrative continues to emphasize their suffering. We experience not Achilles' triumph in killing his friend's killer but the devastating grief of the dead man's mother and father (22.405ff.). Hector's death foreshadows and substitutes for the fall of his city, which the *Iliad* does not include (22.410ff.). The collapse of Hector's wife Andromache upon learning of her husband's death pre-enacts symbolically the fall of Troy itself, which will soon follow.[19] Viewed from the perspective of the devastation that it causes, vengeance seems more vicious than admirable.

An Alternative to Bloodshed

Despite his many killings, Achilles makes no progress in dealing with his grief, but the narrative hints at a possible solution that Achilles as yet fails to appreciate. By refusing to return Hector's body (23.183), Achilles shows not the slightest concern for the grief of Hector's father, but a simile in the narrative foreshadows his eventual moment of compassion. Likening Achilles mourning for Patroclus to a father mourning for his dead son (23.221–225), the simile at first seems peculiar, since Achilles and Patroclus are friends, not father and son. But the analogy makes the audience think of Priam's grief for his son Hector. Prompting the audience to imagine the suffering of an enemy father at the loss of his son, the analogy encourages the audience's capacity for empathy. It suggests that there is something universal about the pain of losing a loved one. Recognition of the universality of human suffering will ultimately prove therapeutic for both Achilles and Priam, but Achilles does not see this yet.

Before spelling out the resolution explicitly, the narrative shows that not even the resumption of political authority among the Greeks can solve Achilles' problem. The funeral games for Patroclus enable Achilles to reestablish his leadership role, but they distract him only temporarily from his grief. He appears surprisingly judicious, diplomatic, and generous, resolving disputes, determining winners, even distributing prizes from his own possessions (23.558ff).[20] He hardly seems like the same Achilles who cared so intensely for prizes that he quarreled so disastrously with Agamemnon over the loss of a single prize. His behavior during the games seems like a complete reversal. But is it? During these funeral games, Achilles' political authority is not in dispute. He is free to be magnanimous and to act on his own whim. For example, he gives a man an extra prize just for praising him, Achilles, as the fastest runner (23.795). This is what autocratic rulers do. They reward and punish based on their own whim, they give and take prizes at will. (That is precisely what infuriated Achilles about Agamemnon's power at the beginning of the epic.) During these games, Achilles seems calm and fully in charge, confident in his unchallenged autocratic authority. But even so, his grief and rage remain undiminished.

Neither the avenging slaughter nor the reassertion of his political authority has in any way lessened the pain of Achilles' loss or enabled him to regain his humanity. After the games, Achilles continues to grieve desperately for his dead friend. He continues to drag Hector's body in the dirt, uselessly seeking to satisfy his desire for revenge by mutilating his enemy's corpse (24.22). Achilles' mother Thetis finds him still "groaning heavily" (24.123). He still cannot sleep. He continues to weep and pace.[21]

Solace comes, ultimately, not from the supernatural realm and not from the qualities that align Achilles with divinity but from Achilles' humanity. Like his aptitude for killing, Achilles' aptitude for autocratic political authority exemplifies the divine side of his nature, since gods, unlike men, can kill with impunity, and Zeus, unlike a mortal king, wields enduring autocratic power. But Achilles finally derives comfort from the capacities that he shares not with gods but with all human beings: the capacity to suffer and the capacity to make moral choices. Following the games, Achilles' behavior continues to be so extreme that even the gods criticize him and insist that human grief must have some limits (24.39–54), but Zeus only makes such limits possible. He does not command them. He does not order or force Achilles to return Hector's body. He only instructs his divine messenger to tell Priam "to bring gifts to Achilles which may move his heart to compassion" (24.119, 176).[22] Zeus instructs his messenger to assure Priam that Achilles will not kill him and will spare a suppliant (24.158–159). But will he? We see that Achilles must make this choice for himself.

The decision is hardly a foregone conclusion. We have recently seen Achilles coldly murder suppliants, and all of Priam's people think that he is going to his death (14.328). Hector's mother Hecuba thinks her husband has lost his mind; she is sure that Achilles will kill him (24.205–207).[23] The desire for revenge still grips

Achilles, but in the end he does spare Priam and he does return the body. Why? Zeus does not compel him. Why does he do it?

The narrative offers another hint with an analogy for Priam as he supplicates Achilles: Achilles marvels at Priam just as people gaze in wonder at a murderer who has come to supplicate a wealthy man (24.476–483). Like the earlier analogy likening Achilles grieving for Patroclus to a father grieving for his dead son (23.221–225), this stunning analogy also seems oddly inappropriate. It likens Priam to a murderer, but Achilles is the killer. The earlier analogy suggested that a friend's grief for a dead friend is like a father's grief for a dead son. This analogy suggests that a grieving father, supplicating the slayer of his son, is just like a murderer seeking refuge. In suggesting that various kinds of terrible human suffering are essentially equivalent, whatever their causes, this analogy, like the earlier one, hints at a fundamental equality between individuals in suffering and sorrow.[24]

And this insight turns out to hold the key. Achilles, looking at Priam and listening to Priam, remembers his own father and grieves for his impending loss. He and Priam weep together, each for his own separate losses (24.507). Achilles suddenly recognizes sorrow as the crucial component separating human beings from gods. He points out that "the gods have spun out the destiny for wretched mortals to live in distress, but they themselves are free from care" (24.525–526). Explaining that Zeus distributes good and bad fates to human beings, giving to some a mixture of good and bad, to others all bad (24.527–533), Achilles realizes that both Priam and his own father received a mixture of good and evil fortune, and that grief will never restore the dead (24.543–550).[25]

Achilles' example reminds us that no one gets all good fortune but that how we cope is not the gods' responsibility but our own. Do our actions make things better for ourselves and others, or worse? Achilles is now willing to return the body, but he remains hot-tempered. When Priam tries to hurry him, Achilles warns Priam not to provoke him (24.559). But Achilles also now understands his own capacity for rage. Consequently, he tactfully instructs his serving women to clean up the body lest the sight of it enrage Priam, for that in turn would provoke Achilles to murderous rage (24.582–586). Achilles now uses foresight and knowledge of causality to forestall his own rage.[26]

As the two enemies grieve together, the audience can appreciate both the power of Achilles' insight and its fragility. Their moment of mutual understanding means that both men can now eat (24.601ff.). Their grief, Priam's for Hector and Achilles' for Patroclus, had earlier prevented either man from eating (24.639ff.). Now, eating marks the end of devastating grief and the restoration of humanity. Achilles' moment of empathy also makes him capable of human compacts. Whereas earlier he had rejected any possibility of striking a deal with Hector, he now agrees to permit twelve days for Hector's burial. Still, his new-found reasonableness seems impermanent. Priam, fearing for his own safety, cannot risk staying the night. The *Iliad*'s conclusion alludes to the conflict at the story's beginning and the devastation at its end: Achilles sleeps beside Briseis (the girl whose loss triggered the events that began Homer's tale), and the epic ends not in the triumphant sack of a city or the accomplishment of vengeance but with the lamentation for and the burial of Hector (24.719–804).[27]

Startling as it is, Achilles' brief moment of insight as he grieves with Priam does not come as a complete surprise to the audience. Throughout the *Iliad*, the narrative has emphasized the essential mortality and humanity of warriors on both sides of the conflict. All have people who care about them. All have families, friendships, prior lives, and agonizing, gory deaths. The stories and similes accompanying the descriptions of bloodshed and slaughter cultivate our understanding that anyone's death is no cause for celebration, that every death is a loss, a cause for sadness not exultation. Homer's tales of dying warriors, like his account of the Greeks' fortifications and the Trojans' assault on them, equate Greek lives with Trojan lives, Greek deaths with Trojan deaths. This equation anticipates for the audience (although not for the characters) the analogy between Priam and Achilles' father, Peleus: one has lost a son, the other soon will.

The *Iliad's* emphasis on the essential equality of all human beings in their mortality and their suffering devalues vengeance and promotes empathy. The epic reveals not only that vengeance dehumanizes the avenger but, more important, that vengeance does not work. It does not bring satisfaction or peace of mind. It only perpetuates and exacerbates destructive rage. Achilles' fleeting identification of Priam with his own father suggests that even bitter enemies can experience empathy, even if only briefly.[28] Achilles' example shows the inadequacy of a moral code that elevates and promotes rage and revenge. His momentary flash of insight suggests that not altruism but self-interest should prompt us to forgo the short-term satisfactions of anger and vengeance and instead to recognize our own needs in the needs of others.

Unquestionably, the *Iliad* describes a rigidly hierarchical society. The characters prioritize honor, success in warfare, helping friends and harming enemies, and, above all, vengeance. The characters feel that it is important to excel in battle but also that it is important to speak effectively. Although they believe that the gods control events, Homer's characters know that human beings differ in their abilities, and they strive to be "best." They know that the community needs talented individuals and talented individuals need the community. They continue to associate martial success with *kleos*, "glory." Some of these ideas are beneficial and admirable, and similar priorities still exist openly and proudly in many parts of the world today, in societies that are not democratic and also in ones that are.

But in depicting these traditional, hierarchical values, the *Iliad* does not simply commend or accept them. Instead, it prompts the audience to question them. Are they constructive? Are they optimal? By giving the audience a perspective different from that of its characters, the *Iliad* permits us to assess the characters' values and to consider other possibilities. The narrative emphatically contradicts the characters' conviction that the gods control events, and the audience sees instead that the characters' choices and actions have predictable consequences. Fierce competition for honor among powerful individuals has a dire impact on everyone. Therefore, competition between powerful individuals prompts each of us to ask ourselves precisely which "achievements" we should honor in others and cultivate in ourselves. The gods admire and validate the human capacity for slaughter, but the narrative makes the audience responsible for determining which abilities and exploits deserve the honor and glory that the community can confer.

Greek myth originates in a spirit of critical self-reflection, a necessary and defining component of any successful life and any life-enhancing community. The *Iliad,* our earliest surviving source for ancient Greek tales, is itself already beginning to evaluate the pros and cons of the value system that produced these stories. Awareness of multiple perspectives and training in logical reasoning promotes recognition of the universality of human suffering. This, in turn, permits empathy. The realization that empathy can replace violence and vengeance (even briefly) may be the most crucial impetus to constructive decision making and successful, stable societies. But empathy, as Achilles' example demonstrates, need not derive from some

extraordinary selflessness. It results, rather, from a clear understanding of our own self-interest.

Despite the *Iliad*'s illuminating message, rage continues
to wreak havoc in the twenty-first century. Rage substitutes for
moral reasoning and promotes violence. Perpetrators exult in
committing atrocities and in exacting violent revenge, and their
communities often celebrate their "achievements." Tyranny,
violence, and intimidation triumph in the absence of empathy,
and communities implode. The *Iliad*, however, reminds its
audience of the value of every individual human life. It points
out that indulging in rage and violent revenge is self-destructive.
The *Iliad* undermines any confidence in the value of vengeance.
By devaluing rage and promoting empathy as a more therapeutic alternative, the *Iliad* reveals the possibility that verbal debate
might replace physical combat.

Internalizing Homer's critique of rage and revenge and
developing these ideas even further, one democratic society, the
world's first *ever*, emerged and flourished 2,500 years ago. Although
citizens in fifth-century Athens continued to embrace warfare in
their conflicts with other citizen-communities, they began to appreciate the value of verbal debate for strengthening their community. In our own violent times, the stakes are even higher. Our
high-tech destructive capacities threaten the entire global community. We need Homer's powerful message now more than ever.

Greek tragedies, produced hundreds of years after the
Iliad first took shape, point the way . . .

5

The Dangers of
Democratic Decision Making
(Sophocles' *Ajax*)

Y ou know the great warrior Ajax as a magnificent defensive fighter and a tremendous asset to the Greek army. Following Achilles' death, Ajax quarreled with Odysseus over Achilles' immortal armor. Odysseus won the armor, but Ajax deserved it. Ajax's rage persisted even after he died; he refused to speak to Odysseus in the underworld.

Your father's father knew of Ajax and his quarrel with Odysseus, as did the many generations before him. Forever, it seems, your ancestors have been telling tales of Troy and the warriors who fought and died there. The events happened long ago, but they are part of your life as you have been hearing these stories ever since you can remember. But today is different. Today the past will become present. Today at the theater in Athens with thousands of other people you will witness Ajax's story as it unfolds.

From your seat, you look down on the encampment of
the Greeks on the shores of Troy. You recognize the goddess
Athena immediately from her distinctive combination of
woman's dress and man's heavy armor. Her helmet, shield,
and long spear glint in the sunlight. Odysseus is there, too,
but you are not sure that he sees Athena. Hearing her voice,
he looks up as she calls to him.

"Always," Athena calls out. "Son of Laertes, I always see
you pursuing some plan against your enemies. I see you now,
hunting around the shelters of Ajax and his men and
calculating from Ajax's tracks whether he is inside. Yes, he's
inside. His head and sword-killing hands are covered with
sweat. But why have you tracked him down?"

"Oh, voice of Athena!" Odysseus exclaims. "Dearest to
me of all the gods, you know me well. I've been hunting for
Ajax, who carries the great shield. We think he has done a
terrible thing, or he may have. We just found all our cattle
slaughtered and the herdsmen, too. Someone said he saw
Ajax bounding over the plains and holding a fresh-reeking
sword. I immediately set off to track him down, but I'm not
certain that I've found him. You have come at the critical
moment. I am always guided by your hand."

Athena assures Odysseus that he has found Ajax and that
Ajax did slaughter the cattle. She explains that Ajax was driven
by rage at not having been awarded the armor of Achilles.

"But why did he attack our herds?" Odysseus asks,
puzzled.

"Thinking he was painting his hands with your blood,"
Athena replies. "He would have succeeded, too. But I
prevented him from killing you, by casting before his eyes
mistaken impressions of his deadly delight. Destroying the
animals, he thought he was murdering you. He slashed and

slaughtered them most cruelly and mercilessly." Athena calmly describes a horrific scene of blood-spattering madness. Ajax thought he was killing Atreus's sons Agamemnon and Menelaus and the other Greek leaders. He still holds some surviving animals bound inside his tent. He continues to torture them, still thinking they are men.

You are appalled. Ajax, distinctive in Homer's tales for protecting the Greeks with his great shield, turned his ruthless sword on his own friends, or tried to? The thought shocks you. "I'll show him to you right now," Athena says. But Odysseus steps back. He begins to turn away. "Wait," Athena continues. "Have courage. I won't let him see you."

"What are you doing?" Odysseus cries in alarm. "Don't call him outside!"

Athena seems annoyed. "Won't you be quiet and not prove yourself a coward?" she says. Since Odysseus continues to protest, begging her to leave Ajax where he is, Athena appears genuinely puzzled. "Lest what occur? Isn't he the same man he was before?" When Odysseus agrees that Ajax is still his enemy, Athena asks, "Isn't it the sweetest laughter to laugh at your enemies?"

If you agree that laughter at an enemy's suffering and humiliation is the sweetest, and you may, Odysseus's response surprises you. He does not want to laugh at Ajax. He must remain and watch him emerge from his shelter, but he wishes that he were anywhere else. Unlike Odysseus, you may be curious to see Ajax in this deluded, blood-coated condition. But Odysseus's reluctance vaguely troubles you.

And, suddenly, there Ajax is, a huge, confident, blood-stained presence. Striding forth from his shelter, Ajax greets Athena and thanks her for her support. He promises her golden spoils from his night of successful hunting. He brags about killing the Greeks. When Athena asks him whether he attacked and killed Agamemnon and Menelaus, Ajax assents boastfully: "So that they will never again dishonor me. Let them try to take my armor away from me now that they're dead!" Still in the grip of the delusion Athena cast upon him, he claims to have his adversary Odysseus, "the practiced fox," bound within his shelter. Calling this prisoner "most welcome" (or "pleasant"), Ajax uses the same word Athena used to describe the pleasure of laughing at an enemy. He adds that he does not want his captive to die yet, not until he is done torturing him. Stalking back toward his shelter, Ajax claims he has work to do. "Always stand beside me as such an ally as you are now," he commands Athena, then disappears inside.

"Do you see how powerful the gods are, Odysseus?" Athena asks, turning back to her favorite. "Was there ever anyone more far-seeing than Ajax and better at doing whatever was necessary at the critical moment?"

"No," says Odysseus. But if you expect him to exult now, you are again disappointed. Odysseus takes no pleasure in seeing his enemy so deluded and disgraced. "I pity him," Odysseus says. "He is altogether wretched, even though he is hostile to me. He is yoked to a ruinous folly. But that could just as easily be me. For I see that we are all nothing, all of us who live. We are nothing except fleeting images, empty shadow."

For Athena, that is the point: mortal life is brief and vulnerable. "Look at his example," she warns, "and never speak arrogantly against the gods. Human affairs can rise or fall in a single day. The gods love those who practice sōphrosunē, 'moderation, restraint, prudence, wisdom,' and hate those who are kakos, 'bad, evil, base.'" You could mistake this for the moral of Ajax's story, but the play doesn't end here. If this play simply illustrates that the gods always punish

human arrogance, why doesn't Odysseus enjoy seeing his
enemy humiliated?

Athena departs, and the Chorus of Ajax's own men
enter. They recall Ajax's illustrious past as ruler of Salamis.
Horrified seeing the Greeks' delight at hearing and spreading
the story of Ajax's humiliation, they recognize it as the
pleasure the small and weak take in the suffering of the great
and powerful. "It isn't possible," they say, "to teach clear
judgment to such fools. We aren't strong enough to defend
ourselves without you, our ruler," they tell Ajax. They
recognize that Ajax must have offended some god or goddess.
He cannot have been in his right mind when he attacked the
cattle. Some divinely sent illness must have fallen on him.
They urge Ajax to go out and defend his reputation.

A young woman emerges from Ajax's shelter. You
recognize Tecmessa. A king's daughter, Tecmessa was
captured by Ajax in a raid. Ajax killed her entire family but
kept her as his bedmate. And yet, she, like the Chorus, seems
dismayed at Ajax's misfortune and at the devastation within
the shelter. The Chorus fear for the future, but Tecmessa tells
them something more troubling still: Ajax has returned to his
right mind. Realizing what he has done, he is in agony. His
pain doubles the pain of his friends, who grieve now not just
for themselves (at having a disgraced and humiliated ruler)
but for him in his misery as well.

Tecmessa explains that Ajax set out in the middle of the
night, silencing her objections. He returned with the animals
and vented his rage on them, attacking them as if they were
men. He slashed some to death and tortured others.
Addressing some shadow, he condemned Odysseus and the
sons of Atreus. He laughed delightedly at the violence he
inflicted on his victims. (You remember that Athena called

laughter at an enemy the sweetest of all, and Ajax thought he was getting revenge. You still wonder why Odysseus couldn't enjoy his enemy's suffering.)

But now Ajax has come to his senses and lies prostrate among his victims, the dead cattle and sheep. He compelled Tecmessa to tell him exactly what he had done (he obviously did not remember), and you hear his terrible moans from within the shelter. He cries out for his son and for his brother. The Chorus and Tecmessa fear what he may be planning.

The gates of the shelter open, and you see Ajax within. He is a bloody mess, surrounded by ravaged animal corpses. He greets his men warmly as his only loyal friends, but he bellows in distress "Look at me now! I was once bold, stouthearted, and fearless in battle against my enemies. Look what I've done to these beasts that no one fears!" Imagining the galling outrage of his enemy's laughter, he begs his men to kill him. Tecmessa objects, asking him to give in and be reasonable. Ajax orders her away.

"Ai ai!" Ajax cries out in his agony. How could he have missed killing his persecutors so completely? "Oh, you who sees and hears all, you most foul, slippery cheat, spawn of Laertes, surely you're laughing now in delight!" Ajax exclaims. (You know that Odysseus is not laughing, but you realize that Ajax, like Athena, thinks he should be.) "Even dishonored as I am, I wish I could see him," Ajax continues threateningly. He prays to Zeus to let him kill Odysseus and the sons of Atreus and then die. He is back in his right mind and knows what he has done, but his murderous rage toward Odysseus, Agamemnon, and Menelaus has not left him. And it never will.

"Ai ai!" Ajax continues to lament. "How can I have come to this? If Achilles, while alive, were to award the mastery of his armor to anyone on the basis of valor, no one else but me would have laid hold of it. But the sons of Atreus, disdaining my powers, awarded the armor to that completely unprincipled Odysseus. If my vision hadn't been distorted, they would never again vote such 'justice' against any other man. But now they've escaped my rage, and they're laughing at me."

"What should I do?" Ajax wonders. "The gods hate me. The Greeks hate me. How can I return home and face my father without any prizes of honor? For the well-born man, it is necessary either to live nobly or to die nobly."

Tecmessa begs Ajax not to abandon her and his son to his enemies. She reminds him that since he enslaved her and made her his bedmate, she has always been well-intentioned toward him. Because he destroyed her home and family, she now relies on him completely. And she has given him pleasure. "A well-born man," she says, "should be mindful of the good he experienced from another."

Demanding to see his little son, Ajax prays that he be luckier than his father but just like him in all other respects. Ajax entrusts the child to the care of his brother Teucrus. The boy's name, Eurysaces, "broad shield," evokes his father's signature weapon in Homer's tales, and Ajax now gives him that very shield, insisting that the rest of his armor be buried with him.

Ajax rejects Tecmessa's pleas and strides out of his shelter. He brandishes his great sword still dripping with the blood of sheep and cattle. "Time changes everything," Ajax announces. "Even I, who was steadfast once, like iron, feel pity at the thought of leaving this woman a widow and my son an orphan among enemies." Ajax says he will go to some remote place to wash away his defilement and ward off the anger of the goddess. He will hide his sword. It was a gift from his most hated enemy, the Trojan Hector. (You might remember that Homer describes this gift exchange in the middle of battle: *Il.* 7.287–312.) "But ever since I got it," Ajax claims, "I've never had anything valuable from the Greeks. It proves the old adage that enemies' gifts are no gifts and not useful. From now on," he continues, "I'll know how to yield to the gods and reverence the sons of Atreus. Even the most terrible and powerful forces of nature yield in honor and office to one another, winter to summer, night to day, storms to calm. Even all-conquering Sleep doesn't hold forever those he has bound. How, then, will we not know how to practice *sōphrosunē*, 'moderation, restraint, prudence, wisdom'?" Ajax's profound understanding of the cyclical processes of nature impresses you as sensible and correct.

But Ajax's next words baffle you. "Now I see," he says, "that an enemy must be hated by me only so far as one hates someone who is one day going to be a friend. And I will wish to benefit a friend only as much as one benefits someone who will not always remain his friend." What can Ajax mean? He recognizes that time changes all things, even friendships and enmities, but the Ajax you remember from Homer's tales remained perpetually loyal to his friends and relentlessly hateful to his enemies. That is the highest goal of every great warrior in Homer's tales: to help friends and harm enemies. (That principle made Achilles' refusal to fight on behalf of the Greeks so wrong, so destructive. That principle made Achilles' empathy for Priam so startling, so fleeting.)

What is Ajax planning now? He orders Tecmessa inside to pray that the gods accomplish his desires. He orders the Chorus to tell his brother Teucrus to take care of him and his people. "Soon you may perhaps learn," he says enigmatically, "that even though I am unfortunate, I have been preserved." Tecmessa and the Chorus assume that Ajax has decided to give up his anger. You are not so certain. You know Ajax as steadfast, unchanging. Has he relented?

Ajax strides off, and a messenger arrives to tell Tecmessa and the Chorus that Ajax must stay inside his shelter for this day only, until Athena's anger has passed. The seer Calchas has explained this. But where is Ajax?

The Chorus and Tecmessa withdraw. The scene changes, and there stands Ajax. He is talking about his sword but no longer holding it. He has stuck its hilt deep in the earth. The razor-sharp blade points skyward. Ajax calls on Zeus to ensure that his brother finds his body first, so that it will not be despoiled by dogs and birds. He calls on Hermes to guide his spirit to the underworld with one swift leap and no struggle. And he calls on the Furies to destroy his enemies, namely the sons of Atreus and the entire Greek army. He calls on the sun to bring news of his death to his parents. Calling on Death itself, he bids farewell to daylight, the plains of his homeland Salamis, and famed Athens with its people, streams, and rivers. With a last farewell to the plains of Troy, Ajax launches himself onto his sword. He is gone.

The Chorus search without success, but Tecmessa finds Ajax. Grieving, she conceals him gently with her cloak, knowing he must not be seen. "No friend could endure seeing him like this," she says, "gushing black blood up toward his nostrils out of the lethal, self-inflicted wound." Despairingly, Tecmessa cries, "What am I to do? Oh, Ajax! Who of your friends will raise you? Where is Teucrus? Oh, ill-fated Ajax! Even among your enemies, you deserve lamentation!"

The Chorus feel certain that Odysseus is laughing now, exulting over Ajax's destruction. Agamemnon and Menelaus will laugh, too, when they hear of it.

"Let them go ahead and laugh," Tecmessa responds. "They did not desire him while he was alive. Perhaps now they may cry out for him dead when they are in need of his spear." You know that she is right. The Greeks have just lost their best warrior.

The final scenes unfold quickly. Teucrus arrives and laments his brother's death. He regrets his failure to protect his brother and fears for his own future, as he expects their father will now cast him out. He marvels at the irony of Ajax's death by Hector's sword, recalling that the belt that Ajax gave Hector in exchange was used by Achilles to drag Hector from his chariot.

The Chorus urge Teucrus to hurry and bury Ajax. But Menelaus arrives and commands that the body be left where it is. He and Agamemnon forbid Ajax's burial. "We brought him here as our ally and friend," Menelaus says angrily. "But he proved a worse enemy than the Trojans. If a god hadn't diverted his violence onto sheep and cattle, he would have killed us all. Therefore, no man is powerful enough to bury him. He will remain stretched out on the sand, food for the birds of the shore." You see his point. Ajax did try to kill him and all of the other Greek commanders.

But Menelaus keeps talking, and you begin to find him pompous and smug. "If we were not able to subdue him while he was alive, we will rule him completely now that he is dead," Menelaus boasts. Then suddenly he waxes philosophical: "Good political order requires fear and respect," he proclaims. "Before, this man was fiery, violent, and overbearing. But now it is my turn to have great thoughts. I warn you not to try to bury him," Menelaus concludes threateningly, "lest in digging his grave you yourself fall into it."

The Chorus warn Menelaus against being violent and overbearing against the dead. But Teucrus becomes furious. "You brought him here, you say?" he screams. "Did he not sail here of his own accord, ruling himself? How are you the one to command him or the men he brought with him? I will bury my brother as is just. He did not come to fight here because of your wife. He came because he had sworn an oath. Your mere sounds will not turn me from my purpose as long as you are such a man as you are," Teucrus sneers.

A mud-slinging, surprisingly petty argument follows. Menelaus accuses Teucrus of being merely an archer, not a real man who fights with spear and shield. "Unarmed, I could defend myself against you, fully armed," Teucrus retorts. When Teucrus claims that he is acting in accordance with justice, Menelaus asks, "Is it just for this man who was killing me to succeed?"

"Killing you?" Teucrus asks mockingly. "What a strange thing you have said, if you are alive having died."

"I would be dead, if a god hadn't saved me."

"Having been saved by the gods, do not dishonor them now," Teucrus insists.

"Is it not fine and noble to prevent the burial of my own enemies?" demands Menelaus.

"Was Ajax ever your enemy in war?" asks Teucrus, not disputing the principle.

"He hated me and I hated him. You knew this."

Teucrus argues that Ajax hated Menelaus only because he was found to have tampered with the votes of the jury that awarded Achilles' armor to Odysseus. But Menelaus accepts no responsibility for the outcome, arguing that the vote was purely the decision of the jurors.

Teucrus points out that such a pretense of a valid procedure could result in a lot of cheating. (You see his point: it is not enough to hold a vote; the voting process must be honest, not corrupt.) The two men return to threatening and insulting one another. Their words achieve nothing. "I'm going away," says Menelaus finally. "It would be shameful if anyone should learn that I have been using words to correct someone whom I could correct using violent force."

"Sneak away now," Teucrus snarls. "For me also it is most shameful to hear a foolish man uttering worthless words."

"Uh oh," says the Chorus (more or less). They lament their loss of Ajax, and they long for home.

Agamemnon now arrives on the scene, and he strikes you as even more pompous and self-satisfied than his brother. Insulting Teucrus for being the son of a barbarian slave woman, he demands, "Are we to hear such objections from slaves?" (Ajax and Teucrus have the same father but different mothers.) Agamemnon denounces Teucrus for his failure to accept that Odysseus was fairly awarded Achilles' armor. It was, after all, a decision made by the majority of the jurors. "How can law survive if decisions made justly can be overturned by the losers?" he asks. "As a slave's son, you are not free to speak at all."

The Chorus helplessly wish that both Agamemnon and Teucrus could act with *sōphrosunē,* "moderation, restraint, prudence, wisdom." You remember that was Athena's advice. But what is the wise or prudent course here?

Teucrus focuses exclusively on the concept of gratitude. He cannot believe how swiftly Agamemnon has forgotten all Ajax did for him in the fighting, risking his own life to protect Agamemnon with his spear. He has forgotten that Ajax drove Hector back from the Greek ships, that he fought Hector in single combat. "And I fought alongside him," Teucrus screams. "Me! The slave, the offspring of a barbarian mother! Don't you know that your own grandfather was a barbarian? And your father fed his nephews to their own father, his brother. Your father had your own mother killed for adultery. You want to criticize my birth? My father was the great Telamon. The army gave him my mother as the greatest prize for his valor." Teucrus concludes with threats. He is quite willing to die fighting for his brother's burial.

Fortunately, Odysseus arrives at just this moment, having heard the yelling from far away. "This man does me a shameful injury," Agamemnon tells him, "saying that he will bury this corpse, using force against me."

"May I speak the truth to you as a friend?" Odysseus asks calmly. "And aid you no less than I have before?" After Agamemnon agrees, claiming to consider Odysseus his greatest friend among the Greeks, Odysseus urges him to permit the burial. You are stunned. Odysseus's inability to enjoy his enemy's humiliation surprised you, but can he possibly think that advocating a proper burial for his greatest foe is the right thing to do?

"Do not in any way let violence conquer you to hate so much that you trample on justice," Odysseus cautions Agamemnon. "This man was once most hateful to me, since the time when I became master of the armor of Achilles. But even so I would not dishonor him so much as to deny that he was the best of all us Greeks who came to Troy, except for Achilles." You realize that even Odysseus admits that Ajax deserved Achilles' armor.

Agamemnon cannot believe that Odysseus is taking Ajax's side against him. "Are you fighting with me, Odysseus, on behalf of this man?" he asks incredulously.

"I am," Odysseus replies evenly. "I used to hate him, when it was noble to hate him."

"But now that he's dead, isn't it necessary for you to trample upon him?" Agamemnon still does not comprehend.

Odysseus persists. "Don't rejoice in gains that are not noble," he cautions. "Honor your friends when they speak well. You will be victorious, you know, by being conquered by your friends," he promises Agamemnon, somewhat paradoxically. "This man was an enemy, but he was once noble. His *aretē*, 'excellence,' counts for more with me than his hatred."

Agamemnon criticizes Odysseus for being "unsteady" or "irresolute." But Odysseus explains that many people are friends now and later bitter enemies. The idea makes Agamemnon uncomfortable. He fears that Odysseus will make them both appear cowardly.

"No," Odysseus assures him. "We will seem just to all of the Greeks."

But Agamemnon cannot wrap his mind around the idea of burying a hated enemy. "Are you then bidding me to allow this corpse to be buried?" he demands.

"I am," Odysseus insists. "For I myself will also arrive at this."

A glimmer of understanding reaches Agamemnon. "Indeed all things are the same. Every man labors on his own behalf." Self-interest is a motive that Agamemnon can appreciate.

"Well, who would it be reasonable for me to work for other than myself?" Odysseus asks.

Agamemnon cannot see the connection between self-interest and compassion. But you can. You realize that Odysseus's humane insistence on burying a fallen enemy emerges directly from his farsighted understanding of his own long-term self-interest. Agamemnon cannot connect the dots. He agrees to permit the burial, but only as a favor to Odysseus. Blinded by hatred, he fails to see that honoring a dead enemy serves his own interest.

After Agamemnon's departure, Odysseus announces that he will now be as great a friend to Teucrus as he was once an enemy. He wants to participate in Ajax's burial, but Teucrus refuses to allow it. He admits that Odysseus has surprised him. Although he was Ajax's greatest enemy among the Greeks, he alone supported him after his death and did not mock him. He alone stood up to Agamemnon and Menelaus and refused to leave Ajax's body unburied. But Teucrus cannot let Odysseus touch the body. It might annoy the dead, he thinks. Teucrus graciously acknowledges that Odysseus has been "noble" toward his brother and himself. And Odysseus, just as politely, departs. Performing the burial with the help of Ajax's son, Teucrus praises his dead brother as "a good man, than whom there was no one better among mortals, when he was alive."

As you try to absorb this new portrait of Ajax and Odysseus, you find your own thoughts conflicted. Ajax's rampage and his suicide trouble you, but surely he was right to be angry. He deserved Achilles' armor. Odysseus was wrong to persuade the jury to award the armor to himself, and his willingness to honor his dead enemy seems weird, but Ajax does deserve honor, doesn't he? You have always admired both men, but can they both be right?

Reinterpreting Traditional Tales

In devising their plays in the democratic Athens of the late sixth century BCE and throughout the fifth, Greek tragic playwrights often retold and revised ancient stories that epic singers had sung for centuries and continued to sing still. The *Iliad* was written down sometime in the mid-sixth century. Singers, accompanying themselves on the lyre, continued to perform the tales, and the form of "Homer's" stories became more stable because they were now based on a fixed written text. But the tragic playwrights could take the traditional myths and rework them. They had to preserve certain basic elements (the fall of Troy, for example, or the death of Hector), but they could change details and emphases.[1]

During this period, performances of tragic plays formed part of a giant, state-sponsored religious festival. The plays were financed by wealthy individuals and performed before thousands of Athenians, resident aliens, and visiting foreigners. They constituted a central feature of Athens's civic structure.[2] The *Iliad* enabled its audiences to reassess the characters' values and their own, and tragedies subsequently made this kind of critical reflection and self-reflection an established component of life in fifth-century Athens. Consequently, by prompting their original audiences to view the traditional stories in new ways, the tragedies encouraged reassessment not only of old ideas but also of new ones.[3]

Most important, ancient Greek myths helped to remove from the judgment process the blinding force of rage. These tales enabled the audience to take an objective, long view in reevaluating priorities. If a story is not your own, you can assess its participants more objectively. If someone harms you or your family, for example, you might, like Achilles or Ajax, feel the urge to retaliate with violence. Anger might make you want to harm the people who injured you as much as or more than they harmed you (even if, in theory, you support the use of civil procedures for peaceful conflict resolution). But if the victim is someone else, your lack of personal involvement might permit you to see that there are healthier and more constructive (and less self-destructive) solutions than violent retaliation. The victim, of course, will not see this in the heat of anger, but you could.

Centuries before the Athenians instituted democratic procedures, Homer emphasized the existence of multiple perspectives and cultivated the audience's capacity for logical reasoning and empirical judgment. Homer's characters continue to view military success and violent revenge as most admirable, but Homer's audience cannot be so certain. The *Iliad* identifies vengeance with justice but presents this equation as problematic. Achilles' experience shows that revenge dehumanizes the avenger and brings him no satisfaction or peace of mind. The *Iliad* promotes empathy as a more constructive alternative.

Hundreds of years later, Greek tragedies enabled the Athenians to reassess their institutional alternative to violent revenge. Without ever abandoning violence in their relations with other states, Athenians were able to reflect on their internal mechanisms for nonviolent conflict resolution. By the mid-fifth century BCE, jury trials had existed in Athens for almost a century and a half. Male citizens also had the right to vote on virtually all political decisions in a general assembly.[4] Democratic institutions made everyone a judge of right and wrong. By continuing to revise the traditional tales and to expose the consequences of the characters' choices, Athenian tragedies continued to develop the audience's ability, as individuals, to make rational moral judgments.

Tragedies enabled their audiences to appreciate that an institutionalized form of group decision making—a jury trial, a vote in an assembly, an election—can help to control individuals' destructive anger, jealousy, even greed. But a jury trial is far from a perfect solution; it is merely better than the eye-for-an-eye alternative.[5] The Greeks knew, as we do, that a democratic process in and of itself does not ensure a just outcome, since a group can vote to commit an injustice. Modern popular elections sometimes elect "presidents for life" or pass laws that violate human rights or suppress individual freedoms that we might expect democratic government to protect. Elections and judicial verdicts may unfairly favor or harm one gender, class, or ethnic group.[6] The processes by themselves cannot ensure a just result, and people frequently will not agree on what constitutes a just decision.

Sophocles' *Ajax* (c. 448 BCE) revisits the problem of rage in the radically democratic Athens of the mid-fifth century BCE.[7] This play warns against overconfidence in the ability of democratic institutions to restrain the passion for violent revenge, since anger and the desire for revenge can persist in spite of, even sometimes because of, democratic political processes. Democratic institutions alone cannot eradicate the burning desire for vengeance, the *Ajax* shows, because they do not address the fundamental problem. How can any nonviolent procedural definition of justice accommodate the fact that people's ideas about what is right and wrong, particularly concerning the big, important questions, tend to be fixed and unchanging? Even in democratic societies, people tend to be highly inflexible on questions that really matter to them. In nondemocratic societies they may be more inflexible still. The *Ajax* shows that a democratic voting process cannot be the whole answer. A group can vote to commit a blatant injustice, as the tribunal does in voting to award Achilles' armor to Odysseus. This suggests that flexible standards cannot simply *replace* absolute ones. On some level we recognize that there is a difference between procedural justice and, well, *justice.*

But the *Ajax* shows that defining justice as a group vote does not merely differ from defining justice as a set of fixed and absolute standards. This play emphasizes that traditional, hierarchical, *aristocratic* ideals of right and wrong and the newer, egalitarian, *democratic* ideals are not merely different; they are antithetical.[8] The very notion of a group of individuals voting to determine what is *aristos*, "best," completely contradicts the concept of "best-ness" that is central to an aristocratic society.[9] Would you hold a group vote to decide who is strongest or who can throw a spear farthest or who is the fastest runner? These are absolute distinctions; they are not a matter of opinion. Democratic political processes make *everything* a matter of opinion. They even risk making the facts irrelevant. And what if a group vote gets it wrong?

In confronting this problem, the *Ajax* reinterprets a well-known ancient tale of a mythical injustice.[10] By adapting traditional material, Sophocles compels the audience to reassess long-admired characters and their choices. Sophocles preserves the characteristics that Ajax displays in Homer's epics, but he revises a tale mentioned only briefly in the *Odyssey*. In the *Iliad*, Ajax appears as a huge, resolute, and valiant Greek warrior, tirelessly defending the Greeks with his great shield.[11] He accompanies Odysseus and Phoenix as they transmit Agamemnon's offer in their attempt to get Achilles back into battle (*Il.* 9). In that scene, Ajax argues that Achilles is betraying his friends and behaving badly. Straightforward, uncomplicated, and practical, Ajax insists that there can and must be material compensation for grievous injury. You accept it, and you move on. What is your problem, he demands of Achilles. You are hurting the very people you should most be helping. You are upset about one girl, but Agamemnon is offering you *seven!* Plus many other things besides. Ajax criticizes Achilles for rejecting Agamemnon's offer and for harming his own friends (9.628–642).

Homer does not relate Ajax's quarrel with Odysseus over the judgment of the armor of Achilles. We know the tale from a later epic called the *Little Iliad,* dating perhaps a hundred years after Homer and surviving only in fragments. But Homer evidently knew the story because the *Odyssey* assumes that it has already taken place. When Odysseus visits the underworld, the shade of Ajax refuses to speak to him. As Odysseus tells it:

> "Alone, the departed spirit of Telamonian Ajax stood apart,
> angered because of the victory which I won beside the ships
> when I was judged for the sake of the arms of Achilles.
> His revered mother set the contest, and the sons of the
>   Trojans
> and Pallas Athena made the judgment.
> How I wish I had not won in such a competition!
> For because of this, the earth covers such a life, Ajax,
> who in regard to his form and his deeds
> had surpassed the other Greeks, after the excellent
>   son of Peleus." (*Od.* 11.543–551)

In the underworld, Odysseus tries to get Ajax to "subdue" his anger, telling him how necessary he was to the Greeks' efforts and how they lamented his death as much as Achilles'. But Ajax stalks away in silence (*Od.* 11.552–567). Wordlessly communicating his utter rejection of Odysseus, the *Odyssey*'s Ajax rages still, even in death.

Despite Ajax's persistent rage and his silence in the underworld, the audience cannot reduce Homer's Ajax simply to a model of brute strength or pure "brawn" in contrast to Odysseus's intellectual and verbal talents. In the *Iliad*, Ajax shares many qualities with Achilles as both are superb warriors, and Homer frequently calls each a "defensive wall" for the Greeks (e.g., Achilles 1.284, Ajax 3.229). But Homer also presents Ajax as thoughtful and articulate, as his arguments to Achilles in *Iliad* 9 show.

Sophocles preserves all of Ajax's admirable qualities: like Homer, he presents Ajax as strong, physically talented, and resolute but also intelligent and articulate. Sophocles' Ajax retains the strength, courage, and resolve of Homer's Ajax. His refusal to give up his anger or to yield recalls not only Homer's portrait of Ajax in the underworld but also Achilles' role in the *Iliad*. But Sophocles also, like Homer, presents Ajax as insightful and eloquent. His Athena asks, "Was there ever found a man more far-seeing?" (*Aj.* 119–120).[12]

Democratic Institutions: Solution or Problem?

Preserving the admirable character traits of Homer's Ajax, Sophocles also conserves the essential theme of his quarrel with Odysseus, but he depicts the contest anachronistically. Homer only hints at the tale, suggesting that Ajax deserved the armor but did not get it. In the *Odyssey*, Odysseus accepts that Ajax was the best of the Greeks, second only to Achilles (*Od.* 11.550–551), and no one disputes this. In the underworld, Odysseus finds Ajax still angry because of the decision about the armor. We learn, too, that Ajax died in consequence of this dispute. But Homer never reveals how Ajax died, nor does he make any mention of madness. Odysseus says that Thetis, Achilles' sea-nymph mother, set the contest for the armor and that "the sons of the Trojans and Pallas Athena made the judgment" (*Od.* 11.547), but in the play, Sophocles implies that the Greeks, not the Trojans, voted, and his description suggests an Athenian judicial process.[13] By the mid-fifth century, political decisions in Athens were made by a vote of all male citizens in a general assembly, but much earlier, since the early sixth century, the Athenians had begun to develop a complicated system of public law courts. The jurors were ordinary citizens, selected at random, and the juries were huge (51 to 1,501 members). Before this, individual aristocratic magistrates had had complete and arbitrary decision-making power (and might be biased and/or easily bribed). By contrast, the jury system, a democratic voting process, seemed a major improvement.[14]

Sophocles anachronistically depicts such a democratic voting process as the method for determining who should get Achilles' immortal armor, but in absolute terms, there is no doubt that the vote was wrong. Ajax views the decision as a monstrous injustice. And he is absolutely right. Everyone agrees that Ajax deserved the armor. In the play, Ajax claims, "And yet, I think I understand so much: if, while he was living, Achilles were to award the mastery of his own arms to anyone on the basis of valor, no one else but me would have laid hold of them. But the sons of Atreus, disdaining my powers, awarded the armor to that completely unprincipled Odysseus" (441–446). In other words, if Achilles were alive, he would have given the armor to *me!* The Chorus call Ajax "noblest of the much-laboring Greeks" (637–638). Although Odysseus won the armor, he too calls Ajax "the best of all of us Greeks who came here to Troy, except for Achilles" (1340–1341). Menelaus and Agamemnon defend the jurors' decision, but they never claim that Ajax was not the Greeks' best surviving warrior.[15]

So there is no doubt that the vote produced the wrong decision, but Ajax's response to it is problematic. He does not accept it. He does not tell himself, "Oh, well, better luck next time." He becomes a sort of ancient terrorist, attempting mass murder and then killing himself. Sophocles begins the play after the vote and after Ajax's violent reaction. Ajax does not "go mad," as many people mistakenly assume. His rage at the injustice of the decision makes him decide to murder all of the leaders of the Greek army (48ff.). Athena prevents this by distorting his vision so that he slaughters cattle and sheep instead of men (60ff.). Even after he recovers from his delusion, his intentions remain unchanged; he simply regrets his failure to kill the Greek leaders (372–376).[16]

Ajax denies the validity of the voting process, certain that Agamemnon and Menelaus manipulated the votes to produce an unjust outcome. If he had succeeded in killing them as he had intended, he would have prevented them from repeating the offense. "If my vision and judgment had not been distorted," he claims, "they would never again vote such 'justice' against any other man" (447–449). Ajax assumes that any such voting procedure will inevitably be corrupt, since in giving his shield to his son, he insists that "no judges of a contest will place [*thēsousi*] my arms before the Greeks, nor will my destroyer" (572–573). Ajax envisions and rejects the possibility of magistrates presiding over any voting process to award *his* armor to the Greeks. By rights, it should go to his son. In Ajax's view, procedural justice is inevitably *not* justice, as his recent experience has shown.[17]

Ajax's rage and suicide reveal the fundamental opposition between traditional archaic values and democratic procedures. It is a mistake to attribute Ajax's attempt at murder to *hybris* and his suicide to weakness, frustration, or shame.[18] *Hybris* in Greek means a sort of reckless arrogance or use of force that brings self-destruction, but it is often mistranslated as "pride." For ancient Greeks, the opposite of *hybris* was not humility but *sōphrosunē,* "prudence, moderation, wisdom, self-restraint." Ajax is indeed arrogant, but he has every right to be. He is the best, and he deserves Achilles' armor, and everyone knows it. Not *hybris* or shame but absolute certainty motivates Ajax to kill himself. Ajax has always pursued traditional goals familiar to Homer's world and to many places in ours: help friends, harm enemies, earn honor for success in battle. But the unjust vote enrages him, and when Athena prevents him from committing murder, Ajax realizes that his traditional talents and priorities no longer suit a society that uses a group vote, not fact, to identify and reward the "best" individual. Ajax attempts murder and then kills himself not out of shame or weakness, but because he refuses to live in a world that no longer recognizes absolute standards of good and bad and right and wrong.[19]

Ajax values achievement and loyalty, and Sophocles' portrait of him suggests that these are both very good and desirable things, but Sophocles also shows that Ajax's inability to change or to evolve is completely self-destructive. Ajax rejects not only the flexibility of democratic values and decision-making procedures but also the cyclical processes of nature and the movement of time itself. Ajax's very name sets him in opposition to time. Ancient Greek has no *j*, so Ajax is *Aias* in Greek. The name evokes the Greek cry of suffering and lamentation (*aiai!*), and it also echoes the Greek word *aei*, "always," the play's first word.[20] Aias "Ajax" embodies both suffering and permanence. He cannot adapt to changes wrought by time. In his brilliant and beautiful speech at the center of the play, Ajax explains exactly how the world works. He sees that time inevitably brings change. The seasons alternate, and so do human loyalties. The Greeks were his friends, and he defended them steadfastly against their Trojan enemies. But a group vote in defiance of the facts has made the Greeks his enemies. Ajax cannot consistently help his friends since friends do not remain friends. He wants no part of a world that cannot recognize and justly reward talent, merit, loyalty, and integrity.[21] Judgments made merely by consensus deprive these ideals of their value.

Sophocles' version of Ajax's story demonstrates that a democratic procedure is as likely to disregard the facts and be unfair any irresponsible magistrate or tyrant who seeks only to suit his own whim. And an unjust democratic decision can cost a society its highest achievers and most talented supporters. This play also suggests that modern efforts to cultivate democratic institutions in traditionally undemocratic societies must somehow recognize and address the incompatibility between absolute, unchanging moral standards and the democratic emphasis on flexibility and group consensus. The play warns against overconfidence in the value of the procedures alone. Unjust democratic decisions can violate individuals' rights and fracture communities. They may produce rather than prevent injustice and conflict.

Moral Flexibility: What Is Lost and What Is Gained?

The *Ajax* shows that aristocratic values cannot simply evolve into democratic values because the two systems are completely opposed. To utterly abandon the old absolute standards and substitute a voting procedure is to surrender all questions of right and wrong to the convenience of the most unscrupulous and manipulative ones among us. Ajax is rigid, old-fashioned, and violent, but he also embodies crucial priorities that even democratic procedures must validate. The play presents Ajax's death as a terrible tragedy. It deprives the Greeks of their greatest warrior and staunchest defender.[22] Ajax's rage and suicide warn against the failure to value facts and the failure to reward high achievement that serves the community.

The problem for the Athenians in the fifth century BCE continues to confront our world: How do you transition from an exclusive, aristocratic power structure to a more inclusive, egalitarian one? How do you create a community of political equals, when people obviously differ in fundamental ways, not merely in appearance but also in physical and intellectual abilities? These differences provoke competition. Competition can result in physical conflict and warfare, but it can also encourage outstanding achievement that benefits others. Homer stresses this dual potential of competition, as rivalries produce bloodshed, but individuals also strive to defend their families and friends.[23] In practical terms, how can a society reward talented individuals and benefit from their achievements without being unfair? And which talents should we reward? Is a talent for compromise admirable? Is flexibility on moral questions admirable? The success of democratic procedures requires that everyone accept their outcome, even those who believe the decision wrong. But does flexibility on important questions of right and wrong make someone a "flip-flopper," an opportunist who does not really care about right and wrong?

Following Ajax's death, the play exposes the double nature of moral flexibility. Ajax is admirable in his strength, loyalty, wisdom, and integrity, but not so admirable in his inability to relent, forgive, or change.[24] Lacking Ajax's absolute standards of right and wrong, Menelaus and Agamemnon seem petty, vicious, and small-minded. Their moral flexibility entails a complete disregard for facts and for individual merit. Ajax sees no value in a democratic procedure. He feels cheated. But Agamemnon and Menelaus see only the value of the process. Neither ever acknowledges that the democratic vote resulted in a mistake, a factual error, an actual injustice. When Ajax's brother Teucrus accuses Menelaus of theft and of tampering with the votes (1135), Menelaus insists that the jurors, not himself, made the decision, claiming "this fell out [*esphalē*] among the jurors, not me" (1136).[25] Like Menelaus, Agamemnon sees only the correctness of the process and ignores the injustice of the outcome. He criticizes Teucrus for his inability to accept the decision "that was pleasing to the majority of the judges" (1239–1243).[26] Agamemnon insists that everyone must accept a lawful, democratically made decision, explaining that no law can ever be secure if decisions made justly can simply be overturned in favor of the losers (1246–1250). Their enthusiasm for the voting process makes both Agamemnon and Menelaus willing to threaten and intimidate others into accepting its results (e.g., 1073–1090; 1138; 1159–1160; 1253–1256). For them, only the procedure matters.[27]

Even Teucrus does not affirm any absolute standard of value. Viewing justice as an exchange of favors, Teucrus criticizes the colossal ingratitude of these smug and vindictive advocates of democratic procedure. Teucrus details Ajax's outstanding prior services to the Greek army (1264ff.). He does not defend the principle that Ajax died for. He does not argue that society must value integrity and loyalty and reward achievement. Teucrus reduces justice to a commercial transaction: look what Ajax did for you; you owe him.

Only Tecmessa, Ajax's spear-won concubine, affirms the traditional, absolute value of friendship and loyalty to friends and relatives. Grieving at Ajax's distress, she asks the Chorus to help prevent him from doing "some evil thing" (326). "O friends!" she cries, "going inside, help him if you can. For such men are conquered by the words of friends" (328–330). Later, finding Ajax's body, she covers it with her cloak (915–919), performing the woman's role, traditional in ancient Greek religious practice, of shrouding dead relatives.[28]

Although valuing, like Ajax, the traditional, absolute obligations of friendship, Tecmessa, surprisingly, introduces a new moral standard. As female characters often do in Greek tragedy, she identifies an obligation that the men seem to be ignoring.[29] Addressing Ajax's corpse, Tecmessa asks, "Who of your friends will give you a proper burial?" (920). But then she suggests, astonishingly, that Ajax is worthy of lamentation even from his enemies (923–924). This novel idea would be incomprehensible to Ajax.

Tecmessa's statement directly contradicts the traditional archaic value system that commends not grief at the destruction of an enemy but laughter and exultation. Both Athena and Ajax take pleasure in an enemy's destruction. Not comprehending Odysseus's reluctance to gloat over his deluded and humiliated enemy, Athena asks incredulously, "Isn't it the sweetest laughter to laugh at your enemies?" (79). And Ajax, we learn, laughed while torturing the animals he mistook for Odysseus and the sons of Atreus (303). Ajax attributes to Odysseus this same lack of compassion, certain that he is now enjoying laughter at Ajax's expense (379–382).[30]

But Ajax is wrong. We know that Odysseus is not laughing. In fact, the *Ajax* directly criticizes laughter at someone else's suffering. To laugh at someone else's misfortune, this play shows, is to completely misunderstand the most basic facts about human life. Both Athena and Ajax assume that an enemy's calamity is something to exult in and laugh at. Athena, as a goddess, can be certain who her friends and her enemies are. Her relationships and affections are unchanging. She consistently loves Odysseus. And she hates Ajax because Ajax offended her twice: he scoffed at his father's advice to "wish to prevail with your spear, but always with a god" (764–765), and later, a messenger reports, he refused Athena's direct offer of help in battle. According to the messenger, Ajax answered his father "arrogantly and foolishly," saying:

> "Father, together with the gods
> even a man who is not at all powerful would prevail.
> But I am persuaded that even apart from the gods I will
>   obtain this glory."
> He made such a boastful remark as this.
> And then, a second time, when divine Athena, urging him
>   on,
> told him to turn his bloody hand against his enemies,
> he answered then a terrible and unspeakable word:
> "Queen, stand near the others of the Greeks.

> The battle line will never break in against me."
> By such words, you know, not thinking as a man should
>   think,
> he acquired the hateful anger of the goddess. (766–777)

In telling Athena, "I'm fine. Go help someone who needs you," Ajax is not boasting but stating the truth. The battle line will never break where Ajax stands. But you cannot speak to a goddess like that. This rudeness earns him Athena's perpetual enmity.[31]

As a goddess, Athena can have perpetual enmities, but Ajax's experience emphasizes that human beings cannot. Unlike the permanent friendships and enmities of gods, human relationships naturally change over time. Ajax helped the Greeks to besiege Troy, but he came to hate them all because of the judgment over Achilles' armor. Ajax destroyed Tecmessa's family and her city and made her his captive and bedmate, but she cares for him and tries to protect him.[32] Ajax fought with his Trojan enemy Hector and then exchanged gifts with him (*Aj.* 661–663 and *Il.* 7.287–312). In a subsequent reversal, each gift proves deadly.[33] Ajax once fought alongside Odysseus but became his enemy because of the decision over Achilles' armor. As his enemy, Odysseus nevertheless supports Ajax's right to a proper burial. Ajax considers "friends" and "enemies" to be absolute categories, but the play prevents the audience from sharing his view.

Ajax does not reject this changeability in human relationships out of ignorance. He recognizes that the entire natural world, including human beings within it, is subject to time (646–692), but he refuses to accept this. He claims sarcastically: "I understand just now that an enemy must be hated by me only so far as one hates someone who is one day going to be a friend. And I will wish to benefit a friend only as much as one benefits someone who will not always remain his friend" (678–682). Ajax has based his whole life on the absolute distinction of friend from enemy and the moral obligations this entails. His very identity (his name, after all, is "Mr. Always") depends on this distinction.

In rejecting flexibility in friendships and enmities, Ajax ultimately rejects human relationships altogether. In his last speech (815–865), he stands alone on stage and addresses only divinities and inanimate things, fixed, enduring features of the natural world. He describes the sword he has "fixed, having buried it well" (821) in the ground. He calls on Zeus, Hermes, the Furies, Helios the sun god, Death. He says farewell to the daylight, to his homeland of Salamis, to Athens, to the plains of Troy.[34] "This is the last *epos*, 'word,' Ajax utters to you," he concludes. "As for other things, *muthēsomai*, 'I will tell the tales,' to the ones below in Hades" (864–865). In contrasting *epos*, "word," the substance of epic poetry, with *muthos*, "myth," these lines mark Ajax's final speech and his suicide itself as his last great achievements, worthy of epic remembrance. His words signal his transition, as a shade, into the realm of *muthos*, "myth." In death, of course, as Sophocles' audience already knows, Ajax remains distinctive not for storytelling but for his absolute silence, as he refuses to speak to his most hated enemy Odysseus (*Od.* 11.543–564). Sophocles' Ajax dies hating his enemies, and he takes his rage and hatred to his grave and beyond.[35]

Cultivating the Humane Imagination

By emphasizing Ajax's changing relationships and his self-destructive refusal to accept friendships and enmities that can change over time, this play suggests that striving to help your friends and harm your enemies cannot be your highest and most absolute principle. It is irrational, just as the enjoyment of the suffering of your enemies is irrational, since "friend" and

"enemy" are not permanent, unchanging categories. They fluc-
tuate with time. Although Ajax's inflexibility matches Athena's,
she provides no admirable moral example. The code of helping
friends and harming enemies works fine for a goddess. Human
beings need a better principle.

Tecmessa intuits such a principle, when she insists that
Ajax deserves to be lamented even by his enemies (923–924).[36]
But it takes Odysseus to spell out the logic: we are all human.
We will all be weak and vulnerable and dead someday. In the
beginning of the play, Athena expects Odysseus to enjoy Ajax's
calamity, but he cannot. Athena invites Odysseus to laugh at his
enemy (79). This should be Odysseus's big moment. He has won
the armor; he is at the top of his game. But Odysseus cannot
celebrate or revel in Ajax's suffering and humiliation. Instead,
he tells Athena,

> I pity him.
> He's altogether wretched, even though he is hostile to me,
> because he is yoked together with a ruinous folly,
> and I recognize that that could just as easily be me.
> For I see that we are all nothing, all of us who live,
> nothing except fleeting images, empty shadow. (121–126)

Odysseus feels pity instead of satisfaction, sadness instead of
delight. He recognizes that what happened to Ajax could happen to anyone, even to himself. As mortals, none of us has any
knowledge or control over miseries the future holds. Later, even
the smug Menelaus can see himself in Ajax's place. He claims,
"Before, this man was fiery, violent, and overbearing. But now
it's my turn to have great thoughts" (1087–1088). But this insight
fails to make Menelaus compassionate. Unlike Menelaus, however, Odysseus makes the connection. His compassion comes

from his understanding that we are all human. Dependency and defeat await us all.[37]

Odysseus's compassion derives from a farsighted understanding of his own self-interest. After Ajax's death, Odysseus insists on the justice of honoring a fallen enemy, explaining, "For I myself will also arrive at this" (1365). Odysseus recognizes that once dead, he too may be vulnerable to his enemies. He will need them to be capable of restraint and respect. Odysseus's example shows that kindness, compassion, and generosity need not come from any extraordinary, selfless altruism. They are, rather, the logical consequence of thinking things through.[38]

In defending Ajax's honor against Agamemnon and Menelaus, Odysseus recognizes that hatred is no longer appropriate, and he is able to give it up. He respects greatness, even in an enemy, telling the sons of Atreus:

> Listen to me. By the gods,
> don't dare to throw this man out so cruelly unburied.
> In no way let violence conquer you
> to hate so much that you trample on Justice.
> This man was also once most hateful to me
> from the time when I became master of the arms of
>   Achilles.
> But still I would not dishonor him so much
> as to deny that I know he was the best
> of all of us Greeks who came here to Troy,
> except for Achilles.
> And so you could not, with justice, dishonor him.
>   (1332–1342)

Odysseus cannot laugh at a fallen enemy. He cannot continue to hate a dead man. Today, in twenty-first-century struggles, combatants still sometimes succumb to the impulse to humiliate a defeated enemy or violate an enemy's corpse. But here a character in a 2,500-year-old play explains just how primitive and dishonorable and foolish that impulse is. Odysseus's example shows that laughing at your enemy's destruction is not an admirable sign of your invulnerability or the correctness of your cause; it is a marker of the inadequacy of your imagination.

Odysseus's awareness of human vulnerability and mortality infuses the concept of justice with humanity and compassion, derived not from grand selflessness but from clear-sighted self-interest. Odysseus does not simply abandon the traditional standards of friend and enemy, good and bad, right and wrong. Ajax rejects moral flexibility and criticizes Odysseus for being *pantourgos phrenas,* "ready to do anything [or "unscrupulous"] as to his thoughts" (445). At the end of the play, we see that Odysseus is indeed "ready to do anything": he will even pity and honor a dead enemy. Flexibility on questions of good and bad underlies the idea of using a voting procedure to determine who is "best," but Odysseus also retains a conception of "bestness" that is independent of majority consensus. He calls Ajax *aristos,* "best" (1340), fully acknowledging his enemy's worth.

Democratic procedures require compromise. Citizens in a democratic society must be able to change. They must be tolerant. They must be able to empathize, even with enemies.[39] The blanket rejection of compromise is the mark of a primitive, undemocratic value system, a system that, like the character of Ajax, may prioritize admirable things like honor and friendship and loyalty and consistency, but, like Ajax, can never evolve, can never incorporate anything better.

Ajax's rage reminds us to approach consensus and compromise carefully, with a farsighted, Odyssean understanding of self-interest. Destructive and despicable compromises, such as the one that allowed the inclusion of slavery in the U.S. Constitution of 1787 or the Yalta Agreement of 1945, when Churchill and Roosevelt agreed to return POWs and civilian refugees to the Soviet Union against their will and to their nearly certain death, demonstrate that the moral flexibility of compromise can permit and even promote evil. Equally double-edged, democratic procedures may promote justice or injustice. A persuasive speaker can manipulate voters into committing injustice and even into voting against their own interests, exactly as Odysseus convinces the Greeks to deny Achilles' armor to Ajax, although everyone knows it should go to Ajax. But an effective speaker can also use persuasive speech to promote justice, as Odysseus succeeds in persuading the sons of Atreus to permit Ajax's burial.[40] By exploiting both the destructive and the constructive potential of persuasive argument, Odysseus shows that democratic procedures require some flexibility on questions of right and wrong, but that moral flexibility also must include and defend some absolute standards of justice and humanity. Without these, moral flexibility risks doing more harm than good.

6

The Abuse of Power
and Its Consequences
(Euripides' *Hecuba*)

Seated at the theater in Athens, you look upon a desolate, foreign shore: a sandy coastline, sparse foliage, a shelter suitable for a king on a military expedition. Euripides' *Hecuba* is about to begin. Having heard the ancient stories from your childhood, you know that Hecuba enjoyed fabulous prosperity as queen of Troy and produced an astounding number of noble sons and daughters. Then catastrophe struck. The invading Greek forces killed her warrior sons, murdered her husband, destroyed her beautiful city, and enslaved her and her daughters.

As the play begins, a young man appears. "I am the phantom of Hecuba's son Polydorus," he says. Surprised at the sight of a phantom, you try to recall this son of Hecuba and Priam. They had so many. You remember Paris and Hector, of course, and others, too, but you may not recall Homer saying anything about Polydorus.

The phantom of Polydorus explains that his father Priam, fearing his city might fall to the Greeks, secretly sent him, his youngest son and still a child, to the home of his guest-friend Polymestor in Thrace. He also sent along much gold for safekeeping. While Troy remained intact, defended by Hector and the Trojans, Polymestor treated Polydorus well. But as soon as Hector died and the Greeks sacked the city, plundering Priam's hearth and killing him at the altar, Polymestor, wanting the gold for himself, murdered Polydorus and cast the boy's body into the sea.

This wild, unfamiliar place is the coast of Thrace, in the Chersonese, on the Greeks' route home from Troy. Polydorus's body has washed up on the sand and lies unwept and unburied. The Greeks with their captives, including Hecuba, have arrived from Troy, and their ships remain drawn up on the beach. The spirit of Achilles, appearing above his own tomb, has demanded a human sacrifice. As a phantom, Polydorus can predict the future: his mother Hecuba will soon see two corpses: his and that of his sister Polyxena.

The phantom disappears before Hecuba, emerging from Agamemnon's shelter, can see him. Departing, he laments Hecuba's extreme misfortune, the exact opposite of the supreme good fortune she once enjoyed. "One of the gods is destroying you," he observes sadly, although Hecuba does not seem to hear, "giving you ill fortune exactly equal to the good fortune you had before." Polydorus blames "some god," and this surprises you; he has just described Polymestor's murderous greed and the monstrous demand of Achilles' ghost.

The stooped old woman coming into view bears no resemblance to the beautiful, prosperous Trojan queen of your imagination. Wearing dirty, torn robes, she walks with difficulty, leaning on her daughter and maidservants for support. Hecuba has just had terrifying night visions about her children Polydorus and Polyxena. She dreamed that Achilles' ghost demanded a virgin sacrifice. Completely distraught, Hecuba can only hope that her last son, Polydorus, still survives safe and sound, protected by his father's guest-friend in Thrace. She prays to the gods to preserve her remaining children.

The Chorus of newly enslaved Trojan women immediately confirm the truth of Hecuba's dream: Achilles' ghost has indeed demanded a virgin sacrifice. Worse, it seemed best to the full assembly of the Greeks to sacrifice Hecuba's daughter. The wording of this pronouncement—"it seemed best to the assembly"—anachronistically echoes the official phrasing of your own Athenian assembly of all male citizens. But the men in this play are not citizens of a democratic citizen-community. They are warriors returning long ago from sacking Troy. And yet they use the official phrase of democratic decision making to announce their intention to kill an innocent young girl.

Oh, there was some debate, the Chorus acknowledge. Agamemnon even advised against the sacrifice, feeling perhaps some human connection to Polyxena since her sister, the prophetess Cassandra, now shares his bed. But others favored making the sacrifice and garlanding the tomb of Achilles with fresh-blooming blood. They refused to value Cassandra's bed over Achilles' spear. Odysseus persuaded them. If they spurned the best of all the Greeks by prioritizing the life of a slave, Odysseus insisted, if they refused to honor Achilles' request, one of the dead in the underworld might say that the Greeks left the plains of Troy ungrateful to those who had died on their behalf. Even now, Odysseus is on his way to take Polyxena from Hecuba. The

Chorus advise Hecuba to supplicate Agamemnon and to pray to the gods to spare her child.

Hecuba cries out in helplessness and despair. She informs Polyxena that "it is the common judgment of the Greeks to sacrifice you over the tomb of Achilles." Hecuba has heard "evil reports" that the decision "seemed best, by a vote of all the Greeks."

Taking the news surprisingly well, Polyxena focuses immediately on her mother's suffering, past, present, and future. "What sort of vicious treatment has some divinity let loose against you?" she wonders. As for herself, she embraces death as a "greater happy chance."

Odysseus hurries into view. He does not appear reluctant to accomplish his dreadful task. He is aware that Hecuba already knows "the judgment of the army and the vote that has been executed." But he repeats it anyway. You continue to find the official language of direct democratic decision making jarring. "It seemed best to the Greeks," Odysseus proclaims, "to slaughter your daughter Polyxena over the burial mound of Achilles." Taking no responsibility for the decision, Odysseus says only that he has been assigned to escort the girl. He advises Hecuba to accept the inevitable, informing her, "It is wise for you to think what is necessary, even in evils."

In desperation, Hecuba reminds Odysseus that he owes her a favor. Doesn't he remember? She saved his life when he snuck into Troy in disguise, attempting to spy. Helen knew him but told only Hecuba. And Hecuba saved him, sending him safely away. Odysseus readily agrees that this story is true. "Aren't you acting basely now?" Hecuba demands. "You who experienced at my hands such things as you admit that you experienced? Ungrateful, you do not treat me well. Instead, you do me as much harm as you are able." Hecuba reviles the

Greeks for their dishonorable, immoral decision-making process. "Believing what clever argument did they let loose this vote of death against my daughter?" (Hecuba uses the same verb for the Greeks' decision as Polyxena had used in identifying "some divinity" as the cause.) "What necessity," she demands, "has led them to sacrifice a human being at the tomb where it is more fitting to sacrifice oxen? If Achilles wants to kill the ones who killed him, does he with justice design murder against this girl? She has done him no evil whatsoever."

Why not pick Helen? Hecuba demands, for it was she who destroyed Achilles and brought him to Troy. Seeking justice, Hecuba begs Odysseus to listen and to repay his debt to her. "Do not drag my child from my hands," she cries piteously. "Don't kill her. Enough people have died. She is my comfort, my city, my staff, the guide of my journey."

Hecuba makes a last effort to appeal to a principle that you may never have thought about before. "The strong and mighty," she cautions Odysseus, "must not exert power which is not right, nor should those who are fortunate think that they will fare well always." She should know, she maintains, since she once enjoyed supreme happiness but lost it all in one day. She asks Odysseus for respect and for pity. She knows that he has more power to persuade the Greeks than anyone else.

Hecuba's words have no effect. Odysseus offers to preserve Hecuba herself because she once protected him. But he will not prevent Polyxena's sacrifice, since "the preeminent man of the army" asks it. Odysseus actually takes pride in satisfying the bloodlust of a dead man, explaining pompously: "In this regard, many other cities are beaten, because their noble and zealous men gain nothing more than those who are evil and cowardly. By contrast, we Greeks

consider Achilles worthy of honor. Dying on behalf of the
Greek land, he was the most excellent man. Is it not shameful
if we use him while he looks upon the daylight, but we have
no further use for him when he has perished? How would
other men be willing to fight wars, if they see the Greeks
failing to honor their dead? As for me, I would wish my own
tomb to be seen as being worthy, for gratitude exists for a
long time." You sense a flaw in his logic, but you cannot quite
identify it. "If we are incorrect in honoring a noble man, we
will be convicted of ignorance," Odysseus adds smugly. "But
you barbarians neither consider friends to be friends nor
admire those who died well. So, Greece is fortunate, but you
barbarians get what you deserve." Rationalizing the murder
of an innocent girl, this brutal, self-satisfied Odysseus
evidently lacks the compassion and humanity of the
Odysseus you remember meeting in Sophocles' *Ajax*.

Polyxena does not even try to appeal to Odysseus's
sense of justice or humanity. She accepts her own death "as a
favor of Necessity," explaining, "If I don't wish it, I will appear
to be a cowardly woman who loves her life too much." As a
slave, she no longer has anything to live for. "Dying I would
be more fortunate than living," she says, "for living ignobly is
great suffering." Urging her mother not to fight against those
in power, Polyxena reassures her that her brother Polydorus
still lives. (Hecuba doubts this, believing herself "so
unfortunate in everything.") With a final farewell, Polyxena
goes bravely to her death.

You witness the grief and despair of Hecuba and the
Chorus. Time passes, and the Greek messenger Talthybius
arrives. Seeing Hecuba prostrate, transformed from
magnificent queen to wretched slave, Talthybius marvels at
the devastating power of *Tuchē*, "Chance/Fortune." "I'm an

old man," he concludes, "but nevertheless, would that I might
die before I am wrecked against some shameful fortune."

Talthybius has come for Hecuba so that she can bury
her daughter. "How did you kill her?" Hecuba asks, desperate
for any solace. "Did you do it respectfully? Or did you do this
terrible thing by killing her as an enemy?"

The messenger speaks reluctantly, "I wept as I saw it.
Now you ask me to weep again in recalling it." Nevertheless,
he describes the scene in heart-wrenching detail. The entire
mob of the Greek army watched as Achilles' son led Polyxena
atop the burial mound. "Chosen youths followed," Talthybius
tells Hecuba, "for the purpose of restraining the leap of your
calf." (Yes, you think, the Greeks really did treat the girl as a
sacrificial animal.) Pouring libations, Achilles' son told the
crowd to preserve a reverential silence as he supplicated his
father's spirit to accept "these appeasing libations as escorts
for the dead." To his father's spirit, he called, "Come, so that
you may drink this virgin's pure blood. And be kindly to us
and ensure the Greek army a safe homecoming." The whole
army echoed the prayer. Yes, it was all very properly done,
you think—if Polyxena had been a calf.

But Polyxena was not a calf, and she had no intention of
going to her death like one. As Achilles' son drew his sword to
cut her throat, she made a speech as no calf ever could. "You
Greeks who sacked my city," she began, "I am dying willingly.
Let no one touch me, for I will provide my neck with stout
heart. Letting me go free, kill me, so that I may die a free
woman, by the gods! For being a princess, I am ashamed to
be called a slave among the dead." The men all shouted
applause, and Agamemnon commanded that it happen so.

You hear the rest with sick fascination: Polyxena pulled
open her robe, baring for the blade her neck and breast

("most noble, as if of a statue," Talthybius observes). She knelt on the ground and told the young man where to strike. Yes, she stayed in control to the end, even as she fell, pulling her robe about her, concealing what needed to be concealed from male eyes. "Ah, Hecuba," Talthybius concludes, "you really are most unfortunate of all women."

Grief devastates Hecuba, but she admires Talthybius's nobility. She is struck by a terrible and strange thought: how the wicked remain wicked while the noble remain noble, no matter what. What is the cause? Heredity or nurture? Well, nobility can be taught, she thinks. Since the well-educated person knows what is shameful, having learned to measure it against what is noble. Hecuba finds her own philosophical musings strange and useless at such a moment, as do you. But you realize that she has left open the alternative possibility: Can a good person learn to become evil?

"Tell the Greeks not to touch my child," Hecuba now commands Talthybius. "Restrain the mob. An unbridled mob in an army of thousands and a naval force without government is stronger than fire. And a man doing nothing evil is evil." You recognize the truth of her words. An unrestrained mob has the freedom and power to do terrible things. Anyone who just goes along with it is complicit. Talthybius has just called the Greek army a mob in describing the warriors watching the sacrifice of Polyxena.

Insisting that she will wash and bury her daughter, Hecuba laments her "once-fortunate home" and her late husband Priam, previously so possessed of the finest things and the best children. "How we all arrive at nothing," she cries, "deprived of our former lofty thoughts. Wealth and honor make us puff with pride, but it's all worthless. The wealthiest person is he who chances on no evil day by day."

Hecuba does seem pitiable, but you have begun to suspect that chance is not responsible.

The Chorus begin to sing: "It was necessary for misfortune and suffering to happen to me, from the time when Paris first cut pines to build his ship." It all started, they explain, when Paris judged the contest between the goddesses. (You recall the tale: as a young boy, Paris was asked to judge whether Athena, Hera, or Aphrodite was the most beautiful goddess. He chose Aphrodite and received Helen as his reward. The Trojan War and all its suffering ensued.) Surprisingly, this Chorus of newly enslaved Trojan women sings of "a Spartan girl weeping in her home and a mother lamenting her dead children." You don't expect the defeated to think of the victors' suffering, but the Chorus remind you of the inevitable suffering of men and women on both sides of a war. Still, you wonder why Polyxena's death had to be part of it.

A maidservant arrives to report still more evil. Hecuba at first thinks she means Polyxena but soon learns that Polydorus's body has been found. The sight of the corpse devastates Hecuba. "I look upon my dead son, whom the Thracian was preserving for me in his halls," she gasps in horror. "Wretched, I am destroyed. I no longer exist."

Polydorus's death corroborates Hecuba's dream, so she instantly knows that her *xenos*, "guest-friend," Polymestor murdered her son instead of protecting him. She knows, too, that he did it for the gold. Appalled by this grotesque violation of the rules of *xenia*, "guest-friendship," Hecuba cries out, "Where is justice for guest-friends?" The Chorus blame "some divinity" for Hecuba's misery, but you think of the murderer's unprincipled, pitiless opportunism.

Agamemnon now arrives and urges Hecuba to hurry up and bury her daughter. "Everything has been done well," he assures her. "If any of these things is well," he adds. Hecuba starts to form a plan. She seems literally beside herself, addressing herself in the second person. "Wretch!" she exclaims. "I mean myself in saying you, Hecuba. What am I to do?" You recognize this as the essential tragic question, the question everyone faces at every moment of their lives: what should I do? The question is most crucial—and painful— when there are no good options. What is Hecuba planning? Should she supplicate Agamemnon, she wonders, or should she endure her troubles in silence? Hecuba knows that she needs Agamemnon's help if she is going to avenge the murders of her children. She sees the attempt as necessary, whether she chances upon success or not. Vengeance is now her only desire.

Hecuba tells Agamemnon that she and her husband entrusted their son to the Thracian for safekeeping, along with the gold. But as soon as he knew of the Trojans' misfortune, this greedy "guest-friend" murdered the boy and threw his body into the sea. "I have perished and there is nothing remaining of evils, Agamemnon," Hecuba wails.

"Ah," exclaims Agamemnon sympathetically. "Was there any woman naturally so unfortunate?"

"There is not," Hecuba agrees, "unless you mean the divinity *Tuchē*, 'Fortune/Chance,' herself." You find this exchange puzzling. The Greeks voted to kill Polyxena, and Polymestor opted to murder Polydorus for the gold. How is Chance responsible?

Hecuba asks Agamemnon to help her take revenge on Polymestor, since that "most unholy guest-friend, fearing neither the ones below the earth nor the ones above, committed a most unholy deed." Polymestor had often received generous hospitality in Hecuba's home. She held him first among her friends and gave him all that she should. And yet, "taking forethought," the man killed her son and did not even think him deserving of burial. Hecuba is Agamemnon's slave and in his power, so it is his responsibility to support *Nomos,* "law/custom/tradition." "By *Nomos* we believe in the gods," she insists, "and we live distinguishing injustice from justice." If someone who destroys guest-friends pays no penalty, there is nothing fair in human relationships. Reiterating her terrible losses, Hecuba begs Agamemnon for respect and for pity.

Agamemnon remains unmoved. Hecuba suddenly realizes that the only really powerful tool that human beings have is persuasion. In seeking success, why do we bother with anything else? She reminds Agamemnon that he enjoys her daughter Cassandra in his bed. Does he not therefore owe Cassandra's dead brother, his brother-in-law, honor? (This seems a bit of a stretch, but you sort of see her point.) "It is the part of a noble man," Hecuba reminds Agamemnon, "to serve justice and to harm evil men always everywhere."

Agamemnon says that he pities Hecuba, her child, and her "fortunes" and wants to help. "Because of the gods and justice," he explains, "I wish the unholy guest-friend to pay this penalty to you." But Agamemnon does not want his soldiers to think that he collaborated in murdering the Thracian king for Cassandra's sake. The Greeks consider the Thracian killer a friend and the dead Trojan boy an enemy. Agamemnon fears the Greeks' accusations. You are surprised to see this great ancient king so enslaved to popular opinion, but you know that the leaders of your own day share his concern.

"No one is free," Hecuba acknowledges. Everyone is enslaved to money or to *Tuchē,* "Fortune/Chance," or the city's multitude or its written laws constrain him to act against his own judgment. "In fear," she tells Agamemnon, "you yield to the mob." But then she reassures him, "Don't

worry. I'll do the planning. You just have to know about it.
You don't have to help in doing it."

Agamemnon cannot imagine how women could be
stronger than males, but Hecuba reminds him of the power of
deception and numbers. "With trickery," she explains, "the
multitude is terrible and difficult to fight with." She reminds
Agamemnon of a legendary mass murder, when a group of
newlywed brides slaughtered their husbands on their wedding
night. You know this ancient story of the daughters of Danaus.
It happened long before the Trojan War. (Homer often calls
the Greek warriors "Danaans, 'descendants of Danaus.'") And
Aeschylus dramatized the tale long ago. Only one of Danaus's
fifty daughters did not kill her husband. Hecuba's use of this
example makes you suspicious of her intentions. Mob action
certainly does have the potential for atrocity.

Hecuba orders the maidservant to tell her "guest-friend"
Polymestor that Hecuba, Troy's former queen, calls him
regarding a debt that is his and his sons' not less than hers.
You admire her crafty double entendre. You know Polymestor
is greedy. Hecuba certainly does owe him something, but will
he come eagerly, seeking a different sort of payment?

Hecuba also asks Agamemnon to delay Polyxena's
burial so that she can bury both of her children together.
Agamemnon agrees, but only because, as it happens, the god
does not send favorable breezes for sailing. Necessity compels
the army to remain in Thrace for now. "Otherwise,"
Agamemnon explains, "I would not be able to grant you this
favor. And may it turn out well. For it is important both to
individuals and to the city that an evil person suffer some
evil, and a useful person encounter good fortune."

As Agamemnon departs, the Chorus sing to their
homeland of Troy, so recently laid waste by Greek spears.

Recounting a woman's experience of the devastation, the Chorus describe a young wife preparing for bed. Her husband, unarmed and unable to see the Greeks attacking, awaited her in the bedchamber. Wearing simple clothing, like a Spartan girl, the young woman left her bed, calling uselessly on Artemis as she watched her husband die. Led away to the sea, she looked back upon her city as the ship divided her from her land. The Chorus conclude by cursing Helen and Paris.

The Choral ode has provided the time for the Thracian Polymestor to arrive. "O Priam, dearest of men, and you, Hecuba, dearest of women," he begins, with astonishingly unctuous insincerity, "I weep looking upon your city and your daughter who died just now." He attributes Hecuba's suffering to the randomness of life. "There's nothing trustworthy," he sighs. "Good reputation, good fortune, good deeds all get reversed. The gods themselves jumble things backwards and forwards making confusion, so that we reverence them out of ignorance." (Knowing his reprehensible deeds, you marvel that he blames human suffering on arbitrary divine action.) Polymestor assures Hecuba that her messenger arrived just as he was already preparing to come see her. (You doubt this very much.)

At Hecuba's request, Polymestor sends his attendants away. He continues to insist on his willingness to help, calling her "friend" and the Greek army "beloved/friendly." When she asks directly whether her son still lives, Polymestor lies boldly: "Certainly," he assures her. "With regard to him you are lucky."

"Oh dearest friend," Hecuba responds, now that Polymestor has removed any possibility for doubt, "how well and worthily you declare yourself."

Hecuba cleverly ensnares the man by playing on his greed. She asks if the gold is safe. He assures her that it is. She says that she has something special to tell him and his sons. "There is—" but she interrupts herself. "O, beloved one, how dear you are to me now."

"What must I and my children know?" His eagerness makes him impatient.

"Ancient caverns full of Priam's gold," she intones solemnly. Oh, you see that she has him now. He peppers her with questions. Should he tell her son? Why must his own children be present? Where is the gold? Is there some marker? She responds easily to each question.

"Is there anything else?" he asks.

Well, yes, it turns out that Hecuba was able to save some "things" from Troy. They are hidden safe inside the slave women's tent, among a mob of spoils. "We women are all alone," Hecuba insists. "Come inside. Having done everything you need to do, you may return with your children to the very place where you settled my son."

Polymestor's greed blinds him to the true meaning of her words.

As the Chorus sing of justice, Polymestor's screams from within the tent punctuate their song. "Ah!" he cries. "I am blinded! My eyes! The light has gone! Wretched!" And a second later, "Ah! Worse! My children! Oh, the wretched slaughter!"

The Chorus exclaim, "Friends, new evils have been done inside the shelter!" But they rush to Hecuba's aid.

You hear Hecuba jeering at Polymestor, "The pupils of your eyes will never again see the light! You will never see alive the sons whom I killed!"

"Did you really destroy the Thracian guest-friend, and do you hold power, Mistress?" the Chorus ask, as Hecuba emerges from the tent. "Have you done the very things you said?"

"You will see him for yourselves in a second, a blind man making his way with a blind, staggering step. And you will see the bodies of two children, whom I killed with the help of the best of the Trojan women. He has paid me justice!" Hecuba screams. You cannot deny the symmetry. Polydorus's ghost knew that his mother would see the bodies of two dead children, his sister's and his own. And she did. Now, there are two more dead children. But can you agree with Hecuba that this is justice?

Stumbling out of the tent in an agony of pain, helplessness, and grief, Polymestor calls on the Greeks and Atreus's sons to come to his aid. Agamemnon appears, having heard his screams.

When Polymestor explains that Hecuba, with the captive women, has blinded him and killed his sons, Agamemnon acts surprised. "What do you mean?" he asks. Then, turning to Hecuba, "Did you do this thing, as he says? Did you dare this impossible boldness?" Polymestor wants to tear Hecuba apart, but Agamemnon restrains him. "Hold on," he says. "Cast this barbarism out of your heart and speak, in order that by hearing you both in turn, I may judge justly what you are suffering these things in return for."

Polymestor insists that forethought made him kill Polydorus out of concern for the Greeks. He wanted to ensure that Priam's son could not one day reestablish Troy and cause another war, as the Greeks would attack again and bring evil again to neighboring Thrace. He describes the treachery of Hecuba and the women. They lured him into the tent, entertained him and played with his children, then stabbed out his eyes and stabbed his little boys to death, using daggers hidden in their robes. "Like a wild beast, I pursued the blood-stained bitches!" he cries. "Eager to do you a favor and killing your enemy, Agamemnon, I suffered these things!" Polymestor despises the entire race of women.

Hecuba gets her turn to respond. She ridicules Polymestor's claim that he sought to do the Greeks a favor, since "a barbarian race could never be dear/friendly to the Greeks." If that had been his motive, why didn't he kill the boy immediately or hand him over to the Greeks? The truth is that he killed her son for the gold as soon as he learned of Troy's fall. If Polymestor actually was a friend to the Greeks, why didn't he give them the gold? No, it's all a lie. If Polymestor had saved her son, he would now have noble glory, "for in troubles, good men are the most certain friends."

Agamemnon accepts Hecuba's version of events. Above all, Polymestor murdered a guest-friend. "Maybe guest-killing is easy among you people," Agamemnon says disdainfully. "But to us Greeks, at any rate, this is shameful. Since you dared to do things that are not beautiful and good, endure also things that are not pleasant or dear."

Hecuba remains certain that Polymestor suffers justly for his crimes, but both she and he grieve for their lost children. Polymestor criticizes her for rejoicing in doing violence against him, and she responds, "Isn't it necessary for me to rejoice in taking my revenge on you?" But Polymestor's blindness appears to give him the power of prophecy, and he predicts that on the voyage home, Hecuba will turn into a dog and climb the ship's mast. She will fall into the sea and drown. Her dog's tomb will become a sign for sailors.

"None of this is a care to me," Hecuba scoffs, "since you have paid me justice." Polymestor proceeds to predict the deaths of Cassandra and Agamemnon. You know the prediction is true, since it refers to an ancient long-familiar tale. But this is too much for Agamemnon, and he orders the blind man gagged, removed by force, and cast out on deserted islands somewhere. Agamemnon bids Hecuba bury her two children. The Greeks must sail homeward, as the breezes are finally favorable. The Chorus head for the ships, knowing full well the life of slavery awaiting them. Their final words slice the air: "Cruel is Necessity!"

A Matter of Perspective

Two decades after Sophocles produced the *Ajax,* Euripides also revisited the world of Homer's characters and used a tool that Homer forged. Like Homer and Sophocles, Euripides, in the *Hecuba* (c. 425 BCE), distinguishes the perspective of the audience from that of the characters and prompts the audience to evaluate events and to determine their causes. As spectators, audience members can recognize flaws in the characters' moral reasoning and question the characters' understanding of causality.

In its portrait of rage, Euripides' *Hecuba* exposes the consequences of people in power failing to respect any obligations toward the powerless.[1] Written and performed a generation after the institution of radical, direct democracy in Athens, the play reminds its audience that democratic decision making, by empowering individuals, simultaneously requires individuals to take responsibility for their actions and to learn to judge and to choose to do what is best. Euripides' characters retain the traditional view that Hecuba's example illustrates the vagaries of Chance, but the audience can see that Chance—or bad luck—is not the causal factor. The audience sees instead that each atrocity results directly from deliberate, arbitrary human choices and actions.[2]

The *Hecuba* takes place in the distant past, in the aftermath of the legendary fall of Troy, but its events and themes were acutely familiar to Euripides' fifth-century audience: cities besieged and sacked, men killed, women and children enslaved. Remarkably, the *Hecuba* presents the fall of Troy from the perspective of the defeated Trojans, who encounter gratuitous cruelty from their conquerors. Sadly, the Athenians failed to internalize the play's message, and brutal warfare remained an ever-present reality for Euripides' contemporaries. The atrocities committed by the victorious Greeks in the play evoke the devastation regularly inflicted by victors on the vanquished in fifth-century conflicts between the Athenians and other citizen-communities.[3]

Such brutality by conquerors toward the conquered, not only then but also now, signals a complete failure of empathy. Empathy enables you to imagine yourself in the situation of others, experiencing what they experience, feeling what they feel. Cruelty, by contrast, entails an inability to recognize or value any perspective other than your own. Anxiety and insecurity often underlie cruelty, since inflicting pain can make perpetrators feel powerful. It reassures them to think, "I'm not experiencing this suffering because I'm causing it." The absence of empathy and the enjoyment of cruelty require that you ignore the fact that human fortunes are precarious and variable. You must fail to see that the situation could reverse without warning, that you could experience tomorrow the very atrocities you are inflicting today. Sociopaths generally have no empathy. But even people with a normal capacity for empathy can cultivate it more fully—or unlearn it. The values of our family and community and the stories that we inherit and transmit can enhance or diminish our ability to empathize.

Greek myths, told in epic and tragic form, began long ago to cultivate their audiences' capacity for empathy. Undeniably, the development of this capacity was imperfect and far from linear: Greek history from the eighth through the fifth centuries and beyond indicates that violence and warfare remained a central feature of Greek life. But although Homer's epics evolved centuries before the institutions of democratic government, they nevertheless show events from various perspectives: Greek, Trojan, male, female, victor, vanquished, young, old. Athenian fifth-century tragedies, by permitting various participants to speak for themselves and articulate their views, similarly encouraged the audience to imagine what the experiences and especially the suffering of others might feel like.

In cultivating the audience's ability to imagine the suffering of others, Homer and the tragedians emphasize the instability of human fortunes. The experiences of Hecuba and Priam and of Troy itself exemplify the fragility and impermanence of success and prosperity.[4] The *Hecuba* exposes the need for moral standards between those who have power and those who have none. The play's setting, Thrace, epitomized, for fifth-century Athenians, a place of wildness and savagery, an inhabited but completely uncivilized land.[5] The barbarous acts committed in this wild, savage space expose the need for humane standards governing all human relationships.

Recognition of the precariousness of good fortune can itself engender morality. In another play by Euripides, a character maintains that you should wish that your enemy be educated and wise because if you were to lose to such an enemy, you would be treated with justice. "Therefore," this character explains, "wise men must pray to join in enmity with a wise person, not with an uneducated mind, for a man would encounter much reverence and justice" (*Children of Heracles* 458–460). The *Hecuba* illustrates the antithesis: the dire consequences of losing to an enemy who is neither wise nor just. Seeking justice (271), Hecuba vainly attempts to remind Odysseus that "the strong and mighty must not exert power which is not right, nor should those who are fortunate think that they will fare well always" (282–283).[6] Once you recognize that human fortunes are variable, the terrible suffering that winners inflict on losers begins to seem both reprehensible and foolish.

Choice, Not Chance

Unlike the rage of Achilles or Ajax, Hecuba's fury seems icy and calculating. But its causes and consequences are no less troubling. Like Homer, Euripides enables the audience to see that the human decisions and actions largely impel events and determine their outcome, although the characters persist in believing that the gods, fate, and chance cause everything. By attributing much suffering to human choices, Homer began, millennia ago, to cultivate his audiences' capacity to make judgments and to take responsibility for their own actions. In reinterpreting Hecuba's story for a democratic age, Euripides, too, features the role of choice over chance and invites the audience to reassess the characters' priorities and their own. Euripides transforms Hecuba into an emblem of the suffering inflicted not by the gods or *Tuchē*, "Chance/Fortune," but by human beings.

Euripides probably invented this particular story, but long, archaic tradition presented Hecuba as a symbol of the instability of prosperity.[7] As the wife of Troy's King Priam and the mother of Paris, Hector, and numerous other sons and daughters (*Il.* 6.242–252, 16.717–718, 24.496), Homer's Hecuba epitomizes the impermanence of fortune: she is a magnificent, prosperous queen, and mother of many glorious children, but ill-fortune then makes her a widow, childless and enslaved.[8]

Like Homer's characters, the characters in the *Hecuba* identify the gods or *Tuchē*, "Chance/Fortune," as the source of Hecuba's suffering. The ghost of Polydorus claims that "some god" is responsible for Hecuba's misery (55–58).⁹ Hecuba and the Greek messenger Talthybius both blame Fortune. Doubting that Polydorus is still alive, Hecuba insists, "I am unfortunate with respect to everything" (429). Talthybius suspects that "Fortune oversees all things among mortals" (491). He wishes that he "might die before I am wrecked against some shameful fortune" (498). After relating the sacrifice of Polyxena, ordered and accomplished by Greek hands, the messenger tells Hecuba, "I see that of all women you are most blessed with good children and most unfortunate" (581–582). Similarly, Odysseus attributes Hecuba's previous rescue of him to Chance (301–302). And throughout the play, Hecuba continues to attribute her ill-fortune to Chance. She maintains that "the wealthiest person is he who chances on no evil day by day" (627–628). When Agamemnon wonders, "Was there any woman naturally so unfortunate?" Hecuba responds, "There is not" (785–786).

Oddly, however, the Chorus and Hecuba also seem to recognize that human choices and human actions drive crucial pieces of this terrible story. The Chorus identifies Paris's choice as the source of the Trojan War, the fall of Troy, and the devastation for brides and mothers in both Greece and Troy (629–656). All of this "public evil," they say, results from "the private folly" (641–642) of one man. Encountering the corpse of Polydorus, Hecuba immediately recognizes that her *xenos,* "guest-friend" (710), is responsible. She is stunned that he has violated "the justice of guest-friends" (715). Hecuba knows that Polymestor killed her son for the gold as soon as he learned that Troy had fallen (774–776). How can she possibly know this? The point is that even she, victim of chance that she claims to be, understands that the murder was a calculated decision. She calls Polymestor a "most wicked guest-friend" (790), who murdered her son "taking forethought" (795) and "did not think him worthy of burial" (796–797). Her fury and her description of Polymestor's violation of *xenia*, "guest-friendship," make nonsense of the claim that her son's death resulted from Chance or Fortune.

The audience sees no supernatural causes for the deaths of Hecuba's children, only opportunistic human greed and brutality. Choice, not the gods or Chance, kills Polyxena no less than it kills Polydorus. Polydorus's ghost, Hecuba, the Chorus, and Odysseus all imply that Achilles' honor is at issue, that the sacrifice will give Achilles his share of the plunder taken from Troy (37–41, 92–95, 114–116, 309–312). The ghost of Polydorus says that Achilles' ghost has risen from his tomb and asked for a virgin sacrifice as his "prize" (41). Hecuba's dream corroborates this (94), and the Chorus repeat it (115). But Odysseus chooses to fulfill this demand. Nothing requires or justifies the decision to honor a dead warrior by slaughtering a live girl.[10] The messenger's vivid, poignant account of the sacrifice underscores Polyxena's suffering and must evoke some sympathy in the audience (518–580). The Greek messenger's own evident sympathy for Polyxena must make the audience question Odysseus's decision and the army's enthusiasm for it. Surely the Greeks might have devised some other "prize" in order to honor their fallen champion.

To a fifth-century audience, the sacrifice of Polyxena seems particularly arbitrary in comparison to the famous tale of Agamemnon's sacrifice of his own daughter in order to launch the Trojan War. The messenger's heart-rending account of Polyxena's sacrifice recalls Aeschylus's powerful, painful description of Iphigenia's death in his tragedy the *Agamemnon* (*Ag.* 228ff.).[11] Knowing this tale well, Euripides' original audience also knew that a goddess forced Agamemnon to choose between the life of his daughter and the lives of his soldiers. If Agamemnon had chosen not to kill his own daughter, the goddess Artemis would have continued to prevent the Greek fleet from sailing, and the

Greek warriors would have died of starvation. Comparison of these two tales of female sacrifice invites the audience's recognition that the Greeks in this play face no such inevitable choice. No god or goddess demands the sacrifice of Polyxena, and no army will starve if the Greeks fail to accomplish it.

In the second half of the *Hecuba,* as in the first, the characters continue to attribute to Chance, the gods, or Luck things that the audience recognizes result from free choice. Agamemnon attributes to the gods his decision to help Hecuba get revenge. He says that he is helping Hecuba only because, as it happens, the gods have not sent a favorable wind for sailing away and the Greeks are forced to wait (898–904). The audience can appreciate that Agamemnon has other options. The Greeks must wait, yes, but can they not wait without assisting in murder? Polymestor, hypocritically calling Priam and Hecuba "dearest" (953), blames the gods for her suffering. "There is nothing trustworthy," he insists. "Good reputation, good fortune, good deeds all get reversed. The gods themselves jumble things backwards and forwards making confusion, so that we reverence them out of ignorance" (957–960). But he incriminates himself by falsely reassuring Hecuba that her son is still alive, insisting, "With regard to him you are lucky" (989). Of course, everyone already knows that Polydorus is dead, killed not by ill-luck but by greed and betrayal. And not bad luck, but rage, retaliation, and treachery, combined with the victim's own greed and stupidity, proceed to destroy Polymestor. Hecuba lures him into the tent by playing on his greed (998ff.), and he thoroughly misses all of her sarcasm and double entendres. Hecuba and the women (not Chance or the gods) blind him and murder his two young sons.[12]

As the play ends, Agamemnon foresees favorable winds to escort the Greeks home (1289–1290) and prays for smooth sailing and an end to their toils (1291–1292). The irony here almost approaches comedy: Euripides' fifth-century audience, familiar with the archaic tales of Homer as well as Aeschylus's more recent versions of the myths, knew the suffering and death awaiting the Greeks on their return journey and Agamemnon upon reaching home. The Chorus conclude by blaming the cruelty of *Anankē*, "Necessity" (1295), but since human choices and actions produced each vicious event in this terrible story, Euripides suggests that the real Necessity, the real constraint, is not a supernatural force but human nature itself.

Arbitrary Cruelty and the Pretense of Moral Action

Far from corroborating the characters' certainty that the gods or chance determine the events in the play, the audience sees instead the arbitrary brutality of powerful human beings who choose to reject or to pervert traditional moral standards.[13] Murdering Polydorus out of greed, the Thracian king Polymestor grotesquely violates the ties of *xenia*, "guest-friendship," that ancient, traditional system of mutual obligations of hospitality between foreigners (16–27). The ghost of Polydorus calls the Thracian king his father's *xenos*, "guest-friend," a full three times in the first twenty-six lines of the play (7, 19, 26). The word specifically evokes Polymestor's moral obligation to help Priam and Hecuba and to protect their son, an obligation he spectacularly fails to fulfill but subsequently pretends to have accomplished.

Like the murder of Polydorus, the killing of Polyxena has only the appearance of moral correctness. In advocating the sacrifice, Odysseus maintains that the Greeks consider Achilles "worthy of honor" (309) because he died on behalf of Greece. He claims that failure to honor a fallen warrior will diminish the willingness of other warriors to risk their lives on behalf of the community. Odysseus insists that he must honor a dead warrior by sacrificing a live girl (299ff.). He asks sarcastically, "Will we do battle or will we love life excessively if we see that the dead are not honored?" (315–316). He claims sanctimoniously that the sacrifice of Polyxena is a moral act that distinguishes Greek from barbarian (328–331).[14] But contemporary Greek religious practice required the sacrifice of animals, not people, as Euripides' fifth-century audience well knew. The messenger, describing the sacrifice, highlights the perversion by calling Polyxena a "calf." To a twenty-first-century audience, a decision to murder one woman in order to honor a warrior who died trying to recover another woman might seem to parody the very idea of a moral incentive structure. But even a fifth-century Athenian audience must find the messenger's heart-rending description of Polyxena's death troubling and perceive Odysseus's distortion of the obligations owed to the dead.

Moreover, Polyxena's death appears not only perverse but pointless. Unlike Agamemnon's sacrifice of his daughter Iphigenia, for example, Polyxena's death achieves nothing. A fifth-century audience familiar with the traditional tales knew that the sacrifice of Polyxena failed to achieve its purpose. In the messenger's description of the sacrifice, Achilles' son asks his father's spirit to ensure a safe homecoming for the Greeks. But Euripides' original audience knew very well that most of the victorious Greeks never made it home at all as they were shipwrecked at sea. And most of those who (like Odysseus) did manage to get home arrived "late and badly," having suffered horribly during long years of wandering and deprivation.

The audience cannot share Odysseus's conviction that morality requires the sacrifice of a live girl to honor a dead man, but Odysseus never doubts the moral correctness of his actions.

His callous moral reasoning in this play contrasts strikingly with the wise compassion that Sophocles attributes to Odysseus in the *Ajax*. Sophocles' Odysseus can take the long view. He recognizes that he will not always be in charge. He knows that he too will die one day, and his corpse will be vulnerable. Unlike the Odysseus of the *Ajax*, the Odysseus in the *Hecuba* fails to recognize that prosperity is impermanent and that his enemy's suffering could easily be his own. Sophocles' Odysseus knows that it is in everyone's interest to observe certain standards (see chapter 5). But Euripides' Odysseus never even suspects this.[15]

Unlike Odysseus, the audience recognizes Polyxena's murder as a perversion of moral obligations and a gratuitous act of cruelty, although Polyxena tries to turn her sacrifice into a noble choice. Preferring death to slavery, Polyxena adheres to traditional, uncompromising standards of nobility, insisting, "I do not weep. For dying happens to be the greater happy chance for me" (214–215). She urges her mother to "agree for me to die before encountering shameful things that are not in accordance with my worth" (373–374). The Chorus, too, identify this decision as a marker of being "noble" and a source of "a greater reputation for nobility for those who are worthy" (379–381). Polyxena offers herself willingly to her murderers, claiming to die "free" (547–552). But the audience cannot accept this as noble, since her death appears senseless and wasteful. Polyxena will die whether she chooses to or not. Her death is no more a noble choice than her brother's was, and the play scarcely differentiates the two murders. Hecuba wants both of her children buried in one grave (894–897).[16]

In this play, as so often in our own violent times, ruthless, unnecessary killing masquerades as moral correctness. But Euripides encourages the audience to see the vicious reality behind the charade of moral probity.

Retaliatory Violence Mistaken for Justice

Similarly, Euripides emphasizes that revenge offers only the illusion of moral action. The *Hecuba* suggests that if individuals with power refuse to protect the powerless, democratic procedures alone will afford the weak and vulnerable no protection. Every violent act, whether initiated by a powerful individual or by a popular vote, will predictably produce further violence. The characters call this "justice," but the audience cannot.

Polymestor and Odysseus both fail to identify and respect any obligations to people they hold in their power, but the *Hecuba* also emphasizes that powerful individuals are not the only source of atrocities. Sophocles' *Ajax* shows that a democratic vote can produce an objectively incorrect decision: the tribunal votes to give Achilles' armor to Odysseus although Ajax rightly deserves it. (The consequences are catastrophic not only for Ajax but also for the Greeks, who lose their best warrior.) Taking this critique a step further, Euripides shows that a democratic vote can produce not merely an unfair decision but even a brutal atrocity. Polydorus's death results from the arbitrary, opportunistic greed and ruthlessness of a king, but Polyxena's murder results from a democratic decision.

In reporting to Hecuba the terrible news that the Greeks have decided to sacrifice Polyxena, the Chorus use the official language of fifth-century Athenian political decision making, explaining, "For it is said that in the full assembly of the Greeks, it seemed best to make your daughter a sacrificial victim to Achilles" (107–109). Hecuba explains to Polyxena that sacrificing her "seemed best by a vote of the Greeks" (195–196). Odysseus, too, refers to "the judgment and the vote of the army," explaining that "it seemed best to the Greeks to slaughter" Polyxena at Achilles' tomb (218–221). The repetition of the formulaic legal language forcefully (and anachronistically) aligns the army's decision with fifth-century Athenian democratic political processes.[17]

By presenting the decision to sacrifice Polyxena as the result of a democratic vote preceded by a debate, Euripides challenges his fifth-century audience's confidence in their own democratic procedures.[18] Calling Odysseus a "wily-minded babbler, a sweet-speaking flatterer of the people" (131–132), the Chorus expose the dark side of persuasive speech and moral flexibility, explaining to Hecuba that Odysseus used his verbal talents to persuade the army to sacrifice Polyxena (130–140). Hecuba criticizes the Greeks' fondness for oratory and debate, denouncing Odysseus as the "ungrateful offspring of all of you who envy public speakers their honors. I wish I didn't know you, you who harm your friends and don't give it a thought, as long as you say something that gratifies 'the many.' Believing what clever argument did they let loose this vote of death against my daughter?" (254–259). Hecuba knows that the Greeks' speeches and democratic voting method produced an injustice.

Rejecting debate and the voting process, Hecuba understands that group consensus alone does not and cannot determine justice. She knows that a large group can easily pervert morality, as she urges Talthybius after the sacrifice of Polyxena to tell the Greeks to "restrain the mob [ochlon]. An unbridled mob [ochlos] in an army of thousands and a naval force without government is stronger than fire. And a man doing nothing evil is evil" (605–608). Hecuba recognizes the dangers of mob action. For Euripides' contemporaries, ochlokratia, "mob rule," constituted the vicious version or dangerous potential of demokratia, "democracy." Fifth-century Greeks knew as well as we do that in a large, unregulated group, no individual can be held accountable. And a failure to act makes you complicit in the mob's destructive actions. In this instance, a democratic group decision results in the slaughter of an innocent young girl. A mob, even by voting, can redefine wrong as right.

But what, in this play, is "right"? Hecuba seems to understand justice as a reciprocal exchange. Enraged at the transgressions of Polymestor and the democratic "mob," Hecuba asks repeatedly for justice.[19] But she defines justice only in terms of equivalences— as she reproaches Odysseus for failing to save Polyxena even though she herself had saved Odysseus when he came to spy on Troy (239–250).[20] Reminding Odysseus of this debt to her, Hecuba criticizes him for ingratitude (251–253). Hecuba sees justice as an exchange. She insists that if a human sacrifice is necessary, then Helen should be the one sacrificed since she caused Achilles' death by leading him to Troy (265–270).

The failure of those in power to protect the vulnerable leaves Hecuba to exact "justice" as she understands it. Vengeance becomes her only object (756–757), and it appears to her in the guise of a moral obligation. Odysseus earlier formulated Polyxena's murder as a moral necessity to honor the dead. Now Hecuba presents her vengeance as necessary to preserve the distinction between right and wrong. "The gods are powerful," she says. "And *nomos*, 'law/ custom/tradition,' rules the gods. By [or, because of] *nomos* we believe in the gods, and we live distinguishing unjust things from just things" (800–801). But, "if those who kill guest-friends pay no penalty" (803–804), she explains, "then there is nothing equal/ fair regarding the affairs among human beings" (805). "It is the part of a noble man," Hecuba tells Agamemnon, "to serve justice and always to harm evil men everywhere" (844–845).[21]

The audience may imagine the agony of Hecuba's terrible losses and may sympathize with her certainty that only revenge can preserve justice and faith in the gods, but in equating justice with revenge, Hecuba reverts to an ancient, traditional idea already challenged in the fifth century.[22] The *Hecuba* suggests that this destructive definition of justice resurfaces in response to deliberate acts of cruelty and murder by people in powerful positions, people who clearly had other options.

Hecuba's motives are understandable, but the play makes the audience question her goals and her methods. The gratuitous atrocities of Hecuba's Thracian guest-friend and her Greek enemies enrage her and drive her to seek vengeance. She needs Agamemnon's help to exact her revenge, and she tries to win him over using first pity (807ff.) and then persuasion (814ff.). Ultimately, she resorts to claiming that Agamemnon owes her because he is sleeping with her daughter Cassandra (824–835). Hecuba, this once-glorious queen, has been reduced, by the brutality of powerful men, to demanding fulfillment of the obligations of kinship from the leader of the army that destroyed her family and city.[23]

Suffering atrocity transforms a once kindly queen into a ferocious avenger, and complicity in atrocity turns a king into a demagogue. In agreeing to help Hecuba, Agamemnon shows that he is ruled by the opinions of his subjects.[24] He accepts Hecuba's definition of justice as revenge and is willing to help her, as long as he can avoid the appearance of plotting the murder as a favor to Cassandra (850–863) since currently the Greeks consider the Thracian king "friendly" (858). In his complete subordination to public opinion, Agamemnon epitomizes the most dangerous sort of demagogue, one who panders to the people he ought to lead. Like many twenty-first-century political leaders, Agamemnon cares most about appearances and about his own susceptibility to blame. Hecuba has his number: "Since you are afraid," she tells him, "you distribute more to the *ochlos*, 'mob'" (868). Instead of leading, Agamemnon subordinates himself to the mob. And we have already seen the mob twist wrong into right.[25]

Hecuba calls this justice, but Euripides makes it difficult for the audience to agree. The Chorus equate justice with vengeance (1023–1033), and Hecuba proudly insists that by blinding Polymestor and murdering his children she has accomplished justice. "You will see him for yourselves in a second, a blind man making his way with a blind, staggering step," she says. "And you will see the bodies of two children, whom I killed with the help of the best of the Trojan women. He has paid me justice!" (1049–1053). The audience may derive some vicarious satisfaction from Hecuba's triumph over Polymestor. An audience confident that vengeance equals justice very likely will. But in male-dominated fifth-century Athens, female deception and violence would horrify men. And Euripides previously challenged the validity of mob action, and Hecuba called the women a mob, too. Moreover, we hear the gruesome tale not from Hecuba but from her victim. In addition, the two dead bodies of innocent young children recall the two bodies of Hecuba's murdered children. As the play begins, Polydorus describes the two corpses that his mother Hecuba will see, his own and his sister's (45–46). We now see two other corpses, the young sons of Polymestor. By what criteria can we judge these new murders more just than the previous ones?[26]

The following "trial" scene both highlights the characters' conviction that revenge equals justice and further undermines the audience's confidence in the equation. Polymestor and Hecuba try to justify themselves before Agamemnon, but Agamemnon has perverted the concept of judicial process in holding the "trial" after the punishment has already been inflicted. Polymestor shamelessly tries to present his murder of Polydorus as a favor to Agamemnon and the Greeks (1136–1139; 1175–1177), and he condemns all women (1178–1182). But his first-person account of his suffering at the hands of Hecuba and the women (1145–1177) must evoke some sympathy for him (particularly, in the fifth century, from a largely if not exclusively male audience). And certainly nothing suggests that Polymestor's sons deserved to die. But Agamemnon accepts Hecuba's claims (1196–1237) because Polymestor violated the obligations of "guest-friendship" (1250–1251). Maybe that is all right for barbarians, sniffs Agamemnon, but we Greeks find it shameful (1247–1248). The audience, however, perceives Agamemnon's astounding hypocrisy: he recognizes the shamefulness of someone else's murder of a guest-friend but ignores his own participation in the murders of three innocent children (Polyxena and Polymestor's two sons), four if you count Agamemnon's daughter Iphigenia.

In consequence of the perversion of the judicial process and Agamemnon's hypocrisy, Hecuba's vengeance-with-interest (another two dead children plus a blinding) begins to seem more like a symptom than a solution, particularly since Euripides makes Hecuba's exultation itself problematic. Hecuba accepts the traditional view that finds not only satisfaction but joy in vengeance. When Polymestor asks, "Do you rejoice in doing violence against me, O you villain?" Hecuba responds, "Shouldn't I rejoice in taking my vengeance on you?" (1257–1258). A generation earlier, Sophocles' *Ajax* had exposed the irrationality of this conviction (see chapter 5). For centuries before that, Homer's *Iliad* had already begun to suggest that revenge might not, in fact, be all that satisfying (see chapter 4). Even if the audience agrees that Hecuba acted "justly," her unqualified elation must raise doubts, for it suggests that she has forgotten the very principle that she herself embodies: the variability of fortune and the transience of success.[27]

Any satisfaction the audience shares with Hecuba will necessarily be brief. Recognizing the traditional equation of vengeance with justice, the audience also has the certainty that reciprocal vengeance will continue, for Polymestor predicts the murders of Cassandra and Agamemnon, once they are back in Greece, by

Agamemnon's own wife (1275–1279). This finally gets to Agamemnon and he orders Polymestor gagged (1283), even as he once gagged his daughter's mouth before sacrificing her (*Ag.* 235–237). But Polymestor closes his mouth himself, saying, "It is shut, for it has been said." And, of course, as Euripides' original audience knew, the story has already been told—by Aeschylus in the *Oresteia* more than a quarter of a century earlier.[28] Polymestor's prediction assures the audience that the equation of vengeance with justice will continue to produce endless and escalating violence.

Cultivating Morality

Homer began to suggest that the experience of extreme and arbitrary brutality could destroy Hecuba's humanity. Identifying Hecuba as *ēpiodōros*, "giving welcome gifts" (*Il.* 6.251), Homer distinguishes her especially for her generosity. Pious to the gods and devoted to her husband and children, Homer's Hecuba helps to define Hector as a responsible son, husband, and father, dedicated to defending his city (e.g., *Il.* 6.253–268; 6.269–312). But after Hector's death (*Il.* 24.194ff.), Hecuba's anger at Achilles and her desire for vengeance take a monstrous form—she wishes that she could eat Achilles' liver (*Il.* 24.212–214). Greek myth defines this impulse as bestial and inhuman. In the *Iliad*, Hecuba's desire to eat Achilles' liver suggests that extreme suffering can destroy the distinction between a person and a beast.[29]

In Euripides' *Hecuba*, however, Hecuba herself suggests that human nature is unchangeable. She marvels that "for men always, the wicked man is nothing other than evil, and the noble man is nothing other than noble, and even under misfortune he does not corrupt his nature but is useful/good always" (595–598). Perhaps she herself is the exception that proves the rule, for Polymestor foretells her subsequent transformation into a dog. Because the headland where her tomb lies will be called *Kunos sema,* "Dog's Tomb" (or "Sign") (1273), her transformation perhaps symbolizes the fact that suffering can turn a human being into a creature like a dog that eats raw human flesh and knows nothing of morality.[30]

If morality can be unlearned, can it also be learned? Hecuba seems to lose her noble nature as a consequence of her terrible sufferings. But even while claiming that character cannot change, Hecuba praises education, saying, "Noble nurturing holds the teaching, however, of what is noble, and if someone learns this well, he knows what is shameful, having learned to measure it against what is noble" (600–602). The tragic playwright must believe in the value of education, or his own efforts are futile. If moral behavior cannot be taught, then audiences cannot learn about morality from the dramatization of ancient myths. The tragic playwright would be offering examples of moral and immoral behavior to no purpose. Why would he waste his time? Hecuba must be right. Morality must be teachable.[31]

At the very least, this play insists that morality can be unlearned, that sufficient cruelty will excise moral behavior from even a noble queen. Hecuba's transformation into a dog emphasizes that cruelty obliterates obligations between people, making even good people degenerate into beasts.[32] Human beings need morality, this play insists. They must respect obligations toward one another, particularly between the powerful and the weak. Both sides must recognize that it is in their interest to play by the rules. Although generally nicer than most people, dogs can become vicious if treated with cruelty. Hecuba does not become a monster. Dogs are not monsters but beasts. They know nothing of justice or morality, but they also do not claim to. If the absence of morality makes someone a dog, then morality must be the thing that makes us human.

The *Hecuba* stresses the gratuitous cruelty and suffering that human beings inflict on one another. This play dramatizes the destructive effects of war on winners as well as on losers.[33] It depicts arbitrary brutality and the retaliation that brutality inevitably provokes. Devastating wars and horrific cruelty flourish in the twenty-first century as in the fifth century BCE, and Euripides reminds us that groups are just as good at committing atrocities as individuals are. That insight cautions us against blind faith in corrupt and biased judicial procedures as well as against overconfidence in the results of so-called free and fair elections in any community that does not particularly value empathy or compassion and has no reliable judicial system to substitute for an eye-for-an-eye definition of justice as revenge.

People in power have the most options. Hecuba's rage demonstrates that the failure of not only powerful individuals but also democratic institutions to protect the weak and the vulnerable will have predictable consequences. Even as Athenians in the late fifth century continued to wield imperial power with brutal force, Euripides exposed the costs to the powerful of behaving with rapaciousness and callous cruelty toward those in their power. In this play the perpetrators bring suffering not only on their victims but also on themselves.[34] The *Hecuba* enables the audience to see that whether power derives from wealth, influence, physical strength, military might, or numerical superiority, it is in the interests of the powerful to exercise restraint and compassion.

Just think of what such a farsighted conception of self-interest might accomplish in our own violent times . . .

Conclusion
The Ends of Self-Government

Rage has been and always will be a force in human life and a threat to the well-being of individuals and groups. Sometimes rage, and the violence it produces, will have comprehensible causes. The loss of a beloved relative or friend due to someone's negligence or malevolence may understandably provoke rage. An insult, injury, or injustice, recent or committed by previous generations, may also incite rage. Other sources of rage may be less comprehensible, such as pathological brutality and cruelty, perhaps dressed up as moral or religious conviction. Rage can simplify moral complexity and mask moral uncertainty. ("Surely I'm right," we may reassure ourselves. "Look how angry I am.") At times we may all be tempted to succumb to rage. Rage can "feel right" and sometimes provide short-term satisfaction, although we may recognize on some level that rage offers no real, lasting solace or remedy. For some, rage may be addictive. Undoubtedly, there will always be bullies and tyrants, thugs and criminals, sociopaths and psychopaths. The question is whether our stories encourage us to admire or condemn them, to emulate or despise them.

The ancient Greeks saw everywhere the horrendous consequences of the brutal, tyrannical use of power. They began
to reject autocracy, and they ultimately developed radically
democratic political institutions out of hierarchical, undemocratic social structures and priorities. But the Greeks also understood, as by now we must, that people do not put down their
weapons and set aside their anger overnight merely because
they suddenly have an opportunity to cast a vote.

As early as Homer and long before democratic ideals
emerged, ancient Greeks began incorporating into their stories
the kind of critical self-reflection essential to individual and
communal success. The ancient Greeks continued to use violence frequently in their dealings with non-Greeks as well as
between (and sometimes even within) Greek *poleis,* "citizen-
communities." But their myths and their experience suggest
that the stories we inherit and transmit determine our values,
and our values determine our ends. By "ends" I mean both our
goals and their consequences, because these are not always
identical. Together they determine the quality of our lives and
the nature of life in our community.

Stories can confront ethical and political challenges in a
representational way because the audience may have no direct
involvement in the events depicted. Lacking an immediate or
overriding personal stake in the stories' outcome, the audience
is likely to experience less anxiety and, above all, less anger than
comparable real-life situations might evoke. In this way, Greek
myths enable the audience to assess the characters' decisions
more objectively and also to think creatively about other options
the characters might have had. Homer gave the audience a
separate perspective from which to critique the characters'
values. Centuries later, tragedy institutionalized self-reflection
and self-criticism as part of Athenian communal life. By

dramatizing the stories and putting the characters onstage, fifth-century Athenian tragic playwrights cultivated the audience's ability to see the ends of power, both good and bad, both intentional and inadvertent.

The Homeric epics and the tragic plays taught the ancient Greeks to look for models to esteem and strive to emulate not in the supernatural realm but in the real world of human beings. The gods' behavior provides no basis for human morality because gods can act without consequences and they often behave very badly. The gods' negative example illuminates, by contrast, the human capacity for love, empathy, and farsighted, mutually supportive relationships. In the *Iliad,* for example, the deceitful and loveless marriage of Zeus and Hera contrasts with the deeper emotional connection possible for mortals such as Hector and Andromache. Achilles' capacity to indulge his rage and to cause chaos and destruction elevates the divine side of his nature at the expense of his humanity. But Achilles regains his humanity by recognizing human vulnerability to suffering and death and by discovering the value of empathy. In the *Ajax,* Odysseus's compassion for his fallen enemy reveals that mortals would be irrational and shortsighted to emulate a god's relentless vindictiveness. In these ancient Greek texts, any admirable choices and constructive deeds are those of mortals, not gods. Impervious to suffering and death, gods are incapable of empathy and have no need for it. Conversely, as these stories show, mortals do have the capacity for empathy, and it is irrational to think that we do not need it. Gods can indulge their passions with impunity. Mortals must recognize the costs *to themselves* of indulging in rage and violent revenge.

Because these stories suggest that human beings, unlike gods, are capable of making good moral choices, the audience cannot share the characters' relentless fatalism and moral certainty. Homer's mortal characters think that the gods and fate determine everything. But at the same time they actively compete for honor and glory. Each strives to be *aristos*, "best," the adjective at the root of our word "aristocracy." They endeavor to excel and to succeed by helping their friends and harming their enemies. Above all, when they feel wronged, they seek revenge. Some of this is admirable, but much of it is mistaken and shortsighted. Since Homer shows that human beings, not gods, cause the progression of events, the audience comes to question the characters' limited definition of "bestness." The characters' choices and their consequences reveal that if your top priority is honor and prestige, then you had better think long and hard about what really deserves honor. Striving to excel is admirable, but your goals, and the arenas in which you struggle to excel, must be optimal as well.

By giving the audience a broader view than the characters themselves have and showing many perspectives on the action, the narrative reveals how narrow the characters' understanding is and how limited and limiting their priorities are. The great war that gives these warriors the opportunity to display their courage and military talents, the magnificent struggle that offers the chance of immortal glory, originates in a trivial dispute—the deeply irresponsible act of a single man—and persists in the continued stupidities of many. The *Iliad* emphasizes that honor and prestige deriving from success in battle comes at great cost in human life and suffering.

By undermining the audience's confidence in the characters' fatalism, Homer encourages us to take responsibility for our own choices. We see that Achilles' rage and his pursuit of vengeance prove self-destructive. Anger at Agamemnon and the Greeks costs Achilles his closest friend. His equation of vengeance with justice, an equation the *Iliad*'s characters all accept, becomes self-defeating. Achilles' experience reminds us that the pursuit of vengeance is unsatisfying, interminable, and ever escalating. His example reveals that self-interest demands self-restraint and that the community bears the responsibility of defining the elements of admirable behavior deserving of honor. The *Iliad* suggests that no community can succeed by honoring "achievements" that bring chaos and destruction.

Successful human relationships and nonviolent political participation require that individuals not only take responsibility for their own choices but also acknowledge the viewpoints and essential humanity of others, including political opponents and enemies. Homer offers multiple perspectives on events, closely describing the experience of many characters, divine, mortal, friend, and foe. Far from demonizing the Trojans, Homer humanizes them, showing that they have feelings, choices, and responsibilities as all human beings do. The *Iliad* encourages us to imagine, and above all to care about, someone else's experience.

Homer begins to develop the audience's capacity to recognize and respect the viewpoints and feelings of others, but for the Greeks, this never meant that all opinions and ideas were equally valid. Rather, acknowledging perspectives other than your own both enables and requires you to evaluate each (yours included) on its merits. The main narrative and the numerous shorter tales and similes within it cultivate the audience's ability to draw parallels and contrasts, to judge, and to try to determine what is "best" in ideals of achievement and leadership. In cultivating the audience's critical judgment, the *Iliad* calls into question its characters' certainty that success in battle is the highest form of human accomplishment. Such questioning undermines the audience's eagerness to celebrate physical combat and violent vengeance above all else.

Depicting the horrors of war, the *Iliad* also critiques the moral calculus of warfare and validates the worth of each individual human life. The characters exult in their ability to slaughter enemies, the more the better, but the narrative emphasizes the equality of all human beings in their mortality and their vulnerability to suffering. The characters understand vengeance as the only satisfying response to violence and bloodshed, but the epic shows the audience that vengeance dehumanizes the avenger and brings him no satisfaction or peace of mind. Only a brief moment of empathy between bitter enemies offers a constructive alternative. The audience begins to see that self-interest demands not the short-term satisfactions of anger and vengeance but the identification of our needs with the needs of others. Without empathy, anger and vengeance inevitably produce violence. Without empathy, verbal argument cannot replace physical combat, and nonviolent political processes cannot function, as twenty-first-century world events surely affirm.

Revisiting the problem of rage in the democratic Athens of the fifth century BCE, Sophocles' *Ajax* warns against overconfidence in the value of democratic institutions alone. Democratic methods like jury trials and verbal persuasion—even, we can add, so-called free and fair elections—while crucial to democracy, are not sufficient. The procedures in and of themselves will not solve the problem since a group can vote to commit a blatant injustice, thereby provoking rather than preventing violent rage. A majority decision may align with our understanding of justice. Or it may not. The *Ajax* exposes the costs of ceding moral judgment to majority consensus, but it equally reveals the risks of absolute moral certainty. Majority consensus can produce injustice. But absolute moral certainty rejects compromise and can even justify violent atrocities. Emphasizing the dangers of both moral flexibility and moral absolutism, the *Ajax* suggests that we need a constructive mixture of both: the capacity for sensible compromise plus the wisdom to uphold absolute standards of compassionate justice and humanity. Democratic decision making gives every individual tremendous power. The *Ajax* demonstrates that self-interest demands both creative flexibility and the foresight to recognize one's own needs in the needs of others.

Produced a generation after the *Ajax,* Euripides' *Hecuba* warns against the failure to uphold such farsighted absolute standards of compassionate justice and humanity. In this play, opportunistic greed and lack of empathy provoke rage and escalating reciprocal violence. The *Hecuba* emphasizes that groups are just as good as individuals at committing violent atrocities. And democratic voting processes provide no protection. Arbitrary brutality produces brutality in return, as Euripides transforms Homer's Hecuba into an emblem of the suffering inflicted not by divine forces or bad luck but by the deliberate failure of people in power to respect any obligations toward the powerless. The characters attribute the atrocities in the play to the actions of the gods or Fate or Chance, but the audience sees that each monstrous act of violence originates in the deliberate, capricious choice of a powerful individual or group. The *Hecuba* suggests that the destructive equation of justice with revenge results from the intentional, murderous cruelty of people in powerful positions, people who clearly had other options.

Confronting the problem of rage, these two tragic plays helped foster within Athens a movement from physical conflict to verbal debate, a transformation still eluding many communities today. Although the Athenians continued to employ violence in their relations with other *poleis,* "citizen-communities," their experience and above all their stories remind us that self-government is necessary for a successful society and a fully realized human life. But an institutional voting process in and of itself will not inevitably achieve just, humane results. Groups can behave as tyrannically as individuals. Greek myths suggest that individual and communal success require not merely a specific set of institutions but also a specific set of ideals. Failure to cultivate these ideals transforms "democracy" into a disguise worn by tyranny, as one form of abusive, tyrannical authority violently replaces another in perpetuity.

The necessary priorities must be understood not as perfected accomplishments but as essential goals or objectives. These include: the intellectual capacity to take responsibility for one's own choices and their consequences and to learn from empirical experience, past and present; the imaginative capacity to acknowledge and value points of view other than one's own; the critical capacity to evaluate ideas and opinions on their merits; the realization that the high-achieving individual needs the community as much as the community needs him or her; the recognition that group decision making and compromise must include rewards for objective merit; the understanding that the powerful and the weak have obligations toward one another, since human fortunes are precarious and individual survival, success, and happiness depend on the community's survival, success, and happiness; above all, the wisdom to censure and restrain rage and to reject revenge as the definition of justice. Without such ideals, no form of political power, whether narrowly held or broad based, military or economic, can avoid tyrannical abuses.

Ancient Greek myths suggest that these essential ideals of individual moral responsibility and farsighted self-interest are not natural but cultivated. Shortsighted, self-destructive values, I think, are much more natural than farsighted life-enhancing ones, and their inadequacy is usually not at all evident to the people who hold them. A preference for rage, violent revenge, and political and social domination can easily corrupt and pervert the use of democratic institutions to serve tyrannical ends.

Greek myths move us viscerally while at the same time promoting the ability and, most of all, the desire to replace violence and intimidation with constructive, verbal conflict. Nonviolent verbal conflict permits evolution as we combine the best ideas and the best parts of ideas to develop new and better strategies.

In the twenty-first century, we have ample evidence that majority rule combined with no constructive change in traditional value systems can have horrific results. As we face the domestic, international, and global crises of our own times we have to resist the seductions of rage. Anger may sometimes prompt constructive action, but violent rage devastates individuals, communities, and states. It blinds us to constructive, creative solutions and produces only escalating violent retaliation. Stories that celebrate violence and vengeance and dull our capacity for empathy (whether in novels, television, film, news media, or shared on the internet) may bring short-term emotional satisfaction, but they only exacerbate the problem.

Ancient Greek myths, however, expose such short-term emotional satisfaction for the corrosive poison that it is. The *Iliad, Ajax,* and *Hecuba* urge us to reject the impulse to consider rage an admirable marker of the rightness of our convictions. They urge us, equally, to reject the impulse to embrace relativism, the theory that all values are equally valid and that liberal democratic ideals are no better than any others. Both of these extreme positions are lethal to the kind of individual and communal flourishing that liberal values have the potential to promote. The twenty-first century needs models of individuals, communities, and states that prioritize informed, nonviolent democratic decision making, intolerance of corruption and racism, respect for law, and respect for universal human rights. Whether we reject or embrace these priorities will depend on the stories we choose to tell.

It is an ironic and deeply tragic fact that sometimes these ideals, including the principle of nonviolent, verbal conflict, require defending by force. Flexibility, adaptability, and broad-mindedness are all essential to individual and group success, but history shows that freedom and tolerance are delicate flowers and vulnerable to obliteration by the forces of the less reasonable, less farsighted, less tolerant. Paradoxically, tolerance itself poses a grave danger, as it may make us perilously inactive. Instead, mindful of Edmund Burke's famous claim that "all that is required for the triumph of Evil is that good men do nothing," we must not, in fact, tolerate everything. We must both cultivate and actively defend the principle of constructive, nonviolent conflict. Unfortunately, however, liberal tolerance, the ability to recognize and value opposing viewpoints, can be as paralyzing as weakness or fear or apathy. Robert Frost facetiously defined a liberal as "a man too broad-minded to take his own side in a quarrel." It is possible to be so broad-minded that you tolerate yourself right out of existence. Conversely, it is a mark of a primitive and tyrannical mind-set to celebrate the use of force as a first resort. While revenge requires that you respond to an aggressor's violence not merely with reciprocal violence but with violence exceeding his, justice requires that you avoid violence whenever possible and that you use no more force than necessary. In defending humane and compassionate justice, we must agonize over whether force is necessary and how it should be used. Tyranny never does.

Ancient Greek myths suggest that we should have no illusions about what it takes to create and preserve a successful society. Moderation, tolerance, and equality have always been and will, I think, always be attacked by the forces of extremism, intolerance, and inequality. Ironically, the desire to return to more primitive social relations of violence, coercion, and intimidation always has at its disposal the most sophisticated technological tools that human beings have developed. In antiquity, it was arrows, clubs, siege engines, and fire. Today, it is guns, computer technology, and knowledge of engineering, physics, and biology. Ancient Greek myths remind us that all human power has ambivalent potential. Science, technology, political science, and the institutions of democratic government are all potent tools. How we use them depends on what we value and strive for.

The ancient Greek evidence reminds us that the stories we tell ourselves have political consequences because they inevitably shape our attitudes toward power and its use. The Athenians were the first people to experiment with democratic government. They had no precedent for it. They had to develop it out of a preexisting social and political structure that was completely *un*democratic. Their democracy lasted just under two hundred years, and no other democracy appeared anywhere in the world until our own republic in the eighteenth century. The framers of the U.S. Constitution rejected the Athenian model of radical democracy as too susceptible, still, to tyranny. But we must know by now that no political structures are immune to tyrannical abuse. The rejection of tyranny, ancient Greek myths show, can only derive from a transformation of attitudes.

By telling and retelling their traditional stories, the ancient Greeks in general and the Athenians in particular permitted and encouraged their understanding of moral and political questions to evolve. Each revision of the ancient tales emphasized the consequences of doing this or valuing that. Storytelling, that is, developed ancient Greek ideas about what people should strive to achieve in their lives and how people ought to behave toward one another. Homer began the conversation. Centuries later, Athenian tragic playwrights revised the ancient stories for their own unprecedented political moment. By retelling traditional stories with new emphases, the tragedies helped the Athenians to appreciate that democracy is, essentially, a tool for balancing individual grievances with communal order. Democratic government has the potential to combine extraordinary individual achievement with fairness, compassion, and empathy.

Long, long ago ancient Greek myths began to cultivate the ability to identify the predictable consequences of human actions and aspirations. Obviously, people will not always agree about their choices and the consequences that result, but in order for individuals and societies to thrive, the oppositions, tensions, and conflicts must be acknowledged, and they must become the subject of reasoned, informed debate. Since many fundamentalist faiths have their own exclusive death grip on morality, the only hope for a pluralistic society must derive from the ancient Greeks' insight that morality is the exclusive province of human beings. Gods may help us to indulge in rage. Rage may make us feel, momentarily, like gods. But because we are mortal and vulnerable to suffering, we need morality as gods do not. Because we are mortal and vulnerable to suffering, only we can see the necessity of controlling our rage and respecting our obligations to one another. Ancient Greek myths remind us that rage provokes rage, brutality begets brutality, and atrocity evokes atrocity. In our own violent times, ancient

Greek myths can develop our discernment and our desire to devise and achieve better ends. Human success requires that we learn to restrain rage, reject violent conflict, and embrace verbal debate. Homer, Sophocles, and Euripides invite us to become *aristoi*, "best." We should take them up on their offer.

Notes

Introduction

1. For the role of fiction in shaping culture, see especially Meier 1993, Redfield 1994, 69–98, and Nussbaum 2010. Nussbaum identifies the political effects of stories (2010, esp. 6–10, 26–29). Pozzi and Wickersham argue that "the *polis* is a state of mind, and that mind expresses itself in myth" (1991, 2). Kurke maintains that "art is a privileged domain for the construction and propagation of ideology (and nowhere more so than in a culture like Archaic and Classical Greece, where all art was produced for public performance)" (1998, 156). Csapo defines myth as "a function of social ideology" (2005, 9), and Graf explains the role of myth in shaping Greek identity (2011). For a good introduction to mythology, see Dowden and Livingstone 2011a.

2. Scholars frequently examine Homer for evidence of historical and political features of the archaic Greek world, but the question of whether or not Homeric epic itself embodies political thought remains controversial. J. H. Finley identifies myth as a "vehicle" for political thought in Attic tragedy (1967, 1–13), and arguably a similar role must apply to archaic versions of myth as well, but Bosley and Tweedale, for example, omit Homer from their *Ancient Political Thought: A Reader* (2014), beginning instead with the pre-Socratics and Solon. Edmunds maintains that Homer is not a political thinker (1989), but cf. Raaflaub 2000. Like Raaflaub, Hammer, too, insists that Homeric epic "is engaged in critical reflection and that this reflection is political in nature" (2002, 5 and passim). Hammer persuasively argues that defining Homer as "pre-political" "creates a perplexing situation in which institutions are political, but the pre-institutional activity of forming these institutions is not" (25; Hammer also provides extensive bibliography, 1–14, 19–48). Ahrensdorf presents Homer as an educator and an exemplar of "a noble and humane rationalism" (2014, 24 and passim).

3. For the definition of *polis* as "citizen-community" rather than the anachronistic "city-state," see Raaflaub 2015, 10–15. Regarding the development of the *polis,* see especially Raaflaub 1989, 1993, 2000, 26–34, 2001b, 73–89, Seaford 1994, 1–29, and Hansen 2006. Raaflaub maintains that "both Homeric epics reflect a form of *polis* that is very early but certainly more developed and complete than is usually assumed" (1993, 76).

The movement away from autocracy was by no means linear. The establishment of oligarchies and tyrannies in many Greek *poleis* (including Athens) during the seventh and sixth centuries BCE contrasts with the complex interaction between people and leaders depicted in the Homeric tales (dating from the eighth century and earlier). See, e.g., Ober 1996 and 1998, Raaflaub 1997 and 1998, and Hammer 2002.

4. Kagan 1991 provides an excellent introduction to fifth-century Athens and Athenian democracy. See also Raaflaub 1998. For the workings of the Athenian democracy, see especially Jones 1986, Stockton 1990, Ober 1996 and 2008, Rhodes 2004, and Osborne 2010.

Athens was not unique among Greek *poleis,* "citizen-communities," in its development of democratic ideas. Kurke 1998, 156 (citing Morris 1996) considers the Athenian democracy part of a broader "panhellenic" process. Seaford identifies the *Iliad*'s role in the movement away from monarchy and in the historical evolution of ideals of reciprocity (1994, 191–234).

For analyses of the archaic and classical periods in Greece and the development of the *polis* and democracy, see especially Forrest 1966, Ostwald 1986, Ober 1989 and 1996, Hansen 1991, Robinson 1997, Raaflaub and Ober 2007, J. Hall 2007, Meier 2012, and Ober 2015. For a recent assessment of the structures of Athenian democracy and the economics of the system, see Rosivach 2014. For a comprehensive discussion of the political, social, and cultural contributions of ancient Greek democracy, see Arnason, Raaflaub, and Wagner 2013. Regarding the Greeks' innovations in political theory and practice, see Raaflaub 2015.

5. Meier maintains that the Athenians' fear of their own capacity for tyranny "haunts tragedies from the 450s onwards" (1993, 133). For Athenian attitudes toward tyranny, see especially Podlecki 1966 and Raaflaub 2003. Concern for the tyrannical potential of the Athenian democracy itself led the Athenians in the late fifth century to enact legislation placing some limits on the power of the people (Raaflaub 2015, 20 and nn. 60–61).

6. See Thucydides' *History of the Peloponnesian War* and Kagan's comprehensive analysis (1969, 1974, 1981, 1987). See also Raaflaub's discussion of the persistent, endemic militarism of fifth-century Athenian culture despite questions raised, e.g., by works of Euripides and Aristophanes (Raaflaub

2001a). Hanson also exposes the relationship between democracy and warfare (Hanson 2001).

7. E.g., Euripides' *Trojan Women* and *Bacchae* and the plays of Aristophanes. Thucydides overtly challenges the moral validity of Athenian atrocities, such as the massacres at Mytilene, 427 BCE (Thuc. 3.50), Scione, 421 BCE (Thuc. 5.32), and Melos, 416 BCE (Thuc. 5.85–113, 116).

8. Chua 2003, 9–14, 193–195. Chua cautions against viewing "democracy as a panacea" (12), explaining that in promoting instant universal suffrage along with free-market capitalism in non-Western nations, the West is "asking developing and post-communist countries to embrace a process of democratization that no Western nation ever went through" (194), since "universal suffrage emerged in the West incrementally, over many generations" (275). Chua concludes with considerable prescience (and understatement) that "if some version of free market democracy is the long-term goal in the Middle East, holding overnight elections is probably not the best way to achieve it" (277).

Zakaria stresses the potential of democratic elections to produce autocratic regimes, commenting that in "autocratic states" with "illiberal societies," elections might, in practice, mean "as the saw has it, one man, one vote, one time" (2007, 121). Zakaria distinguishes "democracy," an electoral process, from "constitutional liberalism," a long-standing, Western tradition "that seeks to protect an individual's autonomy and dignity against coercion, whatever the source—state, church, or society" (2007, 17–19, 101–102, 259–262). Zakaria argues that the introduction of democratic elections prior to the development of capitalism and the rule of law can and has produced tyranny or dictatorships (51–62) and may in fact make constitutional liberalism not more but less likely (99–101, 155–158). Harloe also notes the opposition between individual rights and democracy in contemporary Western societies (2013, 5 and n. 3), and Ober observes that "democracy is much more than a set of institutions; it is a way of thinking and acting in the world" (1998, 83, and, similarly, Hansen 1992, 21).

9. Knox uses the term "dead white European males" ironically in the title of his book examining the importance of classical literature in modern times (1993).

10. E.g., DuBois 2001 and 2010 vs. Hanson and Heath 1998 and Hanson, Heath, and Thornton 2000.

11. Athens in the fifth century BCE, by far the best-known example of ancient Greek democracy, was both much less and much more democratic than the modern United States. Like other political systems throughout the world and throughout history until only recently, the Athenians excluded women, slaves, and foreigners from political participation. (On ancient Greek

slavery, see M. I. Finley 1968, 1980, and 1987, Garlan 1988, and Osborne 2010, 85–103. On women in ancient Greece and in Greek myth, see, e.g., H. P. Foley 1981a and 1981b, Lefkowitz 1986, Fantham et al. 1994, S. Blundell 1995, and Katz 1999. On women in Homeric epic, see especially H. P. Foley 1978 and 2005, Felson-Rubin 1987, and Felson and Slatkin 2004.)

But by the mid-fifth century, Athens's radical, direct democracy gave every male citizen the right to vote on all major political decisions in a general assembly, sit on a jury, and be eligible for administrative offices selected by lottery. By contrast, our own "democracy" in the United States is, technically, a republic containing elements of representative democracy. The framers of the U.S. Constitution in the eighteenth century chose the Roman Republic, not the Athenian democracy of the fifth century BCE, as the model for our own republic because they were appalled by the lack of restraints and protections against tyranny in the Greek political model. (See Wood 1972, Richard 1994 and 2009, and Melton 2013, 79–88.)

Arguably, the fifth-century Athenian democracy was more successful than the framers of the U.S. Constitution acknowledged. (For discussions of ancient democracy, see, e.g., M. I. Finley 1973, Dunn 1979, 1992, 2005a, and 2005b, Hansen 1991, 1992, and 1996, Rahe 1992, Euben et al. 1994, Ober and Hedrick 1996, Arnason and Murphy 2001, Raaflaub 2004 and 2015, Ober 2008, and Meier 2012.) But ancient Greek democracy fell far short of twenty-first-century standards of liberal constitutional democracy. Athens was not a theocracy, but Athenian society did not separate religious life from political life. Moreover, most Athenians saw no contradiction at all between democracy at home and tyrannical imperialism abroad. At the height of their prosperity, the Athenians established and maintained a large empire and compelled other city-states to be subject to Athenian rule. For the relationship between Athenian democratic ideology and imperialism, see Knox 1957, E. Hall 1989, Raaflaub 1994 and 1997, esp. 58–61, Rosenbloom 1995, and Osborne 2010, 306–322. For a discussion of Thucydides' view of Athenian imperialism as distinct from the speeches and actions he attributes to Pericles, see Foster 2010.

Warning against uncritical enthusiasm for Athenian democracy, Osborne cautions: "Athenian democracy went part and parcel with an Athenian way of life which we would judge illiberal, culturally chauvinist and narrowly restrictive. It was, essentially, the product of a closed society. It is not at all clear that democracy, in the Athenian form, is worth celebrating. Observing the narrowness and exploitative nature of Athenian democracy, we should be challenged to stop taking cover behind 'democracy' as a term at which only cheering is allowed, and instead ask seriously how we might attain the political openness (and cultural achievement) of Athens while taking pride in a society that is heterogeneous and determinedly open" (2010, 37).

12. See Nussbaum 1997, 9–11, 85–107 and 2010, esp. 95–120. Regarding the ability of myth to provide moral examples, see, e.g., Redfield 1994, 20–29, Livingstone 2011, and Raaflaub 2012, 474, 488, and n. 44.

13. For Homer's adaptation of earlier tales, see, e.g., Haller 2013. For imitation and allusions to earlier poetry in the tragedies of Aeschylus, Sophocles, and Euripides, see especially Garner 1990. Rinon identifies the "tragic pattern" in the *Iliad* that anticipates Attic tragedy (2008). On the flexibility of Greek myth and its limits, see, e.g., Graf 1993, Woodard 2007, Alaux 2011, and Torrance 2013.

14. Recent books for general readers ignore the myths' evolving critique of rage and violence (e.g., Martin 2003, Woodruff 2011, and Freeman 2012). *D'Aulaires' Book of Greek Myths,* an enchanting, beautifully illustrated children's book of Judeo-Christianized and bowdlerized classical myths, remains popular, as do the ahistorical accounts of Hamilton 1942 and Graves 1955. For the reception of Greece and Rome in children's literature, see Maurice 2015. Popular ahistorical film versions include *Helen of Troy* (Warner Brothers 1956), *Hercules* (Disney 1997), a television mini-series *Odyssey* (Warner Brothers 1997), *Helen of Troy* (Universal Studios 2003), *Troy* (Warner Brothers 2004), and *Hercules* (Paramount 2014).

15. The origins and processes of Homeric epic poetry have long been studied and debated. Seminal works on the topic include Lord 1960, 1991, 1995, Kirk 1976, and Nagy 1979 and 1996. For excellent recent discussions, see, e.g., Cairns 2001b, 1–56, Fowler 2004a, Beck 2005, 273–275, Nagy 2007, 52–82, Dué and Ebbott 2010, 4–29, and Ready 2015. Nagy emphasizes the importance of conceiving of "Homer" as the name for the Greek epic tradition rather than an individual (1996, 20–22). Oral composition and transmission of archaic stories enabled details and emphases to change over time. But cf. West's challenge to "oral theory" and his resurrection of the "analysts' approach" (2011). On this, see also Austin 2011.

Lord identifies the singer of epic poetry as no "mere carrier of the tradition but a creative artist making the tradition" (1995, 13), but the claim is controversial. See, e.g., Page 1959, 222–225 vs. Austin 1975, 70. Nagy challenges "the very idea that Homeric myth is a matter of personal invention" (1996, 114), arguing instead that "from an anthropological point of view, 'myth' is indeed 'special speech' in that it is a given society's way of affirming its own reality" (130). Halliwell proposes an " 'interactionist' model . . . with divine endowment and human motivation imagined as operating in tandem" (2011, 56).

16. Many scholars argue that the epics had a broad (not merely narrowly aristocratic) audience: e.g., Kirk 1962, 275, Scully 1990, and Donlan 1993. For the relationship between poet and audience, see Scodel 2002.

17. See especially M. W. Blundell 1989, 26–31. For "cooperative" vs. "competitive" values in Homer, see Adkins 1960 vs. Long 1970.

18. Schein considers the *Iliad* "an ironic meditation" on "traditional themes" (1984, 1). More emphatically, Rabel (1997, 21–31) identifies an "ironic distance" between the characters' views and that of the narrator, maintaining that "the narrator constructs ... a radical critique of life lived in accordance with traditional views of heroism" (1997, 29). Distinguishing the "poet" from the "narrator," Rabel seeks to separate "the message conveyed by the narrator" from "what the poet wishes to communicate" (30). But cf. de Jong's argument that the pursuit of *kleos*, "glory," motivates the poet as much as it motivates the characters within the epics (2006). We cannot determine the intentions of either the poet or the narrator. But we can discern contrasts between the limited understanding of the characters and the broader understanding accessible to the audience. Ahrensdorf, e.g., explains that Homer affirms the mortal characters' confidence in divine justice and then "proceeds to challenge this conventional piety" (2014, 33–37). But cf. Redfield, who argues that the "greatness" of Homer's mortal "heroes" lies in their "consciousness," their "capacity to act and at the same time comprehend themselves and their situation" (1994, 101–102).

Whether Homeric epic affirmed or challenged traditional aristocratic values remains controversial. See, e.g., Tandy 1997 and Thalmann 1998 vs. Hammer 2002, 144–169 (with extensive bibliography). Hammer emphasizes the nature of epic "as public poetry that was engaged in reflection on the activity of organizing community life" (Hammer 2002, 11 and, similarly, 48). Haller provides ample evidence that Homeric epic is already reinterpreting older tales (citing Peradotto 1990, Reece 1993, Felson-Rubin 1994, 10, Marks 2003, and S. Richardson 2006), but Haller maintains that the poet deliberately selects among variant versions in order to promote an aristocratic ideology (2013, 164). In contrast, Raaflaub argues that although archaic poetry was by and for aristocrats, it both promoted and challenged aristocratic values (1993, 75). Regardless of whether or not the *Iliad* and the *Odyssey* are, in fact, a product of aristocratic intentions, the gap between the characters' understanding and the audience's perspective begins to undermine many aristocratic principles.

19. Some scholars even find a direct connection between warfare and democratic government and society (e.g., Hanson 2001 and Raaflaub 2001a). Maintaining that Athenian culture "conditioned the Athenian citizen from youth on to accept war as inevitable and even desirable" (2001a, 339), Raaflaub

concludes that "the function of the theater was precisely one of balancing the picture without changing it" (341).

20. In adapting ancient myths and in conflating past and present, Athenian tragedy derived from and influenced Athenian cultural attitudes. Knox identifies "tragic myth" as "a people's vision of its own past, with all that such a vision implies for social and moral problems and attitudes in its present" (1979, 23, and, similarly, Euben 1990, 50–52). Meier explains that the tragedies make the ancient stories "present and familiar" and at the same time "problematic," as they were "filtered through the experience and needs of a new age, pervaded by the demands for reason and justice, the tensions and responsibilities of the citizenry" (1993, 125). Goldhill identifies the *paideusis*, "educational function," of tragedy "in the retelling of the myths of the past for the democratic *polis*" (2000, 48). (But cf. Rhodes, who argues for a close connection between drama and the *polis* rather than between drama and democracy [2003].) Sommerstein maintains that by the fifth century, myth was already "a powerful instrument of education and socialization" (2010, 117).

But opinions vary as to the precise nature of tragedy's didactic function. See, e.g., Herington 1985, 67–71 and 1986, 110, Podlecki 1986, 82–86, Euben 1990, 50–58, Meier 1993, 51–61, Thomas 1995, Zeitlin 1996, 72–79, Kurke 1998, Sourvinou-Inwood 2003, Boedeker and Raaflaub 2005, Carter 2007, Barker 2009, 268–270, Goldhill and Hall 2009, Mastronarde 2010, 20–28, Osborne 2010, 368–418, Gregory 2012, 515, 529–530, and Raaflaub 2012.

Concerning the controversial question of whether tragedy "endorses," "constructs," or "questions" "Athenian civic ideology," see especially Saïd 1998, 281–284. For views of the competition between democratic and aristocratic ideology in tragedy, see also Goldhill 1990, 2000, and 2009, Euben 1990, 18, 35–36, and passim, Boegehold and Scafuro 1994, Griffith 1995, esp. 63, n. 3 and 109, n. 143, Cairns 2005, Carter 2007, 36–63, Barker 2009, esp. 268–275, and Mastronarde 2010, 15–21.

Griffith, for example, views Greek tragedy as reinforcing aristocratic privilege in Athens (1995), but others argue that the genre in general questions democratic values and encourages critical reflection (e.g., Goldhill 1986 following Vernant and Vidal-Naquet 1988, Meier 1993, 42–48, Goldhill 2000 and 2009, Grethlein 2010, 74–104, and Burian 2011. But cf. Vickers 1973, 157 and Rabinowitz 2013, 122).

Goldhill finds tragedy's questioning in tension with fifth-century Athenian democratic ideology (e.g., 1990, 124–129 and 2000, 35, 46), but other scholars see questioning democratic values as central to democratic ideology (e.g., Ober 1996, 142–143 and Pelling 1997, 225–235). Euben observes that "tragedy is distinctive in its interrogation of the achievement to which it contributes (1990, 35), and Ober identifies "the symbiosis of democracy and criticism" (1996, 142–143). Barker notes the centrality of debate to ancient Greek literature while cautioning against recent scholars' arguments that "equate debate with democratic procedures" (2009, 1–19 and n. 36). Barker argues that tragedy cultivates the audience's capacity for democratic politics by involving the audience in the process of "managing dissent" (e.g., 278, 372, 368). Grethlein observes that tragedy is "a genre better suited to raising questions and opening up tensions than providing clear cut answers" (2010, 83). For the composition and diversity of fifth-century audiences and the variety of responses, see Roselli (2011).

Nussbaum highlights the role of fifth-century Athenian tragedy in promoting "the narrative imagination" and the capacity for compassion (1997, 85–99). Gregory discusses Homer and Sophocles and the development of empathy (2012, 532–535).

21. See Carter 2007, 1–8, 19, 143–160, and passim. Noting the distance between the characters' understanding and that of the audience, Euben explains that tragedy "helped educate to the task of judgment" (1990, 51–59, 94).

1
Passions and Priorities

1. Walsh identifies anger as "central to the epic's analysis of the forces that lead human beings to destroy each other" (2005, 11). See also Redfield's discussion of the opening lines of the *Iliad* (1979). Muellner examines the role of *mēnis*, "rage," in establishing and maintaining status among "a hierarchy of peers" (1996, 5–18, 25–31, 129). Regarding various Homeric terms for anger, see Harris 2001, 50–70, Cairns 2003, 11–49, and Walsh 2005, 21–29.

2. For the structure of society in Homeric epic, see, e.g., M. I. Finley 1954. For "competitive values" in Homeric society and the strain that they place on the community, see Adkins 1960, 37–52. For the importance of honor to Homer's characters, see especially Nagy 1979, van Wees 1992, Fisher 1992, and D. Wilson 2002. Redfield discusses "Homeric social psychology" and the dangers of projecting modern values onto Homer's characters (1994, 1–29). Regarding Homeric morality, see also Segal 1971a, 8–17, Williams 1993, Yamagata 1994, Zanker 1994, Gill 1996, and Gottschall 2008. Gottschall reverses the standard view of women and possessions as instrumental, arguing instead that for Homer's characters "honor, political power, and social dominance are proximate routes to the ultimate goal of women" (10).

3. Regarding the complex question of the relationship of Greek myth to history, see, e.g., M. I. Finley 1965, Veyne 1988, Calamé 1996, Gotteland 2001,

89–102, and Hertel 2011. Schein identifies "fate" as the "poetic tradition" (1984, 63–64), while Redfield explains that for Homer's original audiences "Fate is history" (1994, 133).

4. See especially Schein 1984, 1–18, Nagy 1990, 17–18, 1992, and 1996, Meier 1993, 14, Seaford 1994, 144–154, Barker 2009, 10, Dué and Ebbott 2010, 4–29, Halliwell 2011, 58–62, and Elmer 2013. Nagy argues for an "evolutionary model of Homeric poetry culminating in a static phase that lasts about two centuries, framed by a relatively formative stage in the latter part of the eighth century and an increasingly definitive stage in the middle of the sixth" (1992, 52).

For the relationship between Greek mythology and ancient Greek religious faith and ritual, see, e.g., Veyne 1988, Versnel 1990 and 2011, 539–559, Seaford 1994, and Mastronarde 2010, 15–18. On Greek religion and the absence of a sacred text, see Parker 2011.

Oral transmission over centuries made the *Iliad* remarkably independent of the kinds of constraints often typical of ancient literature from other societies, that is, literature produced at the demand of a powerful ruler or supernatural being. Although Havelock, e.g., considers epic "didactic" and not "reflective" (1963, 66 and 1978, 6, 13), many others disagree (e.g., Russo 1968, Nagler 1974, Austin 1975, Finnegan 1977, Edwards 1987, Martin 1989, and Raaflaub 1989, to cite only a few).

The paucity of historical information for the society Homer depicts prompts scholars to refer to the period as the Dark Ages (Donlan 1985). Redfield emphasizes the "epic distance" between the world of the characters and that of the audience (1994, 30–36). But Raaflaub argues that the society depicted in the epics remained within "the collective memory" of Homer's original audiences, and, consequently, "the old and the new overlapped and coexisted" (1993, 44–45). Tandy argues that the Homeric epics systematically affirmed and maintained "a self-conscious aristocratic class" (1997, 152–188 and, similarly, Thalmann 1998 and Haller 2013). Some scholars emphasize the powerlessness of the people in the assemblies that Homer depicts (e.g., M. I. Finley 1954, 80 and Andreyev 1991). But other scholars see in the epics a much more complex interaction between leaders and people (e.g., Ober 1996 and 1998, Raaflaub 1997 and 1998, and Hammer 2002).

5. The *Iliad* does contain one story of the Muses wounding a man and taking away his musical ability because he challenges them (2.594–600, Gantz 1993, 55). Elsewhere in the *Iliad* the narrator invokes the Muses only for help recalling vast catalogues of troops, ships, or fallen warriors (2.484–493, 2.761–762, 11.218–220, 14.508–510, 16.112–113).

Singing and dancing are the province of the Muses, in both the divine and the human realm. For the poet's relationship to the Muse, see, e.g., Nagy 1979, 16–17 and Redfield 1994, 39–45. Rabel distinguishes the "poet" from the "narrator" of the epic and identifies the "narrator" with the Muses, arguing that in addressing the Muses, the poet seeks not "inspiration" but "information" (1997, 23). Pucci maintains that the Muse confers on the narrator the power of knowledge of the truth (2002, 19–20), but de Jong argues that the poet also pursues *kleos,* "glory," 2006. See also Halliwell's discussion of Homeric *kleos* and the epic's complex portrait of the relationship between poet and divinity (2011, 25–26, 55–77).

6. E.g., Redfield describes the *Iliad* as "a story of free actors and their free choices" (1994, 133). For the nature of divinity in contrast to mortality and the role of the gods in Homer, see, e.g., Schein 1984, 45–66, Vernant 1991, Redfield 1994, 75–78, 131–147, Pucci 2002, Kearns 2004, and Versnel 2011, 163–179.

7. For connections between Apollo's *mēnis,* "rage," and that of Achilles and Agamemnon, see Muellner 1996, 96–116.

8. Most 2003, 63–64. For the challenge that this assembly poses to the community, see especially Barker 2009, 35–42.

9. But cf. Gottschall's argument that women are not status markers but primary objects of contention (2008). Regarding Agamemnon's status and the fear he inspires, see especially Taplin 1990. See also Walsh's discussion of Calchas (2005, 21–23) and Kozak's discussion of the oath that Achilles swears to protect Calchas (2014b, 213–221).

10. Seaford defines the quarrel as a "crisis of reciprocity," resolved, ultimately, "in an act of revenge followed by the closure imparted to the narrative by properly performed ritual" (1994, 65–66). See also the discussions of Agamemnon's decision to take Achilles' prize in Schein (1984) and Muellner (1996). For an analysis of the confrontation and the escalating anger of Agamemnon and Achilles, see Beck 2005, 206–220.

11. The *Iliad* does not mention the tale of the Judgment of Paris until nearly the end of the epic (24.25–30) and then only briefly (Pucci 2002, 25–26). The reference, late and brief as it is, shows that the *Iliad* is already retelling and revising traditional stories, giving them new emphases and addressing new themes.

12. See especially Lesky, 2001, Dodds 1951, 1–18, Adkins 1960, 2–3, 22–23, Willcock 1970, 1–10, and Edwards 1987, 135. Redfield suggests that the concept of "Zeus's will" encapsulates the understanding of the poet and the characters that "since it happened, Zeus must have willed it" (1994, 105).

13. Regarding Athena's sudden arrival and its implications for human responsibility, see, e.g., Dodds 1951, 14–15, Snell 1953, Edwards 1987, 180–181,

Williams 1993, 21–31, and Ahrensdorf 2014, 38–39. Schein finds Athena's presence as evidence of Achilles' second thoughts "psychologically plausible" (1984, 57–58), and Cook notes the correspondence between Athena's advice and Achilles' own calculation (2003, 191–192).

The relationship between divine action and human agency in the *Iliad* remains a source of scholarly controversy, however. Viewing divine action and human moral responsibility as not mutually exclusive, Schein interprets the gods as "an *ex post facto* explanation, not a cause or agent" of events (1984, 57–61). Hammer, by contrast, argues for a culturally determined relationship between chance and human agency, concluding that the characters' understanding of agency derives from their own cultural assumptions and "appears to reflect a cultural concern with the destabilization of hierarchical gradations of rank" (1998, 140). On this issue, see also Willcock 1970, 6–7, Havelock 1978, 42, 50, Nussbaum 1986, 3–4, Austin 1987, 63–70, Gaskin 1990, 6, Morrison 1997, and Pucci 2002. I suggest only that Homer's narrative affords the audience a broader, more objective understanding of chance vs. choice than the characters have.

14. See especially Hammer 2002, 16–18, 80–92 concerning the political "crisis" that the quarrel provokes (81).

15. For the significance of Homer's phrase "best of the Achaeans," see Nagy 1979, 26–41 and 183–184. On Agamemnon's scepter, see also Griffin 1995, 79 and 87.

16. Such challenges to autocracy in the Homeric epics, tales told throughout Greece in the archaic and classical periods, may help to explain the emergence of oligarchic and democratic ideas not just in Athens but in other Greek *poleis,* "citizen-communities," as well. Kurke hints at this possibility in comparing *epinician* to tragic poetry. Although not discussing Homeric epic poetry, Kurke suggests that "publicly performed poetry that negotiates civic tensions" may be a feature of *poleis,* "citizen-communities," in general and not exclusive to democratic Athens (1998, 163). As "publicly performed poetry," Homeric epic could well have served this function long before the fifth century.

Many scholars identify the Homeric *basileus,* "king," as a sort of warlord or tribal leader possessing authority derived from both heredity and personal achievement (e.g., M. I. Finley 1954, Donlan 1979 and 1993, Raaflaub 1989 and 1993, and van Wees 1992).

17. Benardete 2005, 32–34.

18. But contrast Raaflaub's more positive assessment of Agamemnon's leadership in that he later demonstrates his ability to listen to good advice and correct his mistake (2012, 474).

19. Bradshaw notes that Achilles displays "self-interest," "obsession with individual honor," and an "exaltation of personal worth which entails the destruction of one's comrades" (1991, 112). Redfield identifies Achilles' rage as "tragic error" (1994, 91–98).

20. E.g., Whitman 1958, 161–164, Griffin 1980b, 70–71, and Stanley 1993, 295. But cf. Bowra, who criticizes Achilles for his insubordination (1930, 15–19).

21. I am indebted to an anonymous reader for Yale University Press for this point.

22. See, e.g., Pucci 2002, 18 and Ahrensdorf 2014, 65–66. At first the marital tension between Zeus and Hera seems almost comical, as Zeus claims irritably that Hera is always criticizing him for helping the Trojans in battle (1.518–523). Now at the request of Achilles' divine mother Thetis, a sea nymph, Zeus has agreed to help the Trojans press the Greeks back against their ships while Achilles withdraws from the fighting (1.505ff.). The death of many Greek warriors will make the Greeks realize how much they need Achilles' supreme fighting abilities (1.509–510). Hera, hating the Trojans, resents Zeus's decision to let them prevail over the Greeks for a time (1.555ff.). But Hera's objection has no effect.

23. Schein 1984, 55–56.

24. The gods in Homer regularly provide negative moral examples against which to measure human actions. See especially Griffin 1980b, 162, Schein 1984, 51–57, 61, Pucci 2002, Kearns 2004, 71, Ahrensdorf 2014, 25–72. But cf. Barker, who sees in the *Iliad*'s depiction of divine assemblies a "movement towards the establishment of a divine assembly with ordered dissent under Zeus' ultimate authority" (2009, 75–79).

25. For the question of whether or not Homer's characters display self-awareness and act as autonomous, subjective agents making their own moral choices, see, e.g., Dodds 1951, Snell 1953, Redfield 1994, Cairns 1993, Williams 1993, and Hammer 2002. Frede notes the absence in Homer and long after of "any trace of a reference to, let alone a mention of, a free will" (2011, 2). Homer's characters may or may not see themselves as free agents, but Homer's narrative cultivates the audience's ability to make critical moral judgments.

26. Gantz 1993, 55–56.

27. See, e.g., Walsh's discussion of ethnographic studies of violent aggression (2005, 97–105).

28. Redfield 1994, 99–101.

2

Them and Us

1. Zanker 1994, 31–35. See also Muellner regarding the *mēnis* of Zeus *Xenios* (1996, 37–51) and Ahrensdorf regarding the characters' view of Zeus as the

guarantor of oaths (2014, 33–34). For the importance of guest-friendship, see also Kane 1996, 19 and n. 9 and Walsh 2005, 24–25. On oaths in ancient Greece, see especially Sommerstein and Torrance 2014.

2. Although this oath appears to be part of the tradition, Homer never specifically mentions it. The oath does not affect Achilles since he was too young at the time that it was sworn (Torrance 2014, 49–52, Kozak 2014a, 61–62).

3. Schein 1984, 20–22. Leaf notes that the duel between Paris and Menelaus evokes the origin of the conflict (1886, 87). See also Kozak 2014a, 65.

4. This story receives a lot of scholarly attention (See Alden 1996, 257 and n. 2 and 2000, 112–178). Avery rejects Kirk's suggestion that the tale has been inserted (Kirk 1962, 164–166) and argues that the encounter is not separable from the *Iliad*'s main story but organic to it (1994, 502). Gaisser explains that the poet is adapting a traditional story (1969).

For the interpretive problems posed by the encounter between Diomedes and Glaucus and its apparently "comic" conclusion, see Traill 1989. Traill reads the unequal gift exchange as Homer's way of emphasizing that Diomedes, while behaving properly toward a guest-friend, is in fact the better warrior (304–305). Donlan interprets the gift exchange as Glaucus's open admission of inferiority to Diomedes' military and intellectual superiority (1989 and, similarly, Martin 1989, 127). Harries argues that the gift exchange enables Diomedes to triumph intellectually and to transmit to Glaucus "the notion of the past as a precedent for the present" (1993, 142–144). Alden, however, suggests that Glaucus attempts unsuccessfully to transmit to Diomedes an understanding of the variability of human fortunes and the unreliability of the gods' support (1996, 260–262). Scodel similarly reads the unequal exchange and Zeus's intervention as confirmation of the unpredictability of human life and the unreliability of fortune, providing "a mild and almost funny proof of an important and usually tragic truth" (1992, 84). Arguably, however, in avoiding the fight with Diomedes (Walcot 1969), by receiving the armor of stronger metal and walking away with his life, Glaucus actually does get the better deal, or might be excused for supposing that he had.

5. But see Avery 1994 concerning Diomedes' wondering whether Glaucus is a mortal or a god. Avery notes that "golden armor was more appropriate for gods than for mortals" (1994, 500).

6. Edwards reads this simile as foreshadowing the farewell scene between Hector and Andromache (1987, 204).

7. But cf. Pelliccia (2002, 199) and Ahrensdorf (2014, 59, 185–186), who find instead similarity between the terms of the analogy. Gaisser also considers the analogy "appropriate to the genealogy that follows since a genealogy is in its very nature a reminder of the cyclic quality of human life, and of the relative

insignificance of any one individual" (1969, 168). Gaisser argues that Homer's version of Bellerophon's tale illustrates the simile's depiction of "the transitory nature of mankind" (1969, 174). Griffith also reads the simile as emphasizing "the contrast between human transience and divine permanence" and argues that "the effect is to remind us of the unimportance of a man among the numberless generations" (1975, 76). Scodel agrees that the simile underscores Diomedes' emphasis on the distinction between gods and human beings (1992, 77). These interpretations all ignore the chronological reversal in the analogy since the simile states that leaves decay and then regrow while men flourish and then die, i.e., *leaves die and then flourish, but men flourish and then die.* This chronological reversal suggests that not only are men not like gods, they are not like leaves either. Unlike leaves, men are distinguishable one from another. New ones cannot simply replace dead ones. (When the god Apollo later reiterates the analogy at 21.464–466, he asserts that men are like leaves in that they flourish and then die; he says nothing even about leaves growing again.)

For allusions to this simile in Mimnermus, Simonides, and later classical writers, see Sider 2001. Sider finds implicit already in Homer a contrast between the finitude of human life and the potential durability of human poetry and human glory.

8. Plutarch *Moralia* 241.

9. But cf. Schein's view of Helen as unlike other mortals in that she is essentially "immune" from "the consequences of the war" since she will remain with Paris or return to Menelaus (1984, 23–24).

10. Taplin maintains that "ethnographically," Greeks and Trojans are "virtually indistinguishable" (1992, 112). But cf. Barker's contention that unlike Greek assemblies, Trojan assemblies do not include debate and dissent (2009, 67–74).

11. Katz 1981. Explaining that the Scaean Gates mark the separation between the city and the battlefield, Katz argues that in the meeting of Andromache and Hector, the opposition between the feminine and masculine worlds figures the opposition between the city and the battlefield. Katz maintains that *Iliad* 6 both emphasizes the opposition between the two spheres and explores the interaction between them, ultimately affirming the continuity of the two realms.

12. Seaford argues that the tensions between *polis* and household in Homer are less antagonistic than they are in tragedy, explaining that "this distinction between Homer and tragedy derives from the progressive limitation of the autonomy of the household by the *polis*" (1994, 338–344).

13. For women in Greek myth, see especially Lefkowitz 1986. Regarding women in Homeric epic, see also H. P. Foley 1978, 1981b, and 2005, Felson-Rubin 1987, Easterling 1991, and Felson and Slatkin 2004. For Homer's portrait of Helen, see especially Roisman 2006 and Blondell 2010.

14. Regarding Hector as the protector of Troy and its inhabitants, see Nagy 1979, 146–147. For Hector's resistance to supplication, see Alden 2000, 274–281. Beck argues that the failure of communication between Hector and Andromache underscores the *Iliad*'s emphasis on conflict (2005, 128–129).

15. Good discussions of Hector's role and motives include Redfield 1994, 109–127, Zanker 1994, 53–56, Benardete 2005, 121–124, and Ahrensdorf 2014, 85–133. For the concept of shame in Homeric culture, see especially Dodds 1951, Adkins 1960, Rowe 1983, Cairns 1993, Williams 1993 (and cf. Hooker 1987). Zanker argues that concerns about shame and honor motivate warriors' loyalty (1994, 25–28).

16. Discussing the *Iliad*'s symbolic inclusion of the fall of Troy and its depiction of the city as "a rich human culture and civilization," Schein notes the paradoxical relationship between individual glory (as Homer's characters define it) and the destruction of such a civilization (1984, 168–178 and 190).

17. But cf. Mackie, who focuses particularly on Hector in contrast to Achilles and maintains that "Greeks and Trojans speak differently" (1996, 1) as "Achaeans are proficient at blame, while Trojans perform praise poetry" (83).

3
Cultivating Rational Thought

1. Cf. Odysseus's version of the parting advice of Achilles' father (9.252–259) and Phoenix's version (9.438–443).

2. Regarding the characters' concern for status, see, e.g., M. I. Finley 1954, 75. But cf. Hammer 2002, 59–62.

3. Cairns's assessment of traditional archaic Greek attitudes toward human error may explain Agamemnon's failure to accept personal responsibility (2013a, xxxviii and nn. 124 and 127; but cf. Redfield 1994, 96–98 and Raaflaub 2012, 474). Hammer notes that Agamemnon paradoxically weakens his own authority by asserting it (2002, 86).

4. Whitman 1958, 192, Taplin 1992, 71–72. But cf. Scodel 2003.

5. Donlan 1993 and Redfield 1994, 15–16. Some scholars suggest, however, that Achilles has begun to question the capacity of material objects to confer honor and to compensate for fighting and dying. E.g., Martin 1989, 167–170 and Griffin 1995, 108–110.

6. Redfield 1994, 103–109. Redfield identifies Achilles as "the victim of his own ethic" (106). Important discussions of *Iliad* 9 include Kakridis 1949, Parry 1956, Whitman 1958, Sale 1963, Adkins 1971, Reeve 1972 and 1973, Rosner 1976, Nagy 1979, 49–58, Scodel 1982, Martin 1989, Taplin 1992, Donlan 1993, Redfield 1994, Seaford 1994, Muellner 1996, 138–155 and nn. 17 and 18, D. Wilson 1999

and 2002, 71–108, Walsh 2005, 187–201, and Sammons 2008. For the crucial element of timing in acts of reciprocity, see Widzisz 2012. See also the commentaries on *Iliad* 9 of Griffin 1995 and C. Wilson 1996.

7. See especially Whitman 1958, 192, Donlan 1993, 165, and Griffin 1995, 110–112.

8. But cf. Schein, for example, who argues that Achilles experiences "disillusionment" and "comes to question and contradict the validity of the normative social value system" (1984, 71).

9. See especially Alden 2000.

10. See, for example, the discussion of the tale of Meleagros in Willcock 1964, 147–153, Schein 1984, 112–113, Griffin 1995, 134–141, Muellner 1996, 146–155, Alden 2000, 179–290, Gwara 2007, Nagy 2007, 63–69, and Ready 2011, 67–69.

11. See Gwara 2007, 304.

12. For the complexity of the relationship between a simile and its narrative context, see especially Snell 1953, 199–200, Coffey 1957, 117, Moulton 1974 and 1977, Griffin 1980b, 1–24, Scott 1974, 2006, and 2009, Austin 1975, 115, 118, 129, Muellner 1990, 66, 98–99, Buxton 2004, Benardete 2005, 54–63, J. Heath 2005, 45–46, Nagy 2007, 61–63, and Ready 2011, 11–26 and passim (including extensive bibliography). Silk, following I. A. Richards's distinction, defines the "tenor" as the underlying idea in a poetic image and the "vehicle" as "the other idea, the one brought in from outside, the one to which the tenor is, in logical terms, compared" (1974, 6). Scott explains the audience's active role in the process (2009, 6–10).

13. For contrasts between narrative statements and the statements of the characters, see especially de Jong 1987, Rabel 1997, Bakker 2009, and Ready 2011, 150–210.

14. Austin 1975, 116–118.

15. See, e.g., agriculture (*Il.* 12.421–426) and wall building (*Il.* 16.212–214) as analogies for warfare.

16. Redfield 1994, 186–189. See also Bowra 1930, Coffey 1957, Porter 1972, and Schein 1984, 74–75.

17. Cf. *Il.* 17.657–664. See Ready 2011, 123 and 63, n. 127. For the significance of lions in Homeric similes, see Alden 2005.

18. See Benardete 2005, 55 and Ready 2011, 115, 189–190.

19. On the role reversal, see especially Morrison 1994.

20. For a discussion of this and other such contrasts between tenor and vehicle, see especially Porter 1972. Discussing *Il.* 20.495–503, a simile likening Achilles' destructiveness to the threshing of grain, Schein finds a similar contrast between the destructiveness of the tenor and the constructive activity in the vehicle (1984, 146).

21. Compare the beautiful inverted analogy between leaves and men (*Il.* 6.146–149) and its implicit evocation of the uniqueness of each individual human being (see chapter 2).

22. By contrast, Rood identifies a "parallel between craftsman and poet as men who shape natural material into something beautiful and cultural. The craftsman cuts down a tree and makes it into a cultural instrument: oar, spear, chariot wheel, or ship that helps men fight the wars in which, in turn, they are cut down and made by the poet into cultural heroes" (2008, 30). This argument fails to appreciate the often unsettling contrasts between poetic images and their narrative contexts. On the ambiguity of ships in the *Iliad*, see, e.g., Morrison 1994, 225–226.

23. Porter 1972, 18–21. Assessing similes that contrast with their narrative context, Porter observes that "one powerful effect of these similes is to increase our sense of the violence and destructiveness of the war, perhaps even at times to suggest its senselessness" (18).

24. Cf. Scott 2006 for a discussion of this simile in the context of book 11.

25. Regarding the negative comparison, see Ready 2011, 200–201 and n. 128. But cf. Lonsdale who argues that the animal similes align human beings with animals and emphasize the mortality of even the best warriors (1990, 125–127). Maintaining that animal similes "convey pathos" (11 and 59), Lonsdale finds that comparisons of men and lions "emphasize that both bestial and human appetites spur on the warrior" (65).

26. Ready identifies the insult implicit in comparing Trojans to sheep (2011, 121 and n. 42). J. Heath analyzes the portrait of the distinctively human capacity for speech in Homeric epic and the fifth century (2005).

27. I do not agree with Schein's suggestion that Achilles comes to reject "the normal value system in place" (1984, 104–110, citing Parry 1956). Arieti goes even further in finding Achilles distinct from other characters in his "alienation." Arieti defines this "alienation" as "an entirely new thing in the culture and literature of Europe, and it hints at standards and conceptions of glory different not in degree but in kind from any known up until this point" (1986, 27). I suggest, rather, that Achilles' example prompts the audience to reassess traditional ethical priorities.

28. See especially Schofield 1986. Schofield suggests that a warrior's words can be a form of achievement equivalent to military excellence. Martin maintains that Homer is unusual in this (1989, 146 and n. 1). See also Griffin 1995, 81.

29. See Griffin 1995, 128. Ready discusses Phoenix's relationship to Peleus and Achilles (2011, 145–149). Cf. also Odysseus's version of Peleus's parting advice (9.252–259) and Nestor's version (11.784).

30. For Homer's characters' understanding of the value of effectiveness in council, see M. I. Finley 1954 and Schofield 1986, 16–18. For the meaning of *themis,* "traditional, appropriate, right," and its relationship to *mēnis,* "rage," see Muellner 1996, 35–37. Martin analyzes the distinctiveness of Achilles' use of rhetoric (1989, 146–205).

31. For assessments of Agamemnon's strengths and weaknesses, see especially Whitman 1958, 161–164 and Taplin 1990. Taplin argues that "despite all his power, he is a nasty piece of work" (1990, 65), and Griffin observes that Diomedes' criticism of Agamemnon echoes Achilles' accusations in book 1 (1995, 79). Redfield maintains, however, that in speaking of his own *atē,* "ruinous folly," Agamemnon does accept responsibility for his mistake (1994, 96–98). But cf. Donlan 1993, 75–76 and Versnel 2011, 163–179. Raaflaub contrasts Agamemnon with Hector in arguing that Agamemnon's ability to heed good counsel and rectify his error shows that he ultimately "proves an exemplary leader who is praised for having reached a higher level of justice" (2012, 474). Kozak discusses the "oath-relationship" between Achilles and Agamemnon (2014a, 61–62).

32. See Ready 2011, 35, 140–145. Mills suggests that this and other similes illuminate Achilles' relationship with Patroclus (2000).

33. *Aretē* came to mean the supreme achievement, specific goodness, distinctive capacity, or excellence of a person or thing.

34. Redfield explains that Sarpedon and Glaucus fight "not on behalf of their community but on behalf of their own status within it" (1994, 100).

35. Redfield 1994, 99–101.

36. But cf. Schein 1984, 62–70. Schein describes Homer's gods as "frivolous" (62) and "trivial" (70), whereas Homer's mortal characters face life and death issues, and yet he also argues that human life is "limited and unimportant" in comparison (70). By contrast, Ahrensdorf maintains that in presenting the gods as "unpredictable, whimsical, and capricious beings," Homer glorifies "human excellence" (2014, 57–72).

37. Regarding *Il.* 9.189, Nagy discusses the self-referential aspects of Homeric oral epic poetry and identifies *kleos,* "glory" (and the plural *klea*), from the verb meaning "to hear," indicating "that which is heard" (esp. 2007, 55–58). On *kleos,* see also Redfield 1994, 30–36, Griffin 1995, 98–99, Nagy 1979, 16–18 and 2013, 26–31, 47–58, 102–105, Pucci 2002, Kahane 2005, 190, and Halliwell 2011, 37–39, 72–77. Hammer argues that Achilles' singing demonstrates his isolation and his lack of social support (2002, 97). But cf. Whitman 1958, 193.

38. Scully 1990, 44–45. See also Lynn-George 1988, 260 and Lonsdale 1990, 61–65.

39. Morrison explains that the role reversal, as besiegers become the besieged, enables a Greek audience to imagine the Trojans' experience (1994, 227).

40. E.g., Schein 1984, 68.

4
Violence, Vengeance, and a Glimpse of Victory

1. E.g., Gottschall, employing the lens of evolutionary biology and anthropology, identifies the source of the *Iliad*'s violence in the tendency of males to compete for women (2008). But Gottschall also observes that Homer's characters appear to be especially violent (120).

2. Segal concludes that the epic's repeated motif of the mutilation of the dead exposes "the destruction of civilized values, of civilization itself, by the savagery which war and its passions release" (1971, 33). But cf. Thalmann's observation that the *Iliad* could continue to be read by later generations "as encouraging militaristic values," as Aristophanes' *Frogs* 1019–1042 might seem to imply (1993, 135–136). On the pervasive militarism of fifth-century Athens, see especially Raaflaub 2001a.

3. For the pathos evoked by such scenes, see, e.g., Segal 1971a, 17, Griffin 1980b, 123, 140, 143 and Schein 1984, 72–77.

4. Ready identifies the antithesis between tenor and vehicle in this image (2011, 94–95). Later poets adopted this delicate, moving image to illustrate the anguish of unhappy love (e.g., Catullus 11.21–24).

5. For similar analogies, see Ready 2011, 188, n. 96. Rood identifies similes of warriors falling like trees as part of a larger pattern of "craft similes" establishing a cyclical relationship between "trees, craftsmen, and war instruments" and "men, poet, and heroes" (2008, 25–31).

6. Porter identifies the role of similes in evoking criticism of warfare (1972). Some scholars, however, find the epic less evenhanded. Neal 2006, e.g., finds in the similes evidence that the *Iliad* "privileges the vanquishers" (27) in exposing the "savagery, and ultimately, futility, of battle" (33). Benardete, too, noting the increasing incidence of similes for Trojans as the story progresses, maintains that the *Iliad* emphasizes contrasts rather than similarities between Greeks and Trojans (2005, 21–28). Benardete claims that the poet "wishes to teach us that only the civilized Greeks can both weep and be brave, while the barbarous Trojans, in order to be brave, had to stifle all their humanity" (28). But we cannot know what the poet (or poets) wished or intended. The tragic details of warriors' deaths invite the audience to acknowledge the personhood of both Greek and Trojan victims.

7. Segal observes that in this scene Achilles "experiences fully the final vacuity of death" (1971a, 51–52). Similarly, Schein notes that "in the world of the *Iliad*, there is no significant afterlife" (1984, 68–69). For the role of epic poetry in memorializing human achievements, see especially Redfield 1994, 30–35, Griffin 1980b, 95–102, and Morris 1989, 304–305.

8. Schein observes that the gods enjoy the dramatic spectacle and remain unmoved by human suffering (1984, 60–61). See also Pucci 2002, 20–25.

9. See, e.g., Redfield 1994, 131–136. Redfield explains that "men and cities are the counters in a game played between the gods" (132). Others note that the gods permit one another to destroy entire cities (e.g., Schein 1984, 61, and Ahrensdorf 2014, 52–57). But cf. the claim in the still-popular children's book that the Greek gods "could do no wrong" (D'Aulaire and D'Aulaire 1962, 9).

10. Schein argues that despite Achilles' divine mother and his close relationship to the gods, Homer emphasizes his mortality (1984, 91–96). Grieving and rolling in the dust, Achilles foreshadows his own death (Schein 1984, 130–134 and 144–158). Seaford interprets this foreshadowing in terms of ritual (1994, 166–172).

For Patroclus's role and his relationship to Achilles, see Most 2003, 66–71. Redfield maintains that Achilles "has an absolute obligation to revenge his friend, and this obligation takes from him all further necessity for choice" (1994, 18–19). Zanker views Achilles' motives as a combination of shame, honor, and guilt (1994, 17–19).

11. Beck identifies the reconciliation between Achilles and Agamemnon as inadequate (2005, 221–229). Versnel discusses Agamemnon's explanation for his own behavior (2011, 163–179).

12. Shay considers Achilles "berserk" in books 19–22 (1994, 77–99). Many scholars have found Achilles' behavior depraved and morally repugnant (e.g., Bowra 1930, 20–21). For Achilles' transformation after Patroclus's death, see Schein 1984, 128–160. J. Heath identifies the conversation with his horses as central to Achilles' departure from humanity (2005, 39). Regarding the shield and its significance, see especially Taplin 1980, Edwards 1987, 278–286, Redfield 1994, 187–189, Becker 1995, 87–149, and Nagy 1997. For associations between fighting and eating, see especially Nimis 1988, 23–95 and Neal 2006. Neal discusses Achilles' "bloodlust" and the self-destructiveness of his "insatiable appetite for the blood of men" (30–33). But cf. Ahrensdorf's interpretation of Achilles' role after Patroclus's death as a "return to the life of virtue" (2014, 179–186).

13. See Nagy 1979, 143–144.

14. Redfield 1994, 19. Muellner interprets this scene as evidence of Achilles' identification with Patroclus and awareness of his own mortality (1996,

162–163). See also Beck's discussion of Achilles' encounter with Lycaon and its evocation of Lycaon's perspective in contrast to Achilles' "strange detachment" (2005, 171–177). For the motif of supplication on the battlefield and its characterization of victorious fighters, see Kelly 2014.

15. On the meaning of *kudos*, see especially Kurke 1993. Kurke explains that *kudos* is not synonymous with *kleos* but instead "signifies special power bestowed by a god that makes a hero invincible" (132). See also Schein 1984, 52 and n. 19.

16. Some scholars have considered *Iliad* 10 a later addition to the epic, but as part of the text that we have, its moral challenge to violence remains consistent with the *Iliad* as a whole. See especially Dué and Ebbott 2010, 3–87. Dué and Ebbott reject critics' dismissal of the methods of Diomedes and Odysseus as "un-Homeric" and argue that the tale is part of the epic tradition (e.g., 33–34).

Reassessing the costs and benefits of military conquest hundreds of years later, Virgil reinterpreted Homer's tale of this night raid as a deeply troubling challenge to the celebration of slaughter by any means (*Aen.* 9).

17. Regarding Hector's fear and his sense of nightmare, see Redfield 1994, 158–159. For the confrontation between Achilles and Hector, see, e.g., Segal 1971a, 33–47 and Beck 2005, 184–190.

18. See Ready's discussion of the simile at *Iliad* 22.261–267 (2011, 61–69, 92). Many scholars identify Achilles' distance from and dismissal of the standards of his own society. See, for example, Parry 1956, Moulton 1977, 113, Schein 1984, 98–99, 150–153, Lonsdale 1990, 100, N. Richardson 1993 on 22.260–272, and Hammer 2002, 107, 113.

19. Swooning in her grief, Andromache throws her *kredemnon*, "headband," to the ground (22.467–468). In the plural, *kredemnon* also means the battlements of a citadel (Schein 1984, 176). Segal identifies the cumulative effects of the motif of mutilation (1971a) and discusses Andromache's reaction to Hector's death (1971b).

20. See, e.g., Scott 1997, Beck 2005, 239–244, and Ahrensdorf 2014, 186–189.

21. On Achilles' treatment of Hector's corpse, see especially Segal 1971a and Muellner 1996, 145. Some scholars have suggested that the final book of the *Iliad* is a later addition. But cf. Bowra 1930, 105–106, who considers *Iliad* 24 essential to the effect of the epic as a whole. Macleod identifies precise verbal correspondences between *Iliad* 1 and 24 (1982, 32–34). Redfield also finds connections between *Iliad* 1 and 24 (e.g., 1994, 219). For the controversy, see Barker 2009, 132 and n. 144.

22. Barker 2009, 131.

23. Just as Achilles wished he could eat Hector's flesh raw (22.347), Hecuba now wishes that she could eat Achilles' liver. That would be vengeance

(24.212–214). The desire to eat human flesh marks a departure from humanity, a loss of a crucial and distinguishing feature of human existence. Hecuba's wish affirms the dehumanizing power of vengeance.

See Hesiod's account of the first sacrifice at Mecone (*Theogony* 521–617). In this tale, Prometheus establishes the respective roles of gods, human beings, and animals. Human beings eat cooked animal flesh, and gods consume the smoke from the sacrificial fires. For the role of sacrifice in defining the human condition, see especially Nagy 1979, 216–217, Vernant 1986, 37–38, 47, and Muellner 1996, 84–87. But cf. Redfield's argument that "the line between man and dog is fixed only by culture. On the battlefield, where the rules of culture break down, the warrior may become a raw-meat eater," citing *Iliad* 24.207–208 (1994, 197). For the theme of cannibalism in the epic, see O'Brien 1993, 81–94, J. Heath 2005, 133–147, and Neal 2006.

24. See Redfield 1994, 215–218. But Redfield emphasizes the implicit equation in the "killing power" of Hector and Achilles (215). For the complex associations and implications of the simile at *Il.* 24.480–484, see Macleod 1982, 126–127, Schein 1984, 159–163, Heiden 1998, and Beck 2005, 135–145. Muellner, however, emphasizes Achilles' abiding *mēnis,* "rage," during the encounter (1996, 168–175). For the evocation of the parent-child relationship in Homeric similes, see Mills 2000.

25. See Macleod 1982, 131–135.

26. But cf. Widzisz on the crucial importance of timing in the gift exchange (2012, 161–164).

27. See Macleod 1982, 146–157. Beck identifies the associations between the laments for Hector and for Patroclus (2005, 246–270). Kozak explains that whereas Achilles' hatred previously precluded an oath, now his empathy permits one (2014a, 66). See also Kozak's discussion of Achilles' distinctive relationship to oaths (2014b, 213–221).

28. But cf. Segal's suggestion that Achilles comes to experience a perspective previously only accessible to gods (1971a, 57–71).

Citing this scene in discussing Euripides' *Hecuba,* Gregory identifies empathy as the source of pity, explaining that Priam succeeds by prompting Achilles to connect him to his own father and to all human beings (1991, 103). But cf. Seaford's analysis of the epic's resolution in terms of ritual (1994, 65–73, 159–166). Zanker calls Achilles' brief, provisional moment of perception "the poem's central gift" (1994, 73, 115–130), and D. Wilson argues that the scene depicts Achilles' "reintegration into the human community" (2002, 132–133). See, too, Most's discussion of the epic's movement from rage to pity (2003, 50–75). But cf. J. Heath 2005, 152–155. Ahrensdorf finds that Achilles demonstrates "a certain acceptance of death" that is "limited and fragile" (2014, 189–197).

5
The Dangers of Democratic Decision Making

1. Debnar discusses fifth-century Athenians' relationship to their mythical past (2005). On tragedy's adaptation of ancient, traditional myths, see, e.g., Burian 1997, Grethlein 2007, and Alaux 2011. Sansone identifies the effects on the audience of the tremendous contrast between the performance of oral epic poetry and the dramatic performance of tragedy (2012, 14–15, 80–81, and passim). E. Hall (2010) analyzes tragedy as an "enquiry into suffering" (6).

2. For the structure of dramatic and other competitive festivals in Athens, see Osborne 2010, 325–340. Seaford finds the origins of tragedy in Dionysiac initiation ritual (1994, 385), although, as Garner observes, there is a tension between the unchanging stability of ritual and the novel creations of tragedy (1990, 179). See also Burnett 1998, 65–74 and Scullion 2005.

3. Grethlein explains that in its use of myth, tragedy offers the audience a "safe distance" as well as "familiarity" (2010, 96–97). Although tragedy presents tales distant in space and time, nevertheless, Grethlein argues, "the heroic past is in the firm grip of the present" (2010, 101).

4. On jury trials in Athens, see Garner 1987, 67–75. On Solon's reforms and the principle of majority voting, see Raaflaub 2015, 17–23.

Homer depicts a prototype of a legal trial, as Achilles' immortal shield includes a peacetime murder case presided over by a *histor*, "arbitrator" (*Il.* 18.497–508; see, e.g., Muellner 1996, 153–154 and Nagy 1997, 206). The victim's refusal of material compensation echoes the emotions of Homer's Achilles and Odysseus when each rejects the possibility that any material compensation could satisfy his desire for revenge (*Il.* 9.374–392 and *Od.* 22.61–65. See Barker 2009, 125–126). The arbitration procedure demonstrates that a nonviolent solution will better serve the interests of the community as a whole. In the *Odyssey*, however, Odysseus appears to have no alternative to violent revenge, no recourse to law or a nonviolent communal procedure. Like the *Iliad*, the *Odyssey* equates vengeance with justice but exposes problems in the equation. Odysseus's successful return and his revenge on the suitors show that the gods ensure justice among men, but the conflict escalates because the suitors' families similarly seek revenge. Athena's ultimate intervention suggests that only some superhuman effort of wisdom and self-restraint can prevent vengeance from destroying an entire community.

5. A decade before Sophocles produced the *Ajax*, Aeschylus's *Oresteia* (458 BCE) enabled the audience to reassess vengeance as a political principle. Can it be adequate, since it destroys individuals, families, and communities? Orestes wants vengeance, and he has every right to be angry at the murderer of his father. The *Odyssey* suggests that in killing his father's killer, Orestes acts

admirably, but Aeschylus's reinterpretation shows the audience that Orestes just makes the problem worse.

6. It is a cruel irony today that in consequence of the so-called Arab spring, many women have lost or risk losing liberties they had attained under dictatorships.

7. Regarding the uncertainty of the date of the *Ajax* and the indeterminacy of its contemporary historical and political implications, see, e.g., Rose 1995. Although the view may be controversial, I accept Carter's conclusion that tragedy does not include "full-scale political allegory" (2007, 22 and n. 16). Garvie finds no obstacle to a date in the 440s (1998, 6–8). Raaflaub notes that many scholars opt for the 450s (2012, 474).

I have previously articulated some of the ideas in this chapter in a brief commentary accompanying my translation of *Ajax* 646–692 in Anhalt 2015. I include these here with permission from the editors of *Transference*.

8. In contrast, Aeschylus' *Oresteia* rejects Homer's equation of justice with vengeance but suggests that aristocratic values can *evolve* into democratic ones. See, e.g., Lattimore 1972, Herington 1986, 62–63, 143–156, and Euben 1990, 25–26. But cf. Zeitlin 1996, 87–119. On the function of tragedy and the moral tensions in the *Oresteia*, see especially Nussbaum 1986, 32–50 and Davis 2006.

9. The English words "aristocracy" and "democracy" derive from the Greek *aristokratia* and *demokratia*, which translate literally as "best-power" and "people-power," or "rule by the best" and "rule by the people."

10. Whitman 1958, 62–63. For versions of the tale of Ajax that predate Sophocles' play, see also Bowra 1944, 16–18, Garvie 1998, 1–5, and Hesk 2003, 17–39.

11. For Ajax's association with the shield in Homer, see Bradshaw 1991, 106. For a contrasting assessment of Homer's portrait of Ajax as bestial, "insatiate" of war, "ugly," and without "nobility," see Benardete 2005, 44–46. Garner identifies Sophocles' direct allusions to Homer (1990, 51–64).

12. For Sophocles' reinterpretation of Homer and his evocation of the audience's judgment, see especially Burnett 1998, 94–98 and Barker 2009, 281–324. Barker suggests that Sophocles' Ajax evokes Homer's Achilles (283). Whitman describes the mythical opposition, from Homer through the fifth century (and replicated in contemporary attitudes and politics), between the doer (the man of heroic standards) and the talker (the man of reason), but Whitman finds greater complexity in Sophocles' portrait of the conflict between Ajax and Odysseus (1958, 65–67). Larmore argues that unlike Homer's Ajax, Sophocles' Ajax fails to prioritize bonds of friendship or to recognize "that the relationship between hero and community should be reciprocal" (152).

Knox identifies the speech at the center of the play as Ajax's "moment of unclouded vision" regarding the difference between gods and men in their relationship to time (1961, 134). Bradshaw argues that both Homer and Sophocles present Ajax as a character displaying "*mētis* 'intelligence, cunning' as well as *biē* 'force, strength' " (1991, 105–106).

13. Knox 1961, 146 (and, similarly, Meier 1993, 179). For parallels between the *Ajax* and Athenian legal decisions, see Garner 1987, 109 and Rose 1995, 65–69.

14. For the evolving relationship between Greek law and Greek values, see Garner 1987. Garner details the connections between law and drama (1987, 95–130). For the structures of Athenian democracy, see especially Osborne 2010, 26–38.

15. But cf. Woodruff, who draws on post-Homeric mythical portraits to suggest that, in fact, Odysseus's capacity for innovation might define him as "best" (2011, 12–15). Sophocles' play does invite the audience to consider which high-achiever best serves the community, the strong, stalwart, dependable, unchanging fighter or the clever, flexible, persuasive speaker, but the characters within the play all concur that Ajax was "best" after Achilles.

16. Opinions vary as to the exact nature of Ajax's madness. Knox explains it as a "visual delusion" rather than a mental impairment (1961, 129 and n. 26, 131), and others concur (e.g., Burnett 1998, 81–82). But Lawrence, for example, refers to Ajax's "insanity" and "madness" (2005, 21). Simpson sees the madness inherent in Ajax's murderous objective itself (1969, 89–92), and Davis explains that since Ajax intended to slaughter the Greeks like animals, Athena simply exposes his inability to distinguish men from beasts (1986, 145). Bradshaw argues that Ajax's "tragedy is bound up with his loss of control over his intellectual powers" (1991, 117 and n. 40).

17. In a complicated pun, the verb means not only "to place" or "to set" but also to stack arms or to arm for battle and also to surrender, so Ajax also implies that he will never surrender, not to anyone, and not to a voting process that produces unjust results. Larmore maintains that Sophocles aims at deliberate ambiguity regarding the question of whether the voting process was corrupt (2014, 152), but this seems to miss the point that the process itself is problematic, whether it is corrupt or not.

18. E.g., Mastronarde suggests that Ajax "is strongly motivated by shame (2010, 305, and, similarly, Bradshaw 1991, 117–119, Zanker 1994, 66, Barker 2009, 306 and 316, and Davidson 2012, 253, 261). See also Lawrence (2005) regarding the relationship between honor and courage in Greek ethical thought. Pointing out that "in the heroic culture . . . results count for more than motives" (21), Lawrence identifies Ajax's suicide as, by ancient standards, a "spurious moral gesture" (32).

Garner finds associations between Sophocles' Ajax and Homer's Hector (1990, 51–64). Larmore argues that Sophocles explicitly contrasts Ajax's relationship to his community with the relationship of Homer's Hector to his, arguing that shame motivates both, but Hector prioritizes the community's interests, whereas Ajax prioritizes his own (2014, 146–149).

19. Interpretations of the moral tensions in the *Ajax* vary. Knox finds in Sophocles' portraits of Ajax and Odysseus an opposition between traditional aristocratic warrior values, epitomized by Homer's Achilles, and the flexibility and cooperation necessary in the new fifth-century democracy (1961). But cf. Bradshaw, who challenges the "traditional" interpretation of the *Ajax* as contrasting "old values" with "new values," Ajax's "rigid virtue" with Odysseus's "flexibility" (1991, 99–125). Similarly, M. Heath 1987, 204 and Cairns 1993, 240 find the conflict not between old and new values but within the traditional system itself. On this, see also Kitto 1956 [1939], 183–198, Knox 1964, 17–24, Winnington-Ingram 1980, 57–72, Segal 1981, 109–151, Zanker 1992 and 1994, 64–71, Michelakis 2002, 144–150, Hesk 2003, 124–148, and Barker 2009, 283–291 and 316–318. Barker explains that "Ajax acts according to current moral standards" (2009, 285–286 and n. 18, citing M. Heath 1987, 173 and Garvie 1998, 11–12). Whitman observes that "traditional Greek morality would interpret the fate of Ajax simply as *hybris* and punishment," but Whitman cautions against taking Athena's statement at 127ff. as the moral of the play, noting that the *Ajax* ultimately validates not Athena but Ajax (1958, 67–72).

For "competitive" vs. "cooperative" values in Greek culture, see, e.g., Adkins 1960 vs. Long 1970. For the concept of shame in Homeric culture, see also Dodds 1951, Rowe 1983, Cairns 1993, Williams 1993 (and cf. Hooker 1987), and Zanker 1994. For the essential tenet in traditional Greek morality of helping friends and harming enemies, see especially M. W. Blundell 1989, 26–31.

Many scholars discuss the moral tensions between the world Homer describes and the realities of Sophocles' contemporaries (e.g., Kirkwood 1965, Gould 1983, Easterling 1984, Winnington-Ingram 1980, 15–19, and Goldhill 1986, 138–167). Rose finds fifth-century Athenian class tensions visible in the *Ajax* (1995), while Burnett interprets the play in the context of the Athenian tragic festival (1998, 79–98). Raaflaub identifies the *Ajax*'s evocation of fifth-century Athenian domestic and international political relationships (2012, 476–479).

20. Knox 1961, 141–143. See also Davis 1986.

21. See Knox 1961, 127, 133–141 and Segal 1995, 25. Similarly, Winnington-Ingram argues that Ajax acknowledges but rejects "the principle of mutability in the world" (1980, 54). See also Lawrence 2005, 26 and n. 18. By contrast, Bradshaw, suggesting that Ajax experiences "confusion about absolutes" (1991, 119), argues that Ajax does change in that he betrays his own principle

of loyalty to friends (1991, 118–120, and, similarly, M. W. Blundell 1989, 86 and Meier 1993, 176–183). Simpson (1969, 96–99) identifies Ajax's suicide as his way of yielding without changing, as natural phenomena give place to one another "rather than alter their nature and coexist" (99). Seaford (1994, 392–402) contends that Ajax understands the workings of the universe but "implicitly rejects reciprocity" (396). Many scholars view this speech as deliberately deceptive (e.g., Whitman 1958, 75–77, Goldhill 1986, 189–192, Worman 2001, 239 and 2012, 343, and Finglass 2012, 68–69). Mastronarde maintains that Ajax, "whether he sets out deliberately to deceive or not, tailors the language of his penultimate speech (*Ajax* 646–692) to spare the feelings of Tecmessa and the chorus of his sailors" (2010, 305). Others find lying uncharacteristic of Ajax (e.g., Knox 1961 and Bradshaw 1991). Certainly Homer's Ajax finds deception reprehensible (e.g., *Il.* 9.312–313).

22. Knox observes that "there can be no doubt that Sophocles saw him as heroic" (1961, 126). For a modification of Knox's view, see Finglass 2012, 62–65. And cf. Burnett's argument that Sophocles exposes the peril that Ajax's vengeance poses to the community (1998, 82–85).

23. Hesiod explicitly distinguishes constructive from destructive rivalry. One produces violence and conflict, the other promotes hard work and healthy competition (*Works and Days* 11–29). Aeschylus's *Oresteia* suggests that competition can produce constructive progress, since competing claims of justice enable the community to evolve from equating justice with vengeance to defining justice as a communal voting procedure.

24. But cf. Meier's observation that Ajax prioritizes his ancient conception of honor over his obligations to his *philoi*, "friends" (1993, 176–177 and, similarly, Raaflaub 2012, 476–477).

Scholars remain divided over the apparent division in the play's structure. See, e.g., Taplin 1978, 148, Davidson 1985, and M. Heath 1987, 195–197, 204–208. Finglass 2012 maintains that the play's "diptych structure" serves a unifying role in emphasizing the ambivalence of Ajax's character.

25. *Sphallō* in the passive voice, as here, has the additional meaning "be tripped up, stumble, fall, be deceived," so Menelaus's choice of verb ironically undermines his assertion of the justice of the voting procedure.

26. The Greek *ha tois polloisin ēresken kritais* distinctly evokes fifth-century democratic decision making, as *hoi polloi*, "the many," was the technical term for the democratic majority.

27. For Sophocles' portraits of Agamemnon and Menelaus, see, e.g., Knox 1961, 126, 149–150, Meier 1993, 177–183, Barker 2009, 304–309, Finglass 2012, 61–62, and Raaflaub 2012, 477.

28. Alexiou 1974, 207, n. 21. See also H. P. Foley 2001, 91–92. For Tecmessa's relationship to Ajax, see Scodel 1998, 140–143.

29. H. P. Foley 2001, 276. For a good overview of women in myth, see Lewis 2011. For women in Athenian drama, see especially H. P. Foley 1981a and 2001, Zeitlin 1990 and 1996, 341–374, and S. Blundell 1995, 172–180.

30. Knox 1961, 131–132. Archaic culture knew and enjoyed cruel laughter at the suffering of another. In the *Iliad*, Greek warriors laugh as Odysseus beats a low-born man who dares to speak up in the assembly (*Il*. 2.265–277). The *Odyssey* does begin to criticize laughter at someone else's misfortune. The suitors laugh heartily as Odysseus beats the other beggar to a pulp (*Od*. 18.100), and this laughter comes to appear foolish and shortsighted.

31. See Knox 1961, 126–127, 132–133. Davis argues that by rejecting Athena's help, Ajax shows his inability to distinguish men from gods, just as he was unable to distinguish men from beasts (1986, 145–146). No other surviving sources mention these two offenses against Athena (Whitman 1958, 68). The *Odyssey* indicates that Athena especially loves Odysseus because he is so much like her (e.g., *Od*. 13.291–301). See also Barker 2009, 93–94. Concerning the question of whether Athena is actually visible in Sophocles' play, see Segal 1995, 19 (vs. Taplin 1978, 185, n. 12), M. Heath 1987, 165–166, Garvie 1998, 124, Hesk 2003, 43–44, and Barker 2009, 286–287.

32. For parallels and contrasts between Sophocles' portrait of Tecmessa's relationship with Ajax and Homer's portrait of Andromache's relationship with Hector, see Kirkwood 1965, Easterling 1984, Garner 1990, 51–52 and nn. 8–9, Seaford 1994, 400–401, Burian 1997, 193–196, H. P. Foley 2001, 90–92, Lawrence 2005, 23–24, Mossman 2005, 355–357 and 2012, 492–494, Davidson 2012, 252–253, and Larmore 2014, 158–160. Lawrence argues that in contrast to Andromache, Tecmessa "presents a reasoned moral case" (2005, 23). Larmore maintains that Homer's Hector has the imaginative capacity to empathize with others, whereas Sophocles' Ajax does not (2014, 160).

33. Seeing his brother impaled on Hector's sword, Teucrus laments to his corpse, "Did you not see that in time (or 'by time') Hector, even having died, was going to kill you?" (1026–1027). Teucrus also notes that Hector died by means of the belt Ajax gave him (1028–1035). For Ajax's changing relationships and the symbolism of the sword and the gift exchange, see especially Knox 1961, 138–141 and Kane 1996.

34. Knox 1961, 143–144.

35. Burnett identifies Ajax's curse as a further act of vengeance (1998, 86–93).

36. Meier argues that Tecmessa connects memory to gratitude and true nobility (1993, 177).

37. Worman notes the direct antithesis between Odysseus' "flexible attitude" and "Ajax's rigid assessment of heroic alliances" (2012, 343, and see also Worman 2001 and Knox 1961, 151). Regarding Odysseus's humanity and his recognition of human weakness, see especially Whitman 1958, 71, Knox 1961, 149, Meier 1993, 175–176, and Goldhill 2012, 42. Segal argues that Odysseus's reaction evokes the audience's capacity for pity (1995, 6). On the portrait of pity in Sophocles, see Sandridge 2008, esp. 440–442. Larmore suggests that Odysseus's intervention reintegrates Ajax into the community (2014, 147, 163–165).

38. Gregory interprets Odysseus as a model of "empathy" and sees the scene between Achilles and Priam in *Iliad* 24 as a precursor (2012, 534–535). Winnington-Ingram finds the play's conclusion foreshadowed in the opening scene between Athena and Odysseus (1980, 66–72). On this, see also M. W. Blundell 1989, 60–68, 95–105. Knox identifies Odysseus's "enlightened self-interest" (1961, 149, and, similarly, Worman 2012, 342–347). Meier, however, finds that Odysseus here is "renouncing self-interest" (1993, 173–174). Sandridge suggests that the *Ajax* validates "self-regarding, non-familial, non-merit-based pity" (2008, 446). In my view, Odysseus exemplifies the foresight that enables individual self-interest to align with the interests of all.

39. Segal emphasizes the necessity of Odysseus's skills to the community (1981, 150).

40. Regarding Sophocles' depiction of persuasion and the role of oratory in fifth-century Athens, see especially Worman 2012.

6
The Abuse of Power and Its Consequences

1. Most scholars date the *Hecuba* to 425 or 424 BCE (Nussbaum 1986, 404). See also Collard 1991, 34–35 and Gregory 1999, xii–xv.

Alaux finds criticism of victors' abuse of power in all of Euripides' Trojan War plays (2011, 252). But cf. Zeitlin 1996, 172–216. Zeitlin identifies the escalating savagery of the retaliatory process (210) but interprets the *Hecuba* more narrowly as a dramatization of "the Dionysiac effect of women who are made to take over the power and the plot when men abdicate their roles of moral authority and the most sacred cultural taboos are transgressed" (176). Arguably, however, the play also exposes the more universal obligations of all who possess power toward others within their power.

2. My understanding of the *Hecuba* derives from Gregory 1991, 85–120.

3. Gregory 1999, xiv–xv. For example, in 427 BCE the Athenians besieged Mytilene, a city on the island of Lesbos. Failing in its attempt to rebel from the Athenian League, Mytilene eventually capitulated, and the Athenians voted to

execute the entire male population and sell the women and children into slavery. The next day, after a long debate in the assembly, the Athenians revised their initial brutal impulse. Persuaded, according to Thucydides, not by compassion but by the pragmatic argument that it was impractical to kill everyone, as that would prolong future sieges (the besieged would have no incentive to give up but would fight to the death), the Athenians decided to show leniency. In their view, leniency still entailed slaughtering one thousand men, confiscating all the land, and selling the women and children into slavery (see Kagan 1974, 155–167 on Thuc. 3.26–50). In 421 BCE, just a few years after the *Hecuba* was produced, the Athenians suppressed a rebellion at Scione, murdered all of the men, enslaved the women and children, and confiscated the land (Thuc. 5.32). For parallels between the *Hecuba* and Thucydides' account of the civil war in Corcyra (Thuc. 3.82–83), see Nussbaum 1986, 404–405. For parallels with Thucydides' account of the Melian Dialogue (Thuc. 5.84–116), see Gregory 1991, 112–114.

4. The *Odyssey* emphasizes the constant changeability of human fortunes. Once a powerful king and successful sacker of cities, Odysseus becomes a destitute wanderer. Far from home, hearing tales of the Greeks' sack of Troy, Odysseus even resembles a woman captured and enslaved after the death of her husband and the fall of her city (*Od.* 8.521–532). I agree with Halliwell that this paradoxical analogy does not indicate that Odysseus himself has come to experience "pity for the losers in war" (2011, 88). Instead, the analogy cultivates the audience's capacity for empathy. By the conclusion of the *Odyssey*, Odysseus has become a powerful king again.

5. Zeitlin 1996, 172–174, 178.

6. Gregory 1991, 112.

7. Euripides' *Hecuba* is the earliest surviving literary account of the story. Homer mentions a Polydorus, Priam's youngest son, as one of Achilles' battlefield victims (*Il.* 20.407–418), but Hecuba is not his mother. Polydorus does not appear in the *Odyssey*, and Homer never mentions Polyxena. Sophocles' *Polyxena* survives only in fragments. Euripides later hints at Polyxena's sacrifice (*Trojan Women* 264), but earlier sources do not mention it, or Polydorus's murder by treachery, or Hecuba's retaliation (Gantz 1993, 561, 658–661). In Euripides' *Trojan Women*, Hecuba expects to be made Odysseus's slave (the *Odyssey* never mentions this), but in the *Hecuba*, she belongs to Agamemnon. See Mossman's discussion of the play in relation to the mythical tradition (1995, 19–47).

8. Gantz 1993, 561. Barker calls Homer's Hecuba "the archetypal suffering spectator" (2009, 329 with bibliography).

9. Zeitlin (1996, 172–216) notes the absence of the gods in this play in contrast to their presence in Euripides' *Trojan Women* (211–212) but details the implicit presence of Dionysos (175).

10. Gregory 1991, 91 and n. 12. But cf. G. M. A. Grube's claim that Odysseus's logic is "eminently sensible" (1941, 217–218).

11. Thalmann 1993, 136–148. Luschnig maintains that Talthybius begins to "doubt that there are really gods who concern themselves with human fortunes (488–91)" (1976, 231).

12. For the portrait of Polymestor, see especially Nussbaum 1986, 406–411, Mossman 1995, 184–188, Zeitlin 1996, 178–183, and Burnett 1998, 163–176. Luschnig notes that Polymestor "is so offensive—since we know what he has done and why—that we feel that he deserves whatever he will get. For Euripides leads us on and then shocks us with the inhumanity of the punishment" (1976, 232). Gregory explains that "Hecuba accomplishes her revenge by means of deception, traditionally the last weapon of the weak and helpless" (1991, 108, citing Buxton 1982, 64). For Polymestor's negative view of women, see Rabinowitz 1993, 113–121, Zeitlin 1996, 208–216, and Barker 2009, 329–32. For the *Hecuba*'s evocation of Odyssean elements and the associations between Polymestor and the Cyclops Polyphemos, see Thalmann 1993, 127, Zeitlin 1996, 194–197, and Barker 2009, 346–365.

13. Gregory 1991, 89–94, 108–109.

14. For the role of tragedy in defining the Athenians' view of "self" and "other," see especially E. Hall 1989 and J. Heath 2005, 171–212. Burnett discusses the moral degeneration of Odysseus and the Greek army (1998, 158–162). Barker observes that Odysseus fails to take any responsibility for his role in the assembly's decision and that his arguments echo and reverse themes in the *Iliad* (2009, 332–336).

15. Cf. Sandridge's argument that the vulnerability of Euripides' Odysseus precludes pity (2008, 442).

16. See Gregory 1991, 94–98. Gregory identifies Polyxena's willing self-sacrifice as emblematic of the uselessness of collaboration with a conquering enemy. For the complexity of the depiction of female glory in tragedy and the theme of voluntary female self-sacrifice, see Burnett 1998, 142–149, 157–163, Dué 2006, 120–131, and Mastronarde 2010, 261–270. Regarding evaluation of Polyxena's death, see especially Mossman 1995, 142–163, Barker 2009, 339–340, and Mastronarde 2010, 266–268.

The sacrifice of Polyxena appears especially arbitrary and pointless in comparison to two other well-known mythical tales of virgin sacrifice. Unlike Agamemnon's sacrifice of his daughter Iphigenia (depicted in Aeschylus's *Agamemnon*) and the sacrifice of one of Heracles' daughters (depicted in Euripides' *Children of Heracles*), Polyxena's death is not required by a god, and it serves no purpose. Polyxena's death does not prevent an army from starving, as Iphigenia's murder does, or preserve an illustrious family, as the murder of Heracles' daughter does. On the parallels and contrasts between these three examples of female sacrifice, see Thalmann 1993, esp. 136–148, Mossman 1995, 152–163, and Barker 2009, 343–345. Unlike Heracles' daughter (*Children of Heracles* 474ff.), Polyxena cannot actually volunteer. Heracles' daughter refuses to draw lots to decide who should be sacrificed (*Children of Heracles* 547–548). She thus rejects a democratic process that makes everyone equal in favor of an aristocratic principle that makes her choice, her willing self-sacrifice, distinctively best and worthy of honor. The choice of Heracles' daughter results in her death. By contrast, Polyxena's choice remains irrelevant.

Hecuba refers to the sacrifice of Polyxena as *to deinon*, "terrible/wondrous/strange thing" (516). She also begins her musing about human nature asking, "Is it not therefore *deinon* . . ." (592). And she calls the "multitude" *deinon* with its capacity for deception (884). The word might recall the famous first choral ode in Sophocles' *Antigone* (c. 441 BCE) identifying man as more terrible/wondrous/strange (*deinoteros*) than all the many terrible/wondrous/strange things (*deina*) there are (*Ant.* 332ff.). Undoubtedly, only human beings could accomplish the *deinon*, "terrible/wondrous/strange," deed of sacrificing a live girl to honor a dead man.

17. Kovacz 1987, 86, Gregory 1991, 88, and Barker 2009, 330 and n. 19.

18. But cf. Mossman 1995, 72 and n. 10.

19. See Gregory 1991, 88–89 and 98–102.

20. Other surviving sources mention this spy mission but give no details, and Euripides very likely invented this incident (Gantz 1993, 642). Cf. *Od.* 4.242–258. See also Luschnig 1976, 229–231. Regarding the lack of plausibility of Euripides' innovation, see especially Barker 2009, 336–359 and n. 52 (with bibliography).

21. Regarding the reciprocal nature of Hecuba's revenge, see, especially, Burnett 1973 and Michelini 1987, 170. Gregory suggests that Hecuba's "anachronistic" and unsuccessful appeal to *nomos . . . isos* (*Hec.* 291–292) may both evoke the audience's sympathy and prompt questioning of "the double standard of justice prevailing in fifth-century Athens: within the polis *isonomia;* outside the polis, the ruthless imposition of Athenian power" (1991, 100).

22. Barker notes that reciprocal vengeance aligns with "normative standards of Greek morality" (2009, 346 and n. 81, and, similarly, Mossman 1995, 169–170 and Burnett 1998, 65). But Aeschylus's *Oresteia* critiques the traditional equation of Justice with Vengeance. (See, e.g., Lattimore 1972 and Herington 1986, 62–63 and 143–156.)

Gregory finds in the *Hecuba* a reversal of the *Oresteia*, as vengeance follows the failure of a request for procedural justice (1991, 108), and Nussbaum argues that Hecuba's transformation reverses that of the Furies (1986, 416, but cf. Mossman 1995, 204–205). For the relationship between the *Hecuba* and the *Oresteia*, see also Thalmann 1993. Barker maintains that the *Hecuba* reexamines the *Odyssey*'s portrait of vengeance, whereas Sophocles' *Ajax* reinterprets the *Iliad* (2009, 325–365). Zeitlin contrasts the *Hecuba* with Euripides' later *Trojan Women* (1996, 211–216).

23. Regarding Hecuba's use of persuasive speech in pursuing justice, see especially Gregory 1991, 106–107, Mossman 1995, 94–138, Zeitlin 1996, 203–208, Hesk 2000, 283–284, H. P. Foley 2001, 94–95, 283–286, Barker 2009, 342, and Mastronarde 2010, 229–234. For the debate regarding the morality or immorality of Hecuba's reference to Cassandra in her attempt to persuade Agamemnon, see especially Nussbaum 1986, 414–415, Mossman 1995, 180–183, Scodel 1998, and Barker 2009, 334 and n. 73.

24. Many scholars emphasize the implications of the Odysseus and Agamemnon episodes for undermining the absolute validity of *nomoi*. See, e.g., Luschnig 1976, 232 and Gregory 1991, 102. For the play's relation to the "*nomos* vs. *physis*" debate, see Nussbaum 1986, 402–406.

25. Mob action repeatedly proves destructive in the play. Recounting the sacrifice of Polyxena, the herald Talthybius twice calls the Greek army an *ochlos*, "mob" (*Hec.* 521 and 533). Criticizing the destructiveness of the mob mentality, Hecuba also twice calls the Greeks an *ochlos* (*Hec.* 605–608). She also calls an *ochlos* the captive Trojan women who will, en masse, later collaborate in her terrible vengeance (*Hec.* 880). The term *ochlokratia*, "mob-ocracy," came to define the degenerate form of *demokratia*, "democracy," as a kind of tyranny. See Polybius's *Histories* 6.4.6 (second century BCE).

26. Luschnig finds the murders of all four children "most disheartening" and "senseless" since it "signifies the loss of innocence and hope for the future" (1976, 234). But cf. Mossman's argument that a fifth-century Athenian audience would find the blinding more upsetting than the murders (1995, 190). Zeitlin draws a moral distinction between the deaths of Polyxena and Polydorus, pointing out that Polymestor killed only one of them (1996, 191–194). Regarding the moral validity of Hecuba's revenge, see also Burnett 1998, 166–172 and H. P. Foley 2001, 272–273 vs. Mossman 1995, 184–203.

27. For the portraits of Odysseus and Agamemnon and Agamemnon's pretense of impartiality as judge of the debate, see Mastronarde 2010, 300. Garner notes that despite the legal processes depicted in the play, "legality and justice have no superior authority and little independent force" (1987, 112). Gregory observes that this scene evokes the audience's moral judgment (1991, 109). Similarly, Barker argues that "by removing any institutional security for managing dissent, Euripides puts the onus on his audience to face up to their individual responsibilities for judging action" (2009, 328–329 and 354–365).

28. Barker 2009, 344–345, 361–362 and n. 141.

29. See Hesiod's account of the myth of Prometheus and the origins of sacrifice: animal sacrifice establishes human beings in the middle of a hierarchy. Animals eat raw meat and are sacrificed. Human beings eat animals (cooked), not human flesh. The gods consume the smoke from sacrificial fires (*Theogony* 521–617). For the role of sacrifice in defining the human condition, see especially Nagy 1979, 216–217, Vernant 1986, 37–38, 47, and Muellner 1996, 84–87. But cf. Redfield's argument that "the line between man and dog is fixed only by culture. On the battlefield, where the rules of culture break down, the warrior may become a raw-meat eater," citing *Iliad* 24.207–208 (1994, 197). For the theme of cannibalism in the *Iliad,* see O'Brien 1993, 81–94 and Neal 2006.

30. For various critical assessments of Hecuba's transformation and the significance of the "sign," see, e.g., Luschnig 1976, 227, Nussbaum 1986, 397–421, Gregory 1991, 85–86, 109–112 and n. 62, Burnett 1994 and 1998, 172–176, Zeitlin 1996, 183–191, Dué 2006, 117–122, 131–135, and Barker 2009, 325–326 and nn. 2–3, 341 and n. 61, 357–358, 363. Burnett maintains that Hecuba serves as a moral example for the Greeks (1998, 166). Many critics see Hecuba's vengeance as undermining her moral position and interpret her subsequent transformation into a dog as a symbol of her moral regression to bestiality (e.g., Conacher 1967, 21, 152–154, Luschnig 1976, 232, Reckford 1985, 114 and n. 1, Nussbaum 1986, 414–417, Michelini 1987, 140–141, 172, and Rabinowitz 1993, 108–109, 113). Others find this view anachronistic. For a summary of various scholars' moral assessment of Hecuba's character, see Mastronarde 2010, 203, n. 98.

For a discussion of women and anger in ancient society, see Harris 2001, 264–282. For the portrait of dogs in Homer, see Redfield 1994, 192–199 and Nussbaum 1986, 414. Mossman discusses ancient attitudes toward dogs (1995, 194–202).

31. Regarding the secular status of the tragic poet as teacher, see, e.g., Redfield 1994, 42. Livingstone discusses the function of epic and tragic myth in providing moral examples (2011).

32. Gregory suggests that the character of Hecuba enables us to assess "not only the extremes of misery, but also the point at which victims can be expected to retaliate against their tormenters, asserting the claims of justice at whatever cost to themselves" (1991, 112).

33. Gregory reads the *Hecuba* as a warning against imperialism (1991, 86). Mossman identifies the context as Euripides' portrait of the "collapse" of the *polis* and the family (1995, 204–209). Segal interprets the play more broadly as a "devastating critique of a world that has lost touch with basic moral values" (1993, 210). Discussing the relationship between revenge and lamentation, Dué (2006, 117–135) suggests that the play encourages contemporary Athenians "to

reflect upon the current wartime situation in the 420s B.C. by experiencing that of the heroic past" (134). See also H. P. Foley regarding fifth-century Athenian views of justice between individuals and between states (2001, 289–299).

34. Regarding subsequent Athenian ruthlessness, see, e.g., Thucydides' descriptions of the massacres at Scione in 421 BCE (Thuc. 5.32) and Melos in 416 BCE (Thuc. 5.85–113, 116).

Bibliography

Adkins, A. W. H. 1960. *Merit and Responsibility: A Study in Greek Values.* Oxford: Clarendon.

———. 1971. "Homeric Values and Homeric Society." *Journal of Hellenic Studies* 91: 1–14.

Ahrensdorf, P. J. 2014. *Homer on the Gods and Human Virtue: Creating the Foundations of Classical Civilization.* Cambridge: Cambridge University Press.

Alaux, J. 2011. "Acting Myth: Athenian Drama." In *A Companion to Greek Mythology,* edited by K. Dowden and N. Livingstone, 141–156. Malden, Mass.: Wiley-Blackwell.

Alden, M. J. 1996. "Genealogy as Paradigm: The Example of Bellerophon." *Hermes* 124: 257–263.

———. 2000. *Homer beside Himself: Para-Narratives in the "Iliad."* Oxford: Oxford University Press.

———. 2005. "Lions in Paradise: Lion Similes in the *Iliad* and the Lion Cubs of *Il.* 18.318–22." *Classical Quarterly* 55, 2: 335–342.

Alexiou, M. 1974. *The Ritual Lament in Greek Tradition.* Cambridge: Cambridge University Press.

Andreyev, Y. 1991. "Greece of the Eleventh to Ninth Centuries BC in the Homeric Epics." In *Early Antiquity,* edited by I. M. Diakanoff, translated by A. Kirjanov, 328–348. Chicago: University of Chicago Press.

Anhalt, E. K. 2015. "A Man out of Time." *Transference* 3: 94–97.

Arieti, J. A. 1986. "Achilles' Alienation in *Iliad* 9." *Classical Journal* 82, 1: 1–27.

Arnason, J. P., and P. Murphy, eds. 2001. *Agon, Logos, Polis: The Greek Achievement and Its Aftermath.* Stuttgart: Franz Steiner Verlag.

Arnason, J. P., K. A. Raaflaub, and P. Wagner, eds. 2013. *The Greek Polis and the Invention of Democracy: A Politico-Cultural Transformation and Its Interpretations.* Malden, Mass.: Wiley-Blackwell.

Austin, N. 1975. *Archery at the Dark of the Moon: Poetic Problems in Homer's Odyssey.* Berkeley: University of California Press.

———. 2011. "Homer Who?" *Arion* 19, 2: 121–153.

Avery, H. C. 1994. "Glaucus a God? *Iliad* Z 128–143." *Hermes* 122: 498–502.

Bakker, E. 2009. "Homer, Odysseus, and the Narratology of Performance." In *Narratology and Interpretation: The Content of Narrative Form in Ancient Literature,* edited by J. Grethliein and A. Rengakos, 117–136. Berlin: Walter de Gruyter.

Barker, E. T. E. 2009. *Entering the Agon: Dissent and Authority in Homer, Historiography, and Tragedy.* Oxford: Oxford University Press.

Beck, D. 2005. *Homeric Conversation.* Hellenic Studies Series 14. Washington, D.C.: Center for Hellenic Studies (Harvard University Press).

Becker, A. S. 1995. *The Shield of Achilles and the Poetics of Ekphrasis.* Lanham, Md.: Rowman and Littlefield.

Benardete, S. (posth.) 2005. *Achilles and Hector: The Homeric Hero,* edited by R. Burger. South Bend, Ind.: St. Augustine's.

Blondell, R. 2010. " 'Bitch That I Am': Self-Blame and Self-Assertion in the *Iliad.*" *Transactions of the American Philological Association* 140, 1: 1–32.

Blundell, M. W. 1989. *Helping Friends and Harming Enemies: A Study in Sophocles and Greek Ethics.* Cambridge: Cambridge University Press.

Blundell, S. 1995. *Women in Ancient Greece.* Cambridge: Harvard University Press.

Boedeker, D., and K. A. Raaflaub, eds. 1998. *Democracy, Empire and the Arts in Fifth-Century Athens.* Center for Hellenic Studies, Colloquia 2. Cambridge: Harvard University Press.

———. 2005. "Tragedy and City." In *A Companion to Tragedy,* edited by R. Bushnell, 109–127. Oxford and Malden, Mass.: Wiley-Blackwell.

Boegehold, A. L., and A. C. Scafuro, eds. 1994. *Athenian Identity and Civic Ideology.* Baltimore: Johns Hopkins University Press.

Bosley, R. N., and M. M. Tweedale, eds. 2014. *Ancient Political Thought: A Reader.* Ontario: Broadview.

Bowra, C. M. 1930. *Tradition and Design in the "Iliad."* Oxford: Clarendon.

———. 1944. *Sophoclean Tragedy.* Oxford: Oxford University Press.

Bradshaw, D. J. 1991. "The Ajax Myth and the *Polis:* Old Values and New." In *Myth and the Polis,* edited by D. C. Pozzi and J. M. Wickersham, 99–125. Ithaca: Cornell University Press.

Braund, S., and G. W. Most, eds. 2003. *Ancient Anger: Perspectives from Homer to Galen*. Cambridge: Cambridge University Press.

Burian, P. 1997. "Myth into *Muthos*: The Shaping of Tragic Plot." In *The Cambridge Companion to Greek Tragedy*, edited by P. E. Easterling, 178–208. Cambridge: Cambridge University Press.

———. 2011. "Athenian Tragedy as Democratic Discourse." In *Why Athens? A Reappraisal of Tragic Politics*, edited by D. M. Carter, 95–119. Oxford: Oxford University Press.

Burnett, A. P. 1994. "Hekabe the Dog." *Arethusa* 27: 151–164.

———. 1998. *Revenge in Attic and Later Tragedy*. Berkeley: University of California Press.

Bushnell, R., ed. 2005. *A Companion to Tragedy*. Malden, Mass.: Wiley-Blackwell.

Buxton, R. G. A. 2004. "Similes and Other Likenesses." In *The Cambridge Companion to Homer*, edited by R. Fowler, 139–155. Cambridge: Cambridge University Press.

Cairns, D. L. 1993. *Aidōs: The Psychology and Ethics of Honor and Shame in Ancient Greek Literature*. Oxford: Clarendon.

———. 2001a. "Affronts and Quarrels in the *Iliad*." In *Oxford Readings in Homer's "Iliad,"* edited by D. L. Cairns, 203–219. Oxford: Oxford University Press.

———, ed. 2001b. *Oxford Readings in Homer's "Iliad."* Oxford: Oxford University Press.

———. 2003. "Ethics, Ethology, Terminology: Iliadic Anger and the Cross-Cultural Study of Emotion." In *Ancient Anger: Perspectives from Homer to Galen*, edited by S. Braund and G. W. Most, 11–49. Cambridge: Cambridge University Press.

———. 2005. "Values." In *A Companion to Greek Tragedy*, edited by J. Gregory, 305–320. Malden, Mass.: Wiley-Blackwell.

———. 2013a. "Introduction: Archaic Thought and Tragic Interpretation." In *Tragedy and Archaic Greek Thought*, edited by D. L. Cairns, i–xli. Swansea: Classical Press of Wales.

———, ed. 2013b. *Tragedy and Archaic Greek Thought*. Swansea: Classical Press of Wales.

Calamé, C. 1996. *Mythe et histoire dans l'antiquité grecque: La création symbolique d'une colonie*. Lausanne: Editions Payot.

Carter, D. M. 2007. *The Politics of Greek Tragedy*. Exeter: Liverpool University Press.

———, ed. 2011. *Why Athens? A Reappraisal of Tragic Politics*. Oxford: Oxford University Press.

Chua, A. 2003. *World on Fire: How Exporting Free Market Democracy Breeds Ethnic Hatred and Global Instability.* New York: Random House.

Coffey, M. 1957. "The Function of the Homeric Simile." *American Journal of Philology* 78: 113–132.

Collard, C. 1991. *Euripides: "Hecuba."* Warminster: Aris and Phillips.

Cook, E. F. 2003. "Agamemnon's Test of the Army in *Iliad* Book 2 and the Function of Homeric *Akhos.*" *American Journal of Philology* 124: 165–198.

Csapo, E. 2005. *Theories of Mythology.* Malden, Mass.: Wiley-Blackwell.

D'Aulaire, I., and E. P. D'Aulaire. 1962. *D'Aulaires' Book of Greek Myths.* New York: Doubleday.

Davidson, J. 1985. "Sophoclean Dramaturgy and the *Ajax* Burial Debates." *Ramus* 14: 16–29.

———. 2012. "Epic Sources and Models in Sophocles." In *Brill's Companion to Sophocles,* edited by A. Markantonatos, 245–261. Leiden: Brill.

Davis, M. 1986. "Politics and Madness." In *Greek Tragedy and Political Theory,* edited by J. P. Euben, 142–161. Berkeley: University of California Press.

———. 2006. "Why I Read Such Good Books: Aeschylus, Sophocles, the Moral Majority, and Secular Humanism." In M. Davis, *Wonderlust: Ruminations on Liberal Education.* South Bend, Ind.: St. Augustine's.

Debnar, P. 2005. "Fifth-Century Athenian History and Tragedy." In *A Companion to Greek Tragedy,* edited by J. Gregory, 3–22. Malden, Mass.: Wiley-Blackwell.

Dodds, E. R. 1951. *The Greeks and the Irrational.* Berkeley: University of California Press.

Donlan, W. 1979. "The Structure of Authority in the *Iliad.*" *Arethusa* 12: 51–70.

———. 1985. "The Social Groups of Dark Age Greece." *Classical Philology* 80: 293–308.

———. 1989. "The Unequal Exchange between Glaucus and Diomedes in Light of the Homeric Gift-Economy." *Phoenix* 43: 1–15.

———. 1993. "Dueling with Gifts in the *Iliad:* As the Audience Saw It," *Colby Quarterly* 29, 3: 155–172.

Dowden, K., and N. Livingstone. 2011. "Thinking through Myth, Thinking Myth Through." In *A Companion to Greek Mythology,* edited by K. Dowden and N. Livingstone, 3–23. Malden, Mass.: Wiley-Blackwell.

DuBois, P. 2001. *Trojan Horses: Saving the Classics from Conservatives.* New York: New York University Press.

———. 2010. *Out of Athens: The New Ancient Greeks.* Cambridge: Harvard University Press.

Dué, C. 2006. *The Captive Woman's Lament in Greek Tragedy*. Austin: University of Texas Press.

Dué, C., and Ebbott, M. 2010. *"Iliad" 10 and the Poetics of Ambush*. Hellenic Studies Series 39. Washington, D.C.: Center for Hellenic Studies (Harvard University Press).

Dunn, J. 1979. *Western Political Theory in the Face of the Future*. Cambridge: Cambridge University Press.

———. 1992. *Democracy: The Unfinished Journey, 508 BCE to AD 1993*. Oxford: Oxford University Press.

———. 2005a. *Setting the People Free: The Story of Democracy*. London: Atlantic Books.

———. 2005b. *Democracy: A History*. New York: Atlantic Monthly Press.

Easterling, P. E. 1984. "The Tragic Homer." *Bulletin of the Institute of Classical Studies* 31: 1–8.

———. 1991. "Men's *kléos* and Women's *góos*: Female Voices in the *Iliad*." *Journal of Modern Greek Studies* 9, 2: 145–151.

Edmunds, L. 1989. "Commentary on Raaflaub." In *Proceedings of the Boston Area Colloquium in Ancient Philosophy*, vol. 4, edited by J. Cleary and D. Shartin. New York: University Press of America.

Edwards, M. W. 1987. *Homer, Poet of the "Iliad."* Baltimore: Johns Hopkins University Press.

Elmer, D. F. 2013. *The Poetics of Consent: Collective Decision Making and the "Iliad."* Baltimore: Johns Hopkins University Press.

Else, G. F. 1965. *The Origin and Early Form of Greek Tragedy*. Cambridge: Harvard University Press.

Euben, J. P., ed. 1986. *Greek Tragedy and Political Theory*. Berkeley: University of California Press.

———. 1990. *The Tragedy of Political Theory: The Road Not Taken*. Princeton: Princeton University Press.

Euben, J. P., J. Wallach, and J. Ober, eds. 1994. *Athenian Political Thought and the Reconstruction of American Democracy*. Ithaca: Cornell University Press.

Fantham, E., H. P. Foley, N. B. Kampen, S. B. Pomeroy, and H. A. Shapiro, eds. 1994. *Women in the Classical World*. New York: Oxford University Press.

Felson, N., and L. M. Slatkin. 2004. "Gender and Homeric Epic." In *The Cambridge Companion to Homer*, edited by R. Fowler, 91–114. Cambridge: Cambridge University Press.

Felson-Rubin, N. 1987. "Penelope's Perspective: Character from Plot." In *Homer: Beyond Oral Poetry: Recent Trends in Homeric Interpretation*, edited by J. M. Bremer, I. J. F. de Jong, and J. Kalff, 61–83. Amsterdam: B. R. Grüner.

———. 1994. *Regarding Penelope: From Character to Poetics.* Norman: University of Oklahoma Press.

Finglass, P. J. 2012. "Ajax." In *Brill's Companion to Sophocles,* edited by A. Markantonatos, 59–72. Leiden: Brill.

Finley, J. H., Jr. 1967. "Politics and Early Attic Tragedy." *Harvard Studies in Classical Philology* 71: 1–13.

Finley, M. I. 1954. *The World of Odysseus.* New York: Viking. 2nd ed. 1979.

———. 1965. "Myth, Memory, and History." *History and Theory* 4: 281–302.

———, ed. 1968. *Slavery in Classical Antiquity: Views and Controversies,* 2nd ed. Cambridge: W. Heffer and Sons.

———. 1973. *Democracy Ancient and Modern.* New Brunswick, N.J.: Rutgers University Press. 2nd ed. 1985.

———. 1980. *Ancient Slavery and Modern Ideology.* New York: Viking Press.

———. 1987. *Classical Slavery.* London: Routledge.

Finnegan, R. 1977. *Oral Poetry: Its Nature, Significance, and Social Context.* Cambridge: Cambridge University Press.

Fisher, N. R. E. 1992. *Hybris: A Study of the Values of Honour and Shame in Ancient Greece.* Warminster: Aris and Phillips.

Foley, H. P. 1978. " 'Reverse Similes' and Sex Roles in the *Odyssey*." *Arethusa* 11: 7–26.

———. 1981a. "The Conception of Women in Athenian Drama." In *Reflections of Women in Antiquity,* edited by H. P. Foley, 127–168. New York: Gordon and Breach.

———, ed. 1981b. *Reflections of Women in Antiquity.* New York: Gordon and Breach.

———. 2001. *Female Acts in Greek Tragedy.* Princeton: Princeton University Press.

———. 2005. "Women in Ancient Epic." In *A Companion to Ancient Epic,* edited by J. M. Foley, 105–118. Malden, Mass.: Blackwell.

Foley, J. M., ed. 2005. *A Companion to Ancient Epic.* Malden, Mass.: Blackwell.

Forrest, W. G. 1966. *The Emergence of Greek Democracy, 800–400 BC.* New York: McGraw-Hill.

Foster, E. 2010. *Thucydides, Pericles, and Periclean Imperialism.* Cambridge: Cambridge University Press.

Fowler, R. 2004. "The Homeric Question." In *The Cambridge Companion to Homer,* edited by R. Fowler, 220–232. Cambridge: Cambridge University Press.

Frede, M. 2011. *A Free Will: Origins of the Notion in Ancient Thought.* Berkeley: University of California Press.

Freeman, P. 2012. *Oh My Gods: A Modern Retelling of Greek and Roman Myths.* New York: Simon and Schuster.

Gaisser, J. H. 1969. "Adaptation of Traditional Material in the Glaukos-Diomedes Episode." *Transactions of the American Philological Association* 100: 165–176.

Gantz, T. 1993. *Early Greek Myth: A Guide to Literary and Artistic Sources.* 2 vols. Baltimore: Johns Hopkins University Press.

Garlan, Y. 1988. *Slavery in Ancient Greece,* translated by J. Lloyd. Ithaca: Cornell University Press.

Garner, R. 1987. *Law and Society in Classical Athens.* New York: St. Martin's.

——. 1990. *From Homer to Tragedy: The Art of Allusion in Greek Poetry.* London: Routledge.

Garvie, A. F., ed. and trans. 1998. *Sophocles: "Ajax."* Warminster: Aris and Phillips.

Gaskin, R. 1990. "Do Homeric Heroes Make Real Decisions?" *Classical Quarterly* 40: 1–15.

Gill, C. 1996. *Personality in Greek Epic, Tragedy, and Philosophy: The Self in Dialogue.* Oxford: Clarendon.

Goff. B. E., ed. 1995. *History, Tragedy, Theory: Dialogues in Athenian Drama.* Austin: University of Texas Press.

Goldhill, S. 1986. *Reading Greek Tragedy.* Cambridge: Cambridge University Press.

——. 1990. "The Great Dionysia and Civic Ideology." In *Nothing to Do with Dionysos? Athenian Drama in Its Social Context,* edited by J. J. Winkler and F. I. Zeitlin, 97–129. Princeton: Princeton University Press. Orig. pub. 1987. *Journal of Hellenic Studies* 107: 58–76.

——. 2000. "Civic Ideology and the Problem of Difference: the Politics of Aeschylean Tragedy, Once Again." *Journal of Hellenic Studies* 120: 34–56.

——. 2009. "The Audience on Stage: Rhetoric, Emotion, and Judgment in Sophoclean Theater." In *Sophocles and the Greek Tragic Tradition,* edited by S. Goldhill and E. Hall, 27–47. Cambridge: Cambridge University Press.

Goldhill, S., and E. Hall, eds. 2009. *Sophocles and the Greek Tragic Tradition.* Cambridge: Cambridge University Press.

Gotteland, S. 2001. *Mythe et rhétorique: Les examples mythiques dans le discours politique de l' Athènes classique.* Paris: Les Belles Lettres.

Gottschall, J. 2008. *The Rape of Troy: Evolution, Violence, and the World of Homer.* Cambridge: Cambridge University Press.

Gould, J. 1983. "Homeric Epic and the Tragic Moment." In *Aspects of the Epic,* edited by T. Winnifrith, P. Murray, and K. W. Gransden, 32–45. New York: St. Martin's.

Graf. F. 1993. *Greek Mythology: An Introduction,* translated by T. Marier. Baltimore: Johns Hopkins University Press.

——. 2011. "Myth and Hellenic Identities." In *A Companion to Greek Mythology,* edited by K. Dowden and N. Livingstone, 211–226. Malden, Mass.: Wiley-Blackwell.

Graves, R. 1955. *The Greek Myths.* 2 vols. London: Pelican Books. Revised 1960.

Gregory, J. 1991. *Euripides and the Instruction of the Athenians.* Ann Arbor: University of Michigan Press.

——, ed. 1999. *Euripides: "Hecuba."* Atlanta: Scholars Press.

——, ed. 2005. *A Companion to Greek Tragedy.* Malden, Mass.: Wiley-Blackwell.

——. 2012. "Sophocles and Education." In *Brill's Companion to Sophocles,* edited by A. Markantonatos, 515–535. Leiden: Brill.

Grethlein, J. 2007. "The Hermeneutics and Poetics of Memory in Aeschylus' *Persae.*" *Arethusa* 40, 3: 363–393.

——. 2010. *The Greeks and Their Past: Poetry, Oratory and History in the Fifth Century BCE.* Cambridge: Cambridge University Press.

Griffin, J. 1980a. *Homer.* Oxford: Oxford University Press.

——. 1980b. *Homer on Life and Death.* Oxford: Clarendon.

——, ed. 1995. *Homer: "Iliad" IX.* Oxford: Clarendon.

Griffith, M. 1975. "Man and the Leaves: A Study of Mimnermos fr. 2." *California Studies in Classical Antiquity* 8: 73–88.

——. 1995. "Brilliant Dynasts: Power and Politics in the *Oresteia.*" *Classical Antiquity* 14: 62–129.

Grube, G. M. A. 1941. *The Drama of Euripides.* London: Methuen.

Gwara, S. 2007. "Misprision in the Para-Narratives of *Iliad* 9." *Arethusa* 40, 3: 303–336.

Hall, E. 1989. *Inventing the Barbarian: Greek Self-Definition through Tragedy.* Oxford: Clarendon.

——. 2010. *Greek Tragedy: Suffering under the Sun.* Oxford: Oxford University Press.

Hall, J. M. 2007. *A History of the Archaic Greek World, ca. 1200–479 BCE.* Malden, Mass.: Blackwell.

Haller, B. S. 2013. "Dolios in *Odyssey* 4 and 24: Penelope's Plotting and Alternative Narratives of Odysseus' *Nostos.*" *Transactions of the American Philological Association* 143: 263–292.

Halliwell, S. 2011. *Between Ecstasy and Truth: Interpretations of Greek Poetics from Homer to Longinus.* Oxford: Oxford University Press.

Hamilton, E. 1942. *Mythology.* New York: Little, Brown.

Hammer, D. C. 1998. "The Cultural Construction of Chance in the *Iliad*." *Arethusa* 31, 2: 125–148.

———. 2002. *The "Iliad" as Politics: The Performance of Political Thought*. Norman: University of Oklahoma Press.

Hansen, M. H. 1991. *The Athenian Democracy in the Age of Demosthenes*. Oxford: Blackwell.

———. 1992. "The Tradition of the Athenian Democracy, A.D. 1750–1990." *Greece & Rome* 39: 14–30.

———. 1996. "The Ancient Athenian and the Modern Liberal View of Liberty as a Democratic Ideal." In *Demokratia: A Conversation on Democracies, Ancient and Modern,* edited by J. Ober and C. W. Hedrick, Jr., 91–104. Princeton: Princeton University Press.

———. 2006. *Polis: An Introduction to the Ancient Greek City State*. New York: Oxford University Press.

Hanson, V. D. 2001. "Democratic Warfare, Ancient and Modern." In *War and Democracy: A Comparative Study of the Korean War and the Peloponnesian War,* edited by D. McCann and B. S. Strauss, 3–33. Armonk, N.Y.: M. E. Sharpe.

Hanson, V. D., and J. Heath. 1998. *Who Killed Homer? The Demise of Classical Education and the Recovery of Greek Wisdom*. New York: Free Press.

Hanson, V. D., J. Heath, and B. S. Thornton. 2000. *Bonfire of the Humanities: Rescuing the Classics in an Impoverished Age*. Wilmington, Del.: Intercollegiate Studies Institute.

Hardwick, L., and S. Harrison, eds. 2013. *Classics in the Modern World: A "Democratic Turn"?* Oxford: Oxford University Press.

Harloe, K. 2013. "Questioning the Democratic and Democratic Questioning." In *Classics in the Modern World: A "Democratic Turn"?,* edited by L. Hardwick and S. Harrison, 3–13. Oxford: Oxford University Press.

Harries, B. 1993. "Strange Meeting: Diomedes and Glaucus in *Iliad* 6." *Greece & Rome* 40: 133–146.

Harris, W. V. 2001. *Restraining Rage: The Ideology of Anger Control in Classical Antiquity*. Cambridge: Harvard University Press.

Havelock, E. A. 1963. *Preface to Plato*. Cambridge: Harvard University Press.

———. 1978. *The Greek Concept of Justice from Its Shadow in Homer to Its Substance in Plato*. Cambridge: Harvard University Press.

Heath, J. 2005. *The Talking Greeks: Speech, Animals, and the Other in Homer*. Cambridge: Cambridge University Press.

Heath, M. 1987. *The Poetics of Greek Tragedy*. Stanford: Stanford University Press.

Heiden, B. 1998. "The Simile of the Fugitive Homicide, *Iliad* 24. 480–484: Analogy, Foiling, and Allusion." *American Journal of Philology* 119, 1: 1–10.

Herington, C. J. 1985. *Poetry into Drama: Early Tragedy and the Greek Poetic Tradition.* Berkeley: University of California Press.

———. 1986. *Aeschylus.* New Haven: Yale University Press.

Hertel, D. 2011 "The Myth of History: the Case of Troy." In *A Companion to Greek Mythology,* edited by K. Dowden and N. Livingstone, 425–441. Malden, Mass.: Wiley-Blackwell.

Hesk, J. 2000. *Deception and Democracy in Classical Athens.* Cambridge: Cambridge University Press.

———. 2003. *Sophocles: "Ajax."* London: Gerald Duckworth.

Hooker, J. 1987. "Homeric Society: A Shame Culture." *Greece & Rome* 34: 121–125.

Jones, A. H. M. 1986. *Athenian Democracy.* Baltimore: Johns Hopkins University Press. Orig. pub. 1957.

Jong, I. J. F. de. 1987. *Narrators and Focalizers: The Presentation of the Story in the "Iliad."* Amsterdam: B. R. Grüner.

———. 2006. "The Homeric Narrator and His Own *kleos.*" *Mnemosyne* 59: 188–207.

Kagan, D. 1969. *The Outbreak of the Peloponnesian War.* Ithaca: Cornell University Press.

———. 1974. *The Archidamian War.* Ithaca: Cornell University Press.

———. 1981. *The Peace of Nicias and the Sicilian Expedition.* Ithaca: Cornell University Press.

———. 1987. *The Fall of the Athenian Empire.* Ithaca: Cornell University Press.

———. 1991. *Pericles of Athens and the Birth of Democracy.* New York: Free Press.

Kahane, A. 2005. *Diachronic Dialogues: Authority and Continuity in Homer and the Homeric Tradition.* Lanham, Md.: Rowman and Littlefield.

Kakridis, J. 1949. *Homeric Researches.* Lund: C. W. Gleerup.

Kane, R. L. 1996. "Ajax and the Sword of Hector: Sophocles' *Ajax* 815–822." *Hermes* 124: 17–28.

Katz, M. A. [M. B. Arthur]. 1981. "The Divided World of *Iliad* VI." In *Reflections of Women in Antiquity,* edited by H. P. Foley, 19–44. New York: Gordon and Breach.

———. 1999. "Women and Democracy in Ancient Greece." In *Contextualizing Classics: Ideology, Performance, Dialogue,* edited by T. M. Falkner, N. Felson, and D. Konstan, 41–68. Lanham, Md.: Rowman and Littlefield.

Kearns, E. 2004. "The Gods in the Homeric Epics." In *The Cambridge Companion to Homer,* edited by R. Fowler, 59–73. Cambridge: Cambridge University Press.

Kelly, G. P. 2014. "Battlefield Supplication in the *Iliad.*" *Classical World* 107, 2: 147–167.

Kirk, G. S. 1962. *The Songs of Homer.* Cambridge: Cambridge University Press.

——. 1976. *Homer and the Oral Tradition.* Cambridge: Cambridge University Press.

Kirkwood, G. 1965. "Homer and Sophocles' *Ajax.*" In *Classical Drama and Its Influence: Essays Presented to H. D. F. Kitto,* edited by M. J. Anderson, 53–70. London: Methuen.

Kitto, H. D. F. 1956. *Greek Tragedy: A Literary Study.* London: Methuen. Orig. pub. 1939.

Knox, B. 1957. *Oedipus at Thebes.* New Haven: Yale University Press.

——. 1961. "The *Ajax* of Sophocles." *Harvard Studies in Classical Philology* 65: 1–37 [= 1979, 125–160].

——. 1964. *The Heroic Temper: Studies in Sophoclean Tragedy.* Berkeley: University of California Press.

——. 1979. *Word and Action: Essays on the Ancient Theater.* Baltimore: Johns Hopkins University Press.

——. 1993. *The Oldest Dead White European Males: And Other Reflections on the Classics.* New York: W. W. Norton.

Kovacz, D. 1987. *The Heroic Muse: Studies in the "Hippolytus" and "Hecuba" of Euripides.* Baltimore: Johns Hopkins University Press.

Kozak, L. A. 2014a. "Oaths between Warriors in Epic and Tragedy." In *Oaths and Swearing in Ancient Greece,* edited by A. H. Sommerstein and I. C. Torrance, 60–66. Berlin: Walter de Gruyter.

——. 2014b. "Oaths and Characterization: Two Homeric Case Studies." In *Oaths and Swearing in Ancient Greece,* edited by A. H. Sommerstein and I. C. Torrance, 213–229. Berlin: Walter de Gruyter.

Kurke, L. 1993. "The Economy of *Kudos.*" In *Cultural Poetics in Archaic Greece: Cult, Performance, Politics,* edited by C. Dougherty and L. Kurke, 131–163. Cambridge: Cambridge University Press.

——. 1998. "The Cultural Impact of (on) Democracy: Decentering Tragedy." In *Democracy 2500? Questions and Challenges,* edited by I. Morris and K. A. Raaflaub, 155–169. Dubuque, Iowa: Kendall-Hunt.

Larmore, J. 2014. "Hector and Sophocles' *Ajax*: Heroes and Their Communities." *New England Classical Journal* 41, 3: 145–167.

Lattimore, R. 1972. "Introduction to the *Oresteia.*" In *Aeschylus: A Collection of Critical Essays,* edited by M. H. McCall, Jr., 73–89. Englewood Cliffs, N.J.: Prentice-Hall.

Lawrence, S. 2005. "Ancient Ethics, the Heroic Code, and the Morality of Sophocles' *Ajax.*" *Greece & Rome* 52, 1: 18–33.

Leaf, W., ed. 1886. *The Iliad.* 2 vols. London: Macmillan.

Lefkowitz, M. R. 1986. *Women in Greek Myth.* Baltimore: Johns Hopkins University Press. 2nd ed. 2007.

Lesky, A. 1966. *A History of Greek Literature,* translated by J. Willis. New York: Crowell.

———. 2001. "Divine and Human Causation in Homeric Epic." Reprinted in *Oxford Readings in Homer's "Iliad,"* edited by D. L. Cairns, 170–202. Oxford: Oxford University Press. Abridged, translated version of 1961 orig.

Lewis, S. 2011. "Women and Myth." In *A Companion to Greek Mythology,* edited by K. Dowden and N. Livingstone, 443–458. Malden, Mass.: Wiley-Blackwell.

Livingstone, N. 2011. "Instructing Myth: From Homer to the Sophists." In *A Companion to Greek Mythology,* edited by K. Dowden and N. Livingstone, 125–139. Malden, Mass.: Wiley-Blackwell.

Lloyd-Jones, H. 1983. *The Justice of Zeus,* 2nd ed. Berkeley: University of California Press. 1st ed. 1971.

Long, A. A. 1970. "Morals and Values in Homer." *Journal of Hellenic Studies* 90: 121–139.

Lonsdale, S. H. 1990. *Creatures of Speech: Lion, Herding, and Hunting Similes in the "Iliad."* Stuttgart: B. G. Teubner.

Lord, A. B. 1960. *The Singer of Tales.* Cambridge: Harvard University Press.

———. 1991. *Epic Singers and Oral Tradition.* Ithaca: Cornell University Press.

———. 1995. *The Singer Resumes the Tale,* edited by M. L. Lord. Ithaca: Cornell University Press.

Luschnig, C. A. E. 1976. "Euripides' *Hecabe:* The Time Is Out of Joint." *Classical Journal* 71: 227–234.

Lynn-George, M. 1988. *Epos: Word, Narrative and the "Iliad."* Atlantic Highlands, N.J.: Humanities Press International.

Mackie, H. 1996. *Talking Trojan: Speech and Community in the "Iliad."* Greek Studies: Interdisciplinary Approaches. Lanham, Md.: Rowman and Littlefield.

Macleod, C., ed. 1982. *Homer: "Iliad" Book XXIV.* Cambridge: Cambridge University Press.

Markantonatos, A., ed. 2012. *Brill's Companion to Sophocles.* Leiden: Brill.

Marks, J. 2003. "Alternative *Odysseys:* the Case of Thoas and Odysseus." *Transactions of the American Philological Association* 133: 209–226.

Martin, R. P. 1989. *The Language of Heroes: Speech and Performance in the "Iliad."* Ithaca: Cornell University Press.

———. 2003. *Myths of the Ancient Greeks.* New York: New American Library.

Mastronarde, D. J. 2010. *The Art of Euripides: Dramatic Technique and Social Context.* Cambridge: Cambridge University Press.

Maurice, L., ed. 2015. *The Reception of Ancient Greece and Rome in Children's Literature: Heroes and Eagles. Metaforms,* 6. Leiden: Brill.

Meier, C. 1993. *The Political Art of Greek Tragedy,* translated by A. Webber. Baltimore: Johns Hopkins University Press.

———. 2012. *A Culture of Freedom: Ancient Greece and the Origins of Europe.* Oxford: Oxford University Press.

Melton, B. L. 2013. "Appropriations of Cicero and Cato in the Making of American Civic Identity." In *Classics in the Modern World: A "Democratic Turn"?*, edited by L. Hardwick and S. Harrison, 79–88. Oxford: Oxford University Press.

Michelakis, P. 2002. *Achilles in Greek Tragedy.* Cambridge: Cambridge University Press.

Mills, S. 2000. "Achilles, Patroclus, and Parental Care in Some Homeric Similes." *Greece & Rome* 47, 1: 3–18.

Morris, I. 1989. "Attitudes toward Death in Archaic Greece." *Classical Antiquity* 8, 2: 296–320.

———. 1996. "The Strong Principle of Equality and the Archaic Origins of Greek Democracy." In *Demokratia: A Conversation on Democracies, Ancient and Modern,* edited by J. Ober and C. W. Hedrick, Jr., 19–48. Princeton: Princeton University Press.

Morris, I., and B. Powell, eds. 1997. *A New Companion to Homer.* Leiden: Brill.

Morris, I., and K. A. Raaflaub, eds. 1998. *Democracy 2500? Questions and Challenges.* Dubuque, Iowa: Kendall-Hunt.

Morrison, J. V. 1994. "Thematic Inversion in the *Iliad:* The Greeks under Siege." *Greece, Rome, and Byzantine Studies* 35: 209–227.

———. 1997. "*Kerostasia,* the Dictates of Fate, and the Will of Zeus in the *Iliad.*" *Arethusa* 30, 2: 276–296.

Mossman, J. 1995. *Wild Justice: A Study of Euripides' "Hecuba."* Oxford: Clarendon.

———. 2005. "Women's Voices." In *A Companion to Greek Tragedy,* edited by J. Gregory, 352–365. Malden, Mass.: Wiley-Blackwell.

———. 2012. "Women's Voices in Sophocles." In *Brill's Companion to Sophocles,* edited by A. Markantonatos, 491–506. Leiden: Brill.

Most, G. W. 2003. "Anger and Pity in Homer's *Iliad.*" In *Ancient Anger: Perspectives from Homer to Galen,* edited by S. Braund and G. W. Most, 50–75. Cambridge: Cambridge University Press.

Moulton, C. 1974. "Similes in the *Iliad.*" *Hermes* 102, 3: 381–397.

———. 1977. *Similes in the Homeric Poems.* Göttingen: Vandenhoeck und Ruprecht.

Muellner, L. 1996. *The Anger of Achilles: Mēnis in Greek Epic.* Ithaca: Cornell University Press.

Munro, D. B., and T. W. Allen, eds. 1902. *Homeri Opera,* vols. 1 and 2. Oxford: Oxford University Press.

Murray, G., ed. 1906. *Euripidis Fabulae,* vol. 1. Oxford: Oxford University Press.

Nagler, M. N. 1974. *Spontaneity and Tradition: A Study in the Oral Art of Homer.* Berkeley: University of California Press.

Nagy, G. 1979. *The Best of the Achaeans: Concepts of the Hero in Archaic Greek Poetry,* 2nd ed. Baltimore: Johns Hopkins University Press. Revised 1999.

———. 1990. *Pindar's Homer: The Lyric Possession of an Epic Past.* Baltimore: Johns Hopkins University Press.

———. 1992. "Homeric Questions." *Transactions of the American Philological Association* 122: 17–60.

———. 1996. *Homeric Questions.* Austin: University of Texas Press.

———. 1997. "The Shield of Achilles: Ends of the *Iliad* and Beginnings of the Polis." In *New Light on a Dark Age: Exploring the Culture of Geometric Greece,* edited by S. Langdon, 194–207. Ithaca: Cornell University Press.

———. 2007. "Homer and Greek Myth." In *The Cambridge Companion to Greek Mythology,* edited by R. D. Woodard, 52–82. Cambridge: Cambridge University Press.

———. 2010. *Homer the Preclassic.* Berkeley: University of California Press.

———. 2013. *The Ancient Greek Hero in 24 Hours.* Cambridge: Harvard University Press.

Neal, T. 2006. "Blood and Hunger in the *Iliad.*" *Classical Philology* 101, 1: 15–33.

Nimis, S. 1988. *Narrative Semiotics in the Epic Tradition: The Simile.* Bloomington: Indiana University Press.

Nussbaum, M. C. 1986. *The Fragility of Goodness: Luck and Ethics in Greek Tragedy and Philosophy.* Cambridge: Cambridge University Press.

———. 1997. *Cultivating Humanity: A Classical Defense of Reform in Liberal Education.* Cambridge: Harvard University Press.

———. 2010. *Not for Profit: Why Democracy Needs the Humanities.* Princeton: Princeton University Press.

Ober, J. 1989. *Mass and Elite in Democratic Athens: Rhetoric, Ideology, and the Power of the People.* Princeton: Princeton University Press.

———. 1996. *The Athenian Revolution: Essays on Ancient Greek Democracy and Political Theory.* Princeton: Princeton University Press.

———. 1998. "Revolution Matters: Democracy as Demotic Action (a Response to Kurt A. Raaflaub)." In *Democracy 2500? Questions and Challenges,* edited by I. Morris and K. A. Raaflaub, 67–86. Dubuque, Iowa: Kendall-Hunt.

———. 2008. *Democracy and Knowledge: Innovation and Learning in Classical Athens.* Princeton: Princeton University Press.

———. 2015. *The Rise and Fall of Classical Greece.* Princeton: Princeton University Press.

Ober, J., and C. W. Hedrick, Jr., eds. 1996. *Demokratia: A Conversation on Democracies, Ancient and Modern.* Princeton: Princeton University Press.

O'Brien, J. 1993. *The Transformation of Hera: A Study of Ritual, Hero, and the Goddess in the "Iliad."* Lanham, Md.: Rowman and Littlefield.

Osborne, R. 2010. *Athens and Athenian Democracy.* Cambridge: Cambridge University Press.

Ostwald, M. 1986. *From Popular Sovereignty to the Sovereignty of Law: Law, Society, and Politics in Fifth-Century Athens.* Berkeley: University of California Press.

Page, D. L. 1959. *History and the Homeric "Iliad."* Berkeley: University of California Press.

Parker, R. 2011. *On Greek Religion.* Ithaca: Cornell University Press.

Parry, A. 1956. "The Language of Achilles." *Transactions of the American Philological Association* 87: 1–7.

Pearson, A. C., ed. 1924. *Sophoclis Fabulae.* Oxford: Oxford University Press.

Pelliccia, H. 2002. "The Interpretation of *Iliad* 6.145–9 and the Sympotic Contribution to Rhetoric." *Colby Quarterly* 38, 2: 197–230.

Pelling, C., ed. 1990. *Characterization and Individuality in Greek Literature.* Oxford: Clarendon.

Peradotto, J. 1990. *Man in the Middle Voice: Name and Narrative in the Odyssey.* Princeton: Princeton University Press.

Podlecki, A. J. 1966. "Creon and Herodotus." *Transactions of the American Philological Association* 97: 359–371.

———. 1986. *"Polis* and Monarch in Early Attic Tragedy." In *Greek Tragedy and Political Theory,* edited by J. P. Euben, 76–100. Berkeley: University of California Press.

Porter, D. H. 1972. "Violent Juxtaposition in the Similes of the *Iliad." Classical Journal* 68, 1: 11–21.

Pozzi, D. C., and J. M. Wickersham, eds. 1991. *Myth and the Polis.* Ithaca: Cornell University Press.

Pucci, P. 2002. "Theology and Poetics in the *Iliad." Arethusa* 35, 1: 17–34.

Raaflaub, K. A. 1989. "Homer and the Beginning of Political Thought in Greece." *Proceedings of the Boston Area Colloquium Series in Ancient Philosophy* 4: 1–25.

———. 1993. "Homer to Solon: The Rise of the Polis: The Written Sources." In *The Ancient Greek City State,* edited by M. H. Hansen, 41–105. Copenhagen: Royal Danish Academy of Sciences and Letters: Commissioner, Munksgaard.

———. 1994. "Democracy, Power, and Imperialism in Fifth-Century Athens." In *Athenian Political Thought and the Reconstruction of American Democracy,* edited by J. P. Euben, J. Wallach, and J. Ober, 103–146. Ithaca: Cornell University Press.

———. 1997. "Homeric Society." In *A New Companion to Homer,* edited by I. Morris and B. Powell, 624–648. Leiden: Brill.

———. 1998. "Power in the Hands of the People: Foundations of Athenian Democracy." In *Democracy 2500? Questions and Challenges,* edited by I. Morris and K. A. Rauflaub, 31–66. Dubuque, Iowa: Kendall-Hunt.

———. 2000. "Poets, Lawgivers, and the Beginning of Political Reflection in Archaic Greece." In *The Cambridge History of Greek and Roman Political Thought,* edited by C. Rowe and M. Schofield, 23–59. Cambridge: Cambridge University Press.

———. 2001a. "Father of All, Destroyer of All: War in Late Fifth-Century Athenian Discourse and Ideology." In *War and Democracy: A Comparative Study of the Korean War and the Peloponnesian War,* edited by D. McCann and B. S. Strauss, 307–356. Armonk, N.Y.: M. E. Sharpe.

———. 2001b. "Political Thought, Civic Responsibility, and the Greek *Polis.*" In *Agon, Logos, Polis: The Greek Achievement and Its Aftermath,* edited by J. Arnason and P. Murphy, 72–117. Stuttgart: Franz Steiner Verlag.

———. 2003. "Stick and Glue: The Function of Tyranny in Fifth-Century Athenian Democracy." In *Popular Tyranny,* edited by K. A. Morgan, 59–93. Austin: University of Texas Press.

———. 2004. *The Discovery of Freedom in Ancient Greece,* translated by R. Franciscono. Chicago: University of Chicago Press. First English edition, revised and updated from the German.

———. 2012. "Sophocles and Political Thought." In *Brill's Companion to Sophocles,* edited by A. Markantonatos, 471–488. Leiden: Brill.

———. 2015. "Ancient Greece: The Historical Needle's Eye of Modern Politics and Political Thought." *Classical World* 109: 3–37.

Raaflaub, K. A., J. Ober, et al., eds. 2007. *Origins of Democracy in Ancient Greece.* Berkeley: University of California Press.

Rabel, R. J. 1997. *Plot and Point of View in the "Iliad."* Ann Arbor: University of Michigan Press.

Rabinowitz, N. 1993. *Anxiety Veiled: Euripides and the Traffic of Women.* Ithaca: Cornell University Press.

Rahe, P. A. 1992. *Republics Ancient and Modern.* Chapel Hill: University of North Carolina Press, 1992.

Ready, J. L. 2011. *Character, Narrator, and Simile in the "Iliad."* Cambridge: Cambridge University Press.

———. 2015. "The Textualization of Homeric Epic by Means of Dictation." *Transactions of the American Philological Association* 145: 1–75.

Redfield, J. M. 1979. "The Proem of the *Iliad:* Homer's Art." *Classical Philology* 74: 95–110.

———. 1994. *Nature and Culture in the "Iliad": The Tragedy of Hector,* 2nd ed. Durham, N.C.: Duke University Press. Orig. pub. 1975.

Reece, S. 1993. *The Stranger's Welcome: Oral Theory and the Aesthetics of the Homeric Hospitality Scene.* Ann Arbor: University of Michigan Press.

Reeve, M. 1972. "Two Notes on *Iliad* 9." *Classical Quarterly* 22: 1–4.

———. 1973. "The Language of Achilles." *Classical Quarterly* 23: 193–195.

Rhodes, P. J. 2003. "Nothing to Do with Democracy: Athenian Drama and the Polis." *Journal of Hellenic Studies* 123: 104–119.

———. 2004. *Athenian Democracy.* Oxford: Oxford University Press.

Richard, C. J. 1994. *The Founders and the Classics: Greece, Rome, and the American Enlightenment.* Cambridge: Harvard University Press.

———. 2009. *Greeks and Romans Bearing Gifts: How the Ancients Inspired the Founding Fathers.* Lanham, Md.: Rowman and Littlefield.

Richardson, N. 1993. *The "Iliad": A Commentary. Volume VI: books 21–24.* Edited by G. S. Kirk. Cambridge: Cambridge University Press.

Richardson, S. 2006. "The Devious Narrator of the *Odyssey.*" *Classical Journal* 101: 337–359.

Rinon, Y. 2008. "A Tragic Pattern in the *Iliad.*" *Harvard Studies in Classical Philology* 104: 45–91.

Robinson, E. W. 1997. *The First Democracies: Early Popular Government outside Athens.* Stuttgart: Franz Steiner Verlag.

———, ed. 2004. *Ancient Greek Democracy: Readings and Sources.* Malden, Mass.: Blackwell.

Roisman, H. M. 2006. "Helen in the *Iliad: Causa Belli* and Victim of War: From Silent Weaver to Public Speaker." *American Journal of Philology* 127, 1: 1–36.

Rood, N. 2008. "Craft Similes and the Construction of Heroes in the *Iliad.*" *Harvard Studies in Classical Philology* 104: 19–43.

Rose, P. W. 1995. "Historicizing Sophocles' *Ajax.*" In *History, Tragedy, Theory: Dialogues on Athenian Drama,* edited by B. Goff, 59–90. Austin: University of Texas Press.

Roselli, D. K. 2011. *Theater of the People: Spectators and Society in Ancient Athens.* Austin: University of Texas Press.

Rosenbloom, D. 1995. "Myth, History, and Hegemony in Aeschylus." In *History, Tragedy, Theory: Dialogues on Athenian Drama,* edited by B. Goff, 91–130. Austin: University of Texas Press.

Rosivach, V. 2014. "Classical Athens: Predatory Democracy? Hidden Oligarchy? Neither? Both?" *New England Classical Journal* 41, 4: 168–194.

Rosner, J. A. 1976. "The Speech of Phoenix: *Iliad* 9.434–605." *Phoenix* 30, 4: 314–327.

Rowe, C. J. 1983. "The Nature of Homeric Morality." In *Approaches to Homer*, edited by C. A. Rubino and C. W. Shelmerdine, 248–285. Austin: University of Texas Press.

Rowe, C., and M. Schofield, eds. 2000. *The Cambridge History of Greek and Roman Political Thought.* Cambridge: Cambridge University Press.

Russo, J. 1968. "Homer against His Tradition." *Arion* 7: 275–295.

Saïd, S. 1998. "Tragedy and Politics." In *Democracy, Empire and the Arts in Fifth-Century Athens.* Center for Hellenic Studies, Colloquia 2, edited by D. Boedeker and K. A. Raaflaub, 275–295. Cambridge: Harvard University Press.

Sale, W. 1963. "Achilles and Heroic Values." *Arion* 2: 86–100.

Sammons, B. 2008. "Gift, List, and Story in *Iliad* 9. 115–161." *Classical Journal* 103, 4: 353–379.

Sandridge, N. B. 2008. "Feeling Vulnerable, but Not Too Vulnerable: Pity in Sophocles' *Oedipus Coloneus, Ajax* and *Philoctetes.*" *Classical Journal* 103, 4: 433–448.

Sansone, D. 2012. *Greek Drama and the Invention of Rhetoric.* Malden, Mass.: Wiley-Blackwell.

Schein, S. L. 1984. *The Mortal Hero: An Introduction to Homer's "Iliad."* Berkeley: University of California Press.

Schofield, M. 1986. "*Euboulia* in the *Iliad.*" *Classical Quarterly* 36: 6–31.

Scodel, R. 1982. "The Autobiography of Phoenix." *American Journal of Philology* 103: 128–136.

———. 1992. "The Wits of Glaucus." *Transactions of the American Philological Association* 122: 73–84.

———. 1998. "The Captive's Dilemma: Sexual Acquiescence in Euripides' *Hecuba* and *Troades.*" *Harvard Studies in Classical Philology* 98: 137–154.

———. 2002. *Listening to Homer: Tradition, Narrative, and Audience.* Ann Arbor: University of Michigan Press.

———. 2003. "*Iliad* 9 and *autos apouras.*" *Classical Journal* 98, 3: 275–279.

Scott, W. C. 1974. *The Oral Nature of the Homeric Simile.* Leiden: Brill.

———. 1997. "The Etiquette of Games in *Iliad* 23." *Greece, Rome and Byzantine Studies* 38: 213–227.

———. 2006. "Similes in a Shifting Scene: *Iliad,* Book 11." *Classical Philology* 101, 2: 103–114.

———. 2009. *The Artistry of the Homeric Simile.* Hanover, N.H.: Dartmouth College Library and Dartmouth College Press, University Press of New England.

Scullion, S. 2005. "Tragedy and Religion: The Problem of Origins." In *A Companion to Greek Tragedy,* edited by J. Gregory, 23–37. Malden, Mass.: Wiley-Blackwell.

Scully, S. 1990. *Homer and the Sacred City.* Ithaca: Cornell University Press.

Seaford, R. 1994. *Reciprocity and Ritual: Homer and Tragedy in the Developing City-State.* Oxford: Clarendon.

Segal, C. P. 1971a. *The Theme of the Mutilation of the Corpse in the "Iliad."* Leiden: Brill.

———. 1971b. "Andromache's Anagnorisis." *Harvard Studies in Classical Philology* 75: 33–57.

———. 1981. *Tragedy and Civilization: An Interpretation of Sophocles.* Norman: University of Oklahoma Press.

———. 1995. *Sophocles' Tragic World: Divinity, Nature, Society.* Cambridge: Harvard University Press.

Shay, J. 1994. *Achilles in Vietnam: Combat Trauma and the Undoing of Character.* New York: Scribner.

Sider, D. 2001. "'As Is the Generation of Leaves' in Homer, Simonides, Horace, and Stobaeus." In *The New Simonides: Contexts of Praise and Desire,* edited by D. Boedeker and D. Sider, 272–288. Oxford: Oxford University Press.

Silk, M. S. 1974. *Interaction in Poetic Imagery: With Special Reference to Early Greek Poetry.* London: Cambridge University Press.

Simpson, M. 1969. "Sophocles' *Ajax*: His Madness and Transformation." *Arethusa* 2: 88–103.

Snell, B. 1953. *The Discovery of the Mind in Greek Philosophy and Literature.* New York: Dover. Repr. 1982.

Sommerstein, A. H. 2010. *Aeschylean Tragedy.* London: Gerald Duckworth.

Sommerstein, A. H., and I. C. Torrance. 2014. *Oaths and Swearing in Ancient Greece.* Berlin: Walter de Gruyter.

Sourvinou-Inwood, C. 2003. *Tragedy and Athenian Religion.* Lanham, Md.: Rowman and Littlefield.

Stanford, W. B. 1981. *Sophocles: "Ajax."* London: Bristol. Orig. pub. 1963.

Stanley, K. 1993. *The Shield of Homer: Narrative Structure in the "Iliad."* Princeton: Princeton University Press.

Stockton, D. 1990. *The Classical Athenian Democracy.* Oxford: Oxford University Press.

Tandy, D. 1997. *Warriors into Traders: The Power of the Market in Early Greece.* Berkeley: University of California Press.

Taplin, O. 1978. *Greek Tragedy in Action.* Berkeley: University of California Press.

———. 1980. "The Shield of Achilles within the *Iliad.*" *Greece & Rome* 27, 1: 1–21.

———. 1990. "Agamemnon's Role in the *Iliad.*" In *Characterization and Individuality in Greek Literature,* edited by C. Pelling, 60–82. Oxford: Clarendon.

———. 1992. *Homeric Soundings: The Shaping of the "Iliad."* Oxford: Clarendon.

Thalmann, W. G. 1993. "Euripides and Aeschylus: The Case of the 'Hekabe.'" *Classical Antiquity* 12, 1: 126–159.

———. 1998. *The Swineherd and the Bow: Representations of Class in the "Odyssey."* Ithaca: Cornell University Press.

Thomas, R. 1995. "The Place of the Poet in Archaic Society." In *The Greek World,* edited by A. Powell, 104–129. London: Routledge.

Torrance, I. C. 2013. *Metapoetry in Euripides.* Oxford: Oxford University Press.

———. 2014. "Oaths in Traditional Myth." In *Oaths and Swearing in Ancient Greece,* edited by A. H. Sommerstein and I. C. Torrance, 48–59. Berlin: Walter de Gruyter.

Traill, D. A. 1989. "Gold Armor for Bronze and Homer's Use of Compensatory TIMH." *Classical Philology* 84: 301–305.

van Wees, H. 1992. *Status Warriors: War, Violence, and Society in Homer and History.* Amsterdam: Gieben.

Vernant, J.-P. 1986. "At Man's Table: Hesiod's Foundation Myth of Sacrifice." In *The Cuisine of Sacrifice among the Greeks,* edited by M. Detienne and J.-P. Vernant, translated by P. Wissing, 21–86. Chicago: University of Chicago Press.

———. 1991. "Mortals and Immortals: The Body of the Divine." In *Mortals and Immortals: Collected Essays,* edited by F. I. Zeitlin, 27–49. Princeton: Princeton University Press.

Vernant, J.-P., and P. Vidal-Naquet. 1988. *Myth and Tragedy in Ancient Greece,* translated by J. Lloyd. New York: Zone Books. Orig. published as *Mythe et tragédie en Grèce ancienne* (1972) and *Mythe et tragédie en Grèce ancienne deux* (1986).

Versnel, H. S. 1990. "What's Sauce for the Goose Is Sauce for the Gander: Myth and Ritual Old and New." In *Approaches to Greek Myth,* edited by L. Edmunds, 84–151. Baltimore: Johns Hopkins University Press. 2nd ed. 2014.

———. 2011. *Coping with the Gods: Wayward Readings in Greek Theology.* Leiden: Brill.

Veyne, P. 1988. *Did the Greeks Believe in Their Myths? An Essay on the Constitutive Imagination,* translated by P. Wissing. Chicago: University of Chicago Press. Orig. pub. 1983 as *Les Grecs ont-ils cru a leurs mythes?*

Vickers, B. 1973. *Towards Greek Tragedy.* London: Longman.

Walcot, P. 1969. "ΧΡΥΣΕΑ ΧΑΛΚΕΙΩΝ: A Further Comment." *Classical Review* 19: 12–13.

Walsh, T. R. 2005. *Fighting Words and Feuding Words: Anger and the Homeric Poems.* Lanham, Md.: Rowman and Littlefield.

West, M. L. 2011. *The Making of the "Iliad": Disquisition and Analytical Commentary.* Oxford: Oxford University Press.

Whitman, C. H. 1958. *Homer and the Heroic Tradition.* Cambridge: Harvard University Press.

Widzisz, M. 2012. "Timing Reciprocity in the *Iliad*." *Arethusa* 45, 2: 153–175.

Willcock, M. M. 1964. "Mythological Paradigms in the *Iliad*." *Classical Quarterly* 14: 141–154. Also in *Oxford Readings in Homer's "Iliad,"* edited by D. L. Cairns, 435–455. Oxford: Oxford University Press, 2001.

———. 1970. "Some Aspects of the Gods in the *Iliad*." *Bulletin of the Institute of Classical Studies* 17: 1–10. Also in *Essays on the "Iliad": Selected Modern Criticism*, edited by J. Wright, 58–69. Bloomington: Indiana University Press, 1978.

Williams, B. 1993. *Shame and Necessity*. Sather's Classical Lectures, vol. 57. Berkeley: University of California Press.

Wilson, C. H., ed. and trans. 1996. *"Iliad" Books VIII and IX*. Warminster: Aris and Phillips.

Wilson, D. 1999. "Symbolic Violence in *Iliad* Book 9." *Classical World* 93: 131–147.

———. 2002. *Ransom, Revenge, and Heroic Identity in the "Iliad."* Cambridge: Cambridge University Press.

Winnington-Ingram, R. P. 1980. *Sophocles: An Interpretation*. Cambridge: Cambridge University Press.

Wood, G. S. 1972. *The Creation of the American Republic, 1776–1787*. New York: W. W. Norton.

Woodard, R. 2007. *The Cambridge Companion to Greek Mythology*. Cambridge: Cambridge University Press.

Woodruff, P. 2011. *The Ajax Dilemma*. New York: Oxford University Press.

Worman, N. 2001. "The 'Herkos Achaion' Transformed: Character Type and Spatial Meaning in the *Ajax*." *Classical Philology* 96, 3: 228–252.

———. 2012. "Oedipus, Odysseus, and the Failure of Rhetoric." In *Brill's Companion to Sophocles*, edited by A. Markantonatos, 325–347. Leiden: Brill.

Wright, J., ed. 1978. *Essays on the "Iliad": Selected Modern Criticism*. Bloomington: Indiana University Press.

Yamagata, N. 1994. *Homeric Morality*. Leiden: Brill.

Zakaria, F. 2007. *The Future of Freedom: Illiberal Democracy at Home and Abroad*. New York: W. W. Norton. First published 2003.

Zanker, G. 1992. "Sophocles' *Ajax* and the Heroic Values of the *Iliad*." *Classical Quarterly* 42: 20–25.

———. 1994. *The Heart of Achilles: Characterization and Personal Ethics in the "Iliad."* Ann Arbor: University of Michigan Press.

Zeitlin, F. I. 1990. "Playing the Other: Theater, Theatricality, and the Feminine in Greek Drama." In *Nothing to Do with Dionysos? Athenian Drama in Its Social Context*, edited by J. J. Winkler and F. I. Zeitlin, 63–93. Princeton: Princeton University Press.

———. 1996. *Playing the Other: Gender and Society in Classical Greek Literature*. Chicago: University of Chicago Press.

Index

Zeus (*continued*)
blamed by Agamemnon, 83;
blamed by Helen, 35; called
on by Ajax, 123; as explanation
for Glaucus's behavior, 32; as
guarantor of oaths, 39–40;
Hector and, 33; and Hera, 24,
51–52, 186, 208(n22); Poseidon
allowed to destroy fortification
by, 76; and Sarpedon's death,
82; Trojans aided by, 51–52,
80–81